Investment
Markets

Investment Markets

Gaining the Performance Advantage

Roger G. Ibbotson
Yale School of Management
Ibbotson Associates, Inc.

Gary P. Brinson
First Chicago Investment Advisors

McGraw-Hill Book Company

New York   St. Louis   San Francisco   Auckland   Bogotá
Hamburg   Johannesburg   London   Madrid   Mexico
Milan   Montreal   New Delhi   Panama
Paris   São Paulo   Singapore
Sydney   Tokyo   Toronto

Library of Congress Cataloging-in-Publication Data

Ibbotson, Roger G.
  Investment markets.

  Includes index.
  1. Capital market.   2. Portfolio management.
I. Brinson, Gary P.   II. Title.
HG4523.I23   1987   332.6   86-33740
IBN 0-07-031673-2

1234567890   DOC/DOC   893210987

ISBN 0-07-031673-2

The editors for this book were Martha Jewett and Barbara B. Toniolo,
the designer was Naomi Auerbach, and the production
supervisor was Thomas G. Kowalczyk. It was set in Baskerville
by T.C. Systems.

Printed and bound by R. R. Donnelley & Sons Company.

Contents

Part 4:   Inflation, Tangible Assets, Options, and Futures

Part 5:   Constructing Your Portfolio

Preface

This book provides an analysis and history of capital markets throughout the world. We see the unique contributions of the work as threefold. Although many attempts have been made to assess various investment returns, here, for the first time, the returns are measured consistently on many assets across long periods of time. In addition, both income and capital gain components of these returns are segregated. This careful and detailed record provides an important historical perspective on investment markets. The book's second contribution is an economic analysis of all these investment returns in a single volume. The risks associated with investments in various assets and the effects of diversifying those risks are clearly identified. Based on an assessment of each asset market, expected returns are also shown. The third contribution of this work is that it tells investors how to handle various assets in their portfolios. Sound investment advice is always useful, and we base it on both economic analysis and historical evidence. Advice specific to each asset, such as real estate, is presented at the end of the chapter describing that asset's returns. All advice is then summarized in the last chapters, which cover first institutional and then individual portfolios.

This book is not necessarily intended to be read sequentially from front to back. Those concerned primarily with institutional management will be most interested in Chapter 16, which covers investment advice for those managing tax-exempt portfolios. Advice for managing personal portfolios, with returns subject to tax, is given in Chapter 17. Readers interested in the size and scope of various capital markets will want to turn directly to particular chapters on specific assets, which can be identified through the table of contents or the index. Finally, persons interested in the economic perspective may wish to follow the book's organization, which sets the stage, examines various markets, and then draws conclusions about investment activities based on the analysis.

To provide this compendium on capital markets, we draw upon a variety of secondary sources. Unlike other volumes on the subject, however, this work presents the data in a way that is generally comparable across asset classes. To our knowledge, this is the first time that total returns on a wide variety of assets have been made available and also converted to indexes. Since hundreds of years worth of data are compiled from numerous sources, with varying degrees of reliability, this material is useful primarily to provide a view of broad trends. The interested reader who wishes to make statistical use of the data as a basis for evaluating investment performance or for capital market research is urged to go to the original source and determine its level of reliability.

Academic jargon, mathematical formulas, and statistical terms have been largely avoided in the text; an element of precision is sacrificed in order to make the work readable and understandable by investors generally. Our intended audience is broad. Although primarily designed for individual and institutional investors, the book could also be a reference source for the bookshelves of business writers, financial economists, and libraries.

Acknowledgments

The volume would not have been possible without the dedication, patience, and work of others, to whom we are clearly indebted over the years. Laurence B. Siegel was involved with the manuscript from start to finish; he was absolutely vital in the initial conceptualization and ongoing exposition of ideas, as well as the writing, data analysis, exhibit preparation, and manuscript editing. For research, writing, editing, and coordination of a myriad of publication details, we acknowledge the invaluable contribution of Margaret A. Corwin. Also, Jeffrey J. Diermeier made major contributions to the ideas, drafting, and illustrations in the chapter on the institutional portfolio.

In addition, we wish to thank our editor, Martha Jewett, who gave the book focus, discipline, and moral support throughout the publication process. First Chicago Investment Advisors and Ibbotson Associates provided significant financial support. For research assistance and data analysis, we recognize the contributions of Wilbur John Coleman and L. Randolph Hood, Jr. Over the years, Wendy Freyer, Kathryn Love, Nina Bhosley, and Mary Jo Kringas labored to compile exhibits and put them into final form. Many others at Ibbotson Associates, First Chicago Investment Advisors, The University of Chicago, Yale University, and other institutions also helped in specific ways. We gratefully recognize all this help, without which this book would not exist.

Roger G. Ibbotson and Gary P. Brinson

PART 1

Investing in Multiple Assets

1
The Investment Setting

This book is intended to help both personal investors and institutional money managers improve the returns on their portfolios and reduce their risks. For the first time, investors can compare the returns on a wide variety of assets across long time periods. Here they also obtain a historical perspective on capital markets. These data are then analyzed from an economic point of view to provide the foundation for sensible financial advice.

Whether they be institutional money managers or individuals, investors all face the same basic dilemma: making the best return on their money. Many devote significant amounts of time and effort to choosing particular stocks or selecting bonds with the best yields. Surprisingly, though, the decision having the biggest impact on an investor's profit is the percentage of funds allocated to various asset classes, not the choice of individual securities. Emphasizing stocks as opposed to bonds in the boom years of the 1950s was far more important to an investor's overall performance than the specific stocks selected. Likewise, in the inflationary 1970s, buying real estate rather than other financial assets usually boosted an investor's returns, regardless of which particular properties were purchased.

Many investors have also sought to reduce the risk of their portfolios through diversification. Yet diversification, when properly understood, does not just mean holding a variety of stocks. To gain the performance advantage, investors are advised to take the global approach; they should diversify across asset classes and across the world, as well as across the securities of a particular asset class. The principal asset classes are stocks, bonds, cash equivalents, real estate, monetary metals, and tangible assets; securities are simply investments or assets within these classes. Broad diversification can dramatically reduce the risk of a portfolio.

Three Investment Approaches

Most investors try to make high returns by identifying and acquiring undervalued securities. The work of Benjamin Graham and David Dodd provides rules for ascertaining value, and has become the basis for traditional security analysis. A few renowned investors, such as Lord Keynes, relied on psychological interpretation of market movements, while others, such as Warren Buffett, use their unusual insights about future economic trends. Implicit in these quests are attempts to assign a true value to a security, business, property, or activity.

Modern portfolio theory, with its emphasis on efficient markets and risk, has shifted the focus of some investors from value analysis to risk diversification. Investing in accordance with this theory is the second investment approach. According to its most literal interpretation, skill at identifying value cannot be acquired. Except by luck, no investor can gain an advantage over others. Instead, the theory suggests, investors should buy and hold a diversified set of securities.

Many of the tenets of modern portfolio theory have been proven empirically. Few economists question that there are gains from diversification, or that taking risk is rewarded on average. However, some economists doubt that all securities are priced appropriately. Because investors incur different costs and because capital markets are imperfect, the prices of securities may depart from their underlying values. In such cases, more knowledgeable investors can expect to outperform less knowledgeable ones.

A third investment approach, based on a mix of theory and practice, is the orientation of this book. In this approach, the existence of some underpriced securities is recognized, but because most markets are largely efficient, bargains are believed to be the exception, not the rule. Furthermore, investors may need special skills to identify such securities. The cost of acquiring the skills and information necessary to identify bargain securities must be compared with the expected profits from transacting in these securities. This strategy also incorporates the primary thesis of modern portfolio theory—that investors should usually buy and hold a diversified portfolio. However, diversification here takes on a broader meaning: that investors should diversify not only within an asset class, but also across asset classes and across countries. Furthermore, the weight of these classes should be selectively varied over time in accordance with economic trends and profit opportunities. Finally, this strategy emphasizes that investors must recognize the characteristics that make their situation unique, and tailor their portfolios accordingly.

Investing in Multiple Asset Classes

Today's investment alternatives are many. In this book, nontraditional assets as well as the more traditional stocks and bonds are viewed as essential for both individual and institutional investors. Economic trends such as an increase in inflation rates or an oil crisis can change the attractiveness of some asset classes relative to others; for example, increasing inflation reduces the attractiveness of existing bonds, written at old interest rates, relative to stocks or floating-rate cash equivalents. Hence, investing in various asset classes, including stocks, bonds, cash equivalents, real estate, monetary metals, and tangibles, spreads the risks from such economic changes and increases the overall profit potential of an investor's portfolio. Let's look preliminarily at the past profits on both traditional and nontraditional assets.

Traditional Assets

When most people think of investments, they identify the traditional asset classes of U.S. stocks, bonds, and cash equivalents.

U.S. Stocks. Over the very long run, U.S. stocks have topped the charts as the asset with the highest returns. One dollar invested in 1789 would have earned over an 8 percent annual return, and the money would have doubled roughly every 9 years. Through the magic of compounding, investors would have made almost *5 million* times their money in such equities. Since World War II, returns on the riskiest equities, over-the-counter (OTC) stocks, have even surpassed those of the more sedate New York Stock Exchange (NYSE).

U.S. Bonds. In the United States, bonds beat inflation historically, but they had substantially lower returns than stocks. And following World War II, U.S. Treasuries and long-term U.S. corporate bonds had negative real returns, or returns lower than inflation over the period. After this dismal record, bond returns have made a dramatic comeback in the mid-1980s.

Cash Equivalents. Investors' attitudes toward cash have changed. Cash holdings used to be considered only a temporary parking place for funds until they could be invested in other assets. Since the 1970s, with deregulation of interest rates and high rates of inflation, cash has become a more prominent investment vehicle, with returns that closely match inflation.

Nontraditional Assets

Less traditional asset classes are real estate, tangible assets, and monetary metals.

Real Estate.   Over the long run, investors in real estate have achieved capital gains at about the inflation rate, after allowing for depreciation. (Capital appreciation excludes the rent income and expenses like maintenance, property taxes, etc.) The unleveraged postwar returns on U.S. real estate were almost as high as those of U.S. equities. With leverage, real estate had stellar returns, outshining even stocks. In addition, holding real estate reduces the risk of a portfolio and hedges inflation. Also, under the U.S. tax code, real estate investments have traditionally received preferential treatment, enhancing their after-tax returns. The 1986 tax bill removes some of these preferences and may dampen after-tax real estate returns.

Monetary Metals.   Gold and silver had very high (though volatile) returns in the 1970s, but in the 1980s their prices (and hence returns) have plunged. Over the long term, most gold investors have only broken even in real terms. In general, gold's price fluctuates wildly, adding to risk, but this asset does provide portfolio diversification and a hedge against inflation. Silver, the second most important monetary metal, is traded in a much smaller market than gold, and its prices are even more volatile, and the asset even more risky.

Tangible Assets.   Tangible assets like paintings, furniture, and coins may be attractive to investors who appreciate both their pecuniary and nonpecuniary returns. The nonpecuniary returns are the enjoyment, prestige, and psychological income that holding such assets gives their owners. However, those who do not appreciate both types of benefits will have overpaid for the asset.

During inflationary periods, tangibles often have high financial returns. During deflation, financial returns are low. In addition, tangibles have high maintenance, search, and transaction costs. The numbers say that unless the investor enjoys their nonpecuniary benefits, tangibles are not smart investments.

Use of Options and Futures to Manage Risk

Options and futures provide investors with new ways to manage risk. Although commodity futures have been traded for more than a century, new varieties of financial options and futures are being continuously introduced, and trading activity is rapidly increasing. Options and futures are typically used in combination with traditional and nontraditional assets to hedge, to speculate, or to time the market.

Investing Internationally

Why Invest Internationally?

The world's political borders impose costs on all of us by impeding the flow of resources, capital, and people. Investors who allocate money to international as well as domestic assets surmount the barriers which others hesitate to climb. Thus they may capture profits that others miss, and reduce the risk of losing their capital because of local political and economic circumstances.

American investors have traditionally believed that the United States alone provided an adequate range of investment possibilities. But this has become less and less true. Today, foreign economies make up about half of the investment value of the developed world. The amount of U.S. investment in foreign capital markets now runs in the tens of billions of dollars. Furthermore, the proportion of U.S. funds invested abroad is likely to soar in the future.

International Assets

To achieve a truly diversified portfolio, investors should hold assets from the major industrial countries. The investor who has the sophistication and knowledge (or who hires those with knowledge) to handle international investments will be at an advantage over others in the years to come. Let's look briefly at the historical record of such returns.

Foreign Stocks. In the past quarter century, returns on foreign equity markets surpassed returns on the markets of the United States. For example, Asian equities had a compound annual return of over 16 percent per year, compared with about 10 percent on the NYSE. Over the last 200 years, however, many foreign equity markets were wiped out by wars or government upheavals. Many investors who bet on only one country lost everything. Thus, history suggests that international diversification is essential.

Foreign Bonds. Since World War II, investors in foreign bonds have been rewarded with higher returns than investors holding U.S. bonds. Although accelerating inflation generally dampened bond returns, some bond markets, such as Japan, have done extremely well.

Economic Changes and Investment Opportunities

Economic changes have significant effects on different asset classes. Two important changes are shifts in the level of business activity and changes in the inflation rate. Investors should vary the percentage of holdings in different asset classes depending on economic conditions. Likewise, investors will want to adjust their portfolios to take advantage of special investment opportunities.

Inflation

In the postwar period, inflation appeared to be inevitable. But in the 1980s, inflation has moderated in almost every country. Sustained inflation is a relatively recent phenomenon. Over the last several centuries, there has been very little inflation, except during wars or economic expansion. The period since World War II is unusual because inflation persists throughout the world.

Inflation has significant effects on equity returns. If decreases in the rate of inflation could be predicted even 1 year in advance, potential gains to the prognosticator would be large. Both stocks and (especially) bonds do well during falling inflation. Gold and silver are good but unpredictable hedges against rising inflation. Cash equivalents and real estate largely track inflation; both are less volatile than monetary metals.

Level of Business Activity

The degree of expansion or recession in the economy has an important effect on the returns of certain assets. Equities, in particular, are sensitive to the level of activity in the economy as a whole. U.S. stocks dramatically rise and fall upon changing expectations of corporate profits. Likewise, returns on Japanese stocks have reflected the tremendous growth of the Japanese economy. Human capital, or the collective skills and knowledge of human beings, is also higher in countries that have enjoyed more economic success. Even for workers with the same skills, wages are higher in the developed than in the underdeveloped world.

Special Opportunities

Some types of stocks have consistently outperformed the average. That is, some sectors of the equity market have offered extraordinary returns for their level of risk. For example, stocks of companies with smaller capitalizations have had higher risk-adjusted returns than those with larger capitalization. New equity issues (initial public offerings) are another case in point. When these have been bought at the offering price, investors in the past have achieved extraordinarily high returns. While investors have taken advantage of such special opportunities to earn high returns, financial economists do not always understand why such returns exist. Unfortunately, there is no guarantee that such high returns will continue in future periods.

The Global Perspective

Investing across asset classes and across borders can be thought of as a global approach to investing. The word *global* is used here to mean more than "across geographical space"; it describes a comprehensive or all-encompassing perspective on investment markets. In Figure 1.1, the global approach is portrayed; the three "dimensions" of the global perspective are

- Assets
- Geography
- Time

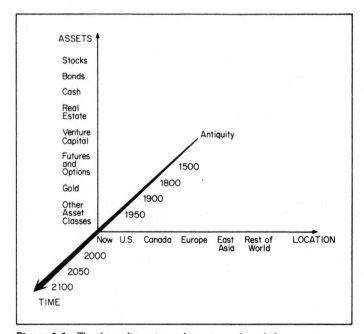

Figure 1.1. The three dimensions of investment knowledge.

The global approach to investing makes sense from the point of view of financial theory, and history shows that it offers the highest long-run returns per unit of risk. Such an approach to investing is the thesis, the argument, of this book. By taking the global approach, and varying the emphasis on asset classes when appropriate, investors gain the performance advantage.

2

A World Economy: Population, GNP, and Capital Markets

Investment markets operate in the context of the world and its economy. While the rest of the book focuses on capital market returns—the payoffs for holding assets with various risk and nonrisk characteristics—this chapter has a macroeconomic perspective. Here the political and economic framework that encompasses capital markets is examined. The discussion moves from a broad view of world population and production to a specific consideration of the wealth inherent in human capital, the skills and knowledge of human beings. Only then does it make sense to take up physical and financial capital, the types found in investment markets.

The Economic Map of the World

A world map is presented in Figure 2.1. The nations of the world may be classified according to their per capita gross national product (GNP) into developed (or rich), middle-income, and poor categories. Both market—or capitalist—countries and centrally planned—or communist—countries are represented in every wealth category.

The Geography of Industrialization

The traditional workshops of the world—the regions having a history of concentrated industrial activity—were located in temperate zones. Peo-

Figure 2.1. Map of the world.

ple who lived in these areas worked in spring, summer, and fall to store
enough food and other necessities to survive the bitter winters. Economic historians suggest that these men and women collectively developed a "plan for tomorrow" attitude, rather than the "live for today"
attitude of tropical areas. Gradually, these conservative habits evolved
into a culture of saving and investment that resulted in the economic
growth of temperate zones.

Through most of history, industrial work was physically taxing, and
required a bracing climate. This pattern, however, is changing. The
decreasing physical difficulty of work is opening up tropical regions to
industrial growth. In fact, Singapore—one of the steamiest locales on
Earth—is now Asia's second wealthiest economy. With the advent of air
conditioning, the hotter regions of rich countries, such as the southern
states of the United States, have also been industrialized.

The Geography of Wealth and Poverty

A country's geographic size is not related to its economic well-being. On
the other hand, developed countries do have significant empty lands.
Large areas of Australia, Canada, Greenland, the United States, and the
Soviet Union are unpopulated deserts or arctic wastes within the territo-

rial borders of these rich countries, making the developed world look larger than it really is. Although many poor countries also contain empty lands, the exaggeration of land area is greater for rich countries.

This does not mean that spaciousness makes for wealth, or crowding for poverty. The world's greatest accumulations of wealth are in the fabulously crowded cities of New York, London, Paris, and Tokyo; these cities provide many opportunities for interaction, leading to the development of knowledge and the matching of human skills to economic needs. It is the very wealth of the cities that attracts the poor. Cities also breed wealth because they enable the urban poor to improve their economic status, while the rural poor have fewer opportunities. On a world scale, there is no relationship between wealth level and crowding, the wealthy Netherlands and impoverished Bangladesh both having very high population density, and rich Australia and extremely poor Chad having very low density.

Population, Production, and Economic Growth

Where the People Are

The world map in Figure 2.2 shows each country in proportion to its population. This map looks quite unfamiliar, since conventional maps portray countries in proportion to their land areas. In this map, however, the world is dominated by China and India. Although North and South America, Europe, Africa, and the Pacific rim of Asia all have substantial populations, they sum to little more than half the world's total.

Population and world influence have been related throughout history. The "population scale" map makes clear why China, despite its poverty, is a superpower ranking behind only the United States and the Soviet Union. Population trends suggest that the power of the United States and Soviet Union may be declining, while China and India may gain influence in the future.

In the past, the Old World—Asia and Europe—has had the largest populations. From ancient times until less than two centuries ago, the two cultures of the West (Europe) and the East (Asia) also produced most of the world's science, literature, technology, and wealth. Slowness of travel and communication kept the East and West apart, so that their development proceeded along different paths. Beginning about 1800, North America's population began to grow rapidly and contribute significantly to Western culture. Now, Western civilization is as much American as European.

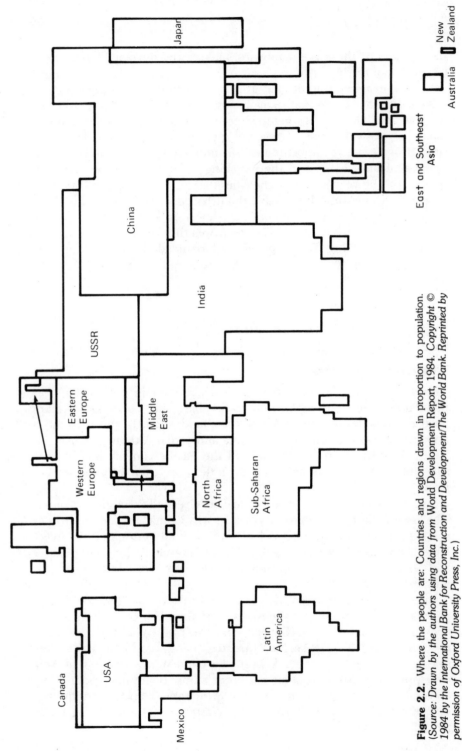

Figure 2.2. Where the people are: Countries and regions drawn in proportion to population. (*Source: Drawn by the authors using data from World Development Report, 1984. Copyright © 1984 by the International Bank for Reconstruction and Development/The World Bank. Reprinted by permission of Oxford University Press, Inc.*)

14

Where the Money Is

The world map in Figure 2.3 shows each country in proportion to its GNP. The United States, Western Europe, the Soviet Union, and Japan are the dominant areas, while China, India, South America, and Africa are small. This strange-looking map shows Great Britain to be larger than either India or Africa. From this perspective, it is easy to see why Britain was able to rule the world for a century.

Comparison of the GNP and population maps brings political and economic conflicts into focus. The population map shows why the Soviet Union might feel political rivalry with China. Similarly, the GNP map explains China's economic rivalry with the Soviet Union, and suggests that both may be overwhelmed by the giant capitalist countries, particularly nearby Japan.

Total population, relative population shares, and relative GNP shares for major world regions and principal countries are listed in Table 2.1. A quarter of the world's people, who live in developed countries with both capitalist and communist economies, earn over 80 percent of world GNP. This wealth distribution mimics that found internally in many countries. Because the GNP figures ignore subsistence, poor countries command a somewhat larger share of true production than is indicated by the proportionate-share numbers.

When population and GNP are considered together over time, a clearer picture of the relative importance of nations and regions emerges. Europe dominated the world in GNP, was high in relative population, and ruled the world in the nineteenth century. In the twentieth century, the GNP/population profile of North America generally dominated the world, and some might say that the world was ruled for a time from the United States. Today Asia is moving into a position of superiority, and possibly the world of the twenty-first century will be ruled in some sense from that continent. As the world becomes more economically integrated, however, the importance of "who rules whom" may decline, so that Asian dominance of the world economy, if it occurs, will be of a different character than the past dominance of other regions.

The relative production shares of the United States, the United Kingdom, and the rest of the world in 1850, 1950, and today are shown in Figure 2.4. These output measures confirm previously mentioned trends. The United Kingdom, which was rightly called the workshop of the world in 1850, yielded that position to the United States in the ensuing hundred years. Since 1950, the output of the rest of the world has grown at the expense of both America's and the United Kingdom's relative shares.

The United States and Europe will probably decline not in absolute

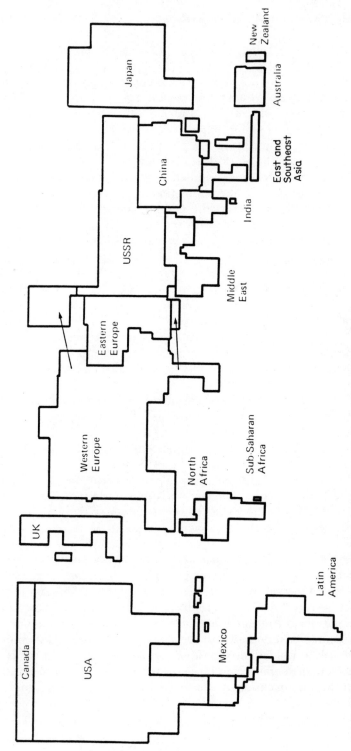

Figure 2.3. Where the money is: Countries and regions drawn in proportion to GNP. (*Source: Drawn by the authors using data from World Development Report, 1984. Copyright © 1984 by the International Bank for Reconstruction and Development/The World Bank. Reprinted by permission of Oxford University Press, Inc.*)

Table 2.1. The World: Population and GNP

	Population (millions)	Population as % of World	GNP as % of World
DEVELOPED WORLD			
Developed Free World			
United States	232	5.1 %	25.1 %
Western Europe	350	7.8	26.8
Japan	118	2.6	9.8
Canada/Australia/others	_43_	_1.0_	_3.9_
Subtotal	743	16.5	65.6
Developed Communist World			
USSR	270	5.9	12.4
Eastern Europe	_136_	_3.0_	_2.9_
Subtotal	406	9.0	15.3
Total Developed Free & Communist	1,149	25.5	80.9
THIRD WORLD			
Noncommunist			
East/Southeast Asia	352	7.8	2.6
Indian Subcontinent	929	20.6	2.0
Latin America	362	8.0	6.2
Middle East/N. Africa	234	5.2	2.8
Sub-Saharan Africa	_393_	_8.7_	_2.2_
Subtotal	2,270	50.3	15.8
Communist			
China	1,008	22.3	2.7
Other	_85_	_1.9_	_0.2_
Subtotal	1,093	24.2	2.9
Total Third World	_3,363_	_74.5_	_18.7_
WORLD TOTAL	**4,512**	**100.0 %**	**100.0 %**

Note: 1982 estimates, except where unavailable, in which case 1980 estimates were used.
Sources: *The World Almanac and Book of Facts,* 1982 & 1984 editions, copyright © Newspaper Enterprise Association, 1981 and 1983, New York, N.Y. 10166; and from *World Development Report, 1984,* copyright © 1984 by the International Bank for Reconstruction and Development/The World Bank. Reprinted by permission of Oxford University Press, Inc.

wealth, but only in relative terms. A decline in absolute wealth would indicate that these countries made up a declining share of a fixed "world pie." If the pie of world wealth expands, as it probably will, the Western nations may retain or even expand their absolute wealth by producing goods and services in which they have a comparative advantage. Today, that advantage is in the fields of communications, agriculture, education, health care, computer technology, and finance. The West's fields of comparative advantage in the next century are yet unknown, but these dynamic societies will undoubtedly have growth fields.

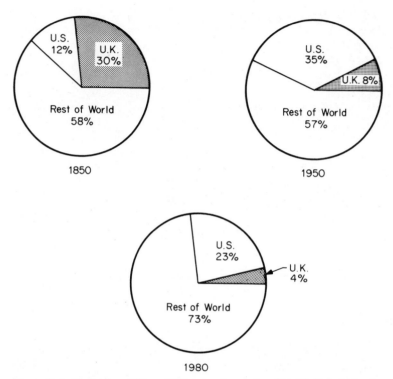

1850

1950

1980

Figure 2.4. Production: U.K. and U.S. percentages of world total. (Industrial output, 1850 and 1950; GNP, 1980. World total includes Soviet Union for 1980.) U.K. production shrinks from 30 percent to 8 percent to 4 percent. U.S. production grows from 12 percent to 35 percent and then drops to 23 percent. (*Sources: Philip E. Bagwell and G. E. Mingay, Britain and America 1850–1939: A Study of Economic Change, Routledge & Kegan Paul, London, 1970, for 1850 and 1950; 1980 GNP proportions from Laurence B. Siegel, "Why You Should Invest Internationally," address given to Chase Global Strategy Seminar, New York, 1983.*)

The Dynamics of Population and Wealth

Thomas Malthus made two observations about the building of wealth. First, he noticed that as people reproduced they obliterated wealth gains in per capita terms and thereby condemned themselves to subsistence living. Second, he observed that when individuals reproduced less, their wealth accumulated over time. As the first observation is most closely associated with Malthus, a growing population that obliterates its wealth gains is called "Malthusian." Eventually, though, Malthus's second observation overcame the first in importance. As the nineteenth century passed, it became clear that whole societies, not just a few individuals, had raised their wealth level above subsistence by careful control of population.

Malthus did not understand that societies could, in fact, raise their standard of living by *increasing* their population. The authors believe that people tend to perceive correctly whether they can gain more by reproducing (investing in the quantity of people) or by education, training, and control of reproduction (investing in the so-called quality of people). Both activities are investments in human capital. The Nobel-Prize-winning economist Theodore W. Schultz has formalized this observation into a theory, although the idea has been familiar to economists since the 1700s. In the Schultz framework, an additional person may be a net boon or burden to society, while Malthus saw additional people only as social burdens.

There is some evidence that people do make wealth-maximizing decisions about human capital. Most citizens of rich countries invest in human "quality" through education and population limitation. The Irish, without the help of the government, have limited their population in the twentieth century through late marriage and by downplaying religious proscriptions against contraception. Citizens of poor countries, however, have found that investing in the quantity of people sometimes makes sense. In India, for example, having another child may be the best investment certain individuals can make. Thus, human beings in a society can increase their human capital by investing in the quantity or quality of other human beings.

Human Capital as a Component of World Wealth

Human beings, then, are a form of capital. Their bodies, skills, and knowledge are part of the capital stock of the world. This concept, while familiar to most economists, is often unknown or even discomforting to many persons. Humanists usually prefer to separate the world of money and capital from the world of sentient beings and their emotions. Yet economists of the past as well as those of today recognize the existence of human capital.

Human Capital as a Percentage of the World's Wealth

Human capital comprised all of the world's wealth at one time. Early *homo sapiens* had no possessions and certainly no investments. As centuries passed, physical and financial capital increased slightly more rapidly than human capital. The value of human capital, usually represented by wage levels, has increased many times. Physical and financial capital adds value to human capital because a more sophisticated business environment requires more skilled and consequently more highly paid workers. Likewise, human capital engenders more physical and financial capital; it is people who invent machines, start new businesses, and construct new buildings.

The proportion of national income attributed to workers and assets over different time periods and between countries is shown in Table 2.2. The changing proportions are consistent with the concept that physical and financial capital adds value to human capital. In the latter half of the nineteenth century, the United Kingdom was just beginning to industri-

Table 2.2. Distribution of National Income among Factor Shares, Selected Countries, Long Periods

	Compensation of Employees	Income from Assets
United Kingdom		
1860-1869	54 %	46 %
1905-1914	54	46
1920-1929	66	34
1954-1960	75	25
France		
1853	56	44
1911	66	34
1920-1929	71	29
1954-1960	81	19
Germany		
1895	53	47
1913	61	39
1925-1929	79	21
1954-1960	71	29
Switzerland		
1924	65	35
1954-1960	74	26
Canada		
1926-1929	81	19
1954-1960	81	19
United States		
1899-1908	76	24
1919-1928	73	27
1954-1960	81	19

Source: Simon Kuznets, <u>Modern Economic Growth</u>, Yale University Press, New Haven, 1966, pp. 168-170.

Table 2.3. Human, Physical, and Financial Capital of the Developed Free World, 1984

		Amount in $Trillions	Percent of Total
Human Capital			
	U.S.	$ 42.0	31.2
	Foreign	64.8	48.2
Physical and Financial Capital			
	U.S.	10.5	7.8
	Foreign	16.2	12.1
	Gold	0.9	0.7
Total		$134.4	100%

Note: The developed free world here includes the U.S., Western Europe, Japan, Hong Kong, Singapore, Australia, and Canada. Gold is a component of physical capital but cannot be allocated to the U.S. or foreign countries; it is a "world" asset. Human capital is estimated to be 4 times the value of physical and financial capital (excluding gold), drawing on the finding that labor income averages 80% of all income (Table 2.2).

Source: Physical and financial capital as of 1984 were estimated by the authors using methods described in Roger G. Ibbotson and Laurence B. Siegel, "The World Market Wealth Portfolio," *Journal of Portfolio Management*, Winter 1983.

alize. As workers created more physical and financial capital, their human capital became more valuable, resulting in higher wages. Since the late 1920s, the compensation for human capital relative to other capital has changed little, although the absolute size of both compensation amounts has grown substantially.

According to the more recent estimates in Table 2.2, human capital earns about 80 percent of national income among the various nations. If human capital earns this percentage of the world's income, this suggests that human capital represents 80 percent of the world's wealth. Then it follows that if human capital has earned this percentage of the free world's wealth, the value of the world's human capital can be estimated from its physical and financial capital. A rough estimate of the wealth of the developed free world is presented in Table 2.3. Using such an approach, the total wealth of the free world is in the range of $134 trillion.

The entire world's wealth can then be approximated using GNP figures. The developed free world has about 65.6 percent of the world's per capita GNP, while the developed communist world has 15.3 percent and the third world has 19.1 percent. Consequently, while the developed free world's human, physical, and financial capital was approximately $134 trillion in 1984, the wealth of the developed communist world was about $31 trillion, and the third world's wealth was around $39 trillion.

Adding world metals, total world wealth was very approximately $205 trillion by the beginning of 1985. With 4.5 billion people in the world, this wealth is about $45,500 per capita, of which $9100 per person is physical or financial (nonhuman) capital.

Human Capital and Borders

Human capital is not as well integrated across borders as most other types of assets. That is, the compensation for human capital is not uniform across countries. Despite the similarity of specialized skills, workers in different places are not always paid the same for similar tasks. For example, in Table 2.4, the salaries of bus drivers in various cities around the world are listed. Although the ability to drive a bus is virtually the same anywhere, almost a fifteenfold difference exists between the wages of Zurich bus drivers and those of Manila drivers. (While data were not collected for China or India, salaries are probably much lower in those countries.) If anything, it takes more skill to drive a bus in Manila than in Zurich; at any rate, this skill can be learned relatively quickly anywhere. The varying ratios of human to physical and financial capital over time cannot explain the differences in compensation between countries at any one point.

Markets for various trades and professions can be very segregated or only somewhat integrated. Because of immigration restrictions, language barriers, and cultural differences, bus drivers can seldom move across national boundaries to take advantage of higher salaries elsewhere. The fact that the salaries of bus drivers are not equalized between countries demonstrates that the market for drivers is very segregated.

Table 2.4. Annual Gross Salary of Bus
Drivers around the World in 1980

	U. S. Dollars
Zurich	$25,510
Duesseldorf	21,000
New York	19,250
Tokyo	15,688
London	9,577
Athens	6,450
Mexico City	4,910
Hong Kong	4,800
Bangkok	2,095
Manila	1,796

Source: *World Paychecks: Who Makes What, When & Why.*
© 1982 by David Harrop. Reprinted by permission from
Facts on File, Inc., New York.

The market for doctors is more integrated than that for bus drivers. Doctors have highly developed skills for which all countries pay well. Doctors also have greater information about international job opportunities. Finally, physicians, unlike bus drivers, have less to prevent them from moving: they can afford to travel and are more welcome to settle anywhere. The end result is that some doctors migrate to high-wage areas, although many originate in poor countries such as India. Nevertheless, doctors with the same training do not always receive the same compensation for similar work; even they experience barriers to entry that prevent the complete equalization of their wages throughout the world.

Regardless of the trade or profession, salaries in more-developed countries are higher for several reasons. Most importantly, skills are more valuable in the presence of more physical and financial capital. Although part of the salary differential between countries is due to the higher cost of living in rich countries, Zurich drivers' wage levels are still eight times higher than Manila drivers' after adjusting for this cost of living. If the cost of travel continues to decline and if immigration is permitted more freely, wage differentials for many trades and professions can be expected to decline.

Quality of Life as a Wealth Measure

Aside from wage levels, another measure of a population's wealth is its quality of life. The Overseas Development Council has constructed an international index of the physical quality of life (PQLI) using an average of infant mortality, life expectancy at age 1 year, and literacy level. The PQLI compares countries' abilities to keep individuals alive and literate at a basic level. For comparison purposes, this index is presented in Table 2.5 along with per capita GNP. As might be expected, developed countries with high GNPs rank high on the index. Yet the broad range of PQLIs among countries with similar wealth is surprising; Sri Lanka rates 81 while India scores only 43.

The PQLI is an imperfect index of quality because it measures survival-based achievements of countries, not their advanced accomplishments. Because two of the three inputs are life-span measures, it is as much a quantity as a quality index. In a broader sense, quality of life may include values such as personal and political freedom, high levels of literacy, consumption of material goods, financial security, and access to social goods like parks, universities, and legal institutions. Per capita GNP may be a better approximation of quality of life, since when a country has high GNP, its government can convert some pecuniary wealth into nonpecuniary well-being by investing in social goods. Never-

Table 2.5. Per Capita GNP and Quality of Life Indexes

Continent/Country	GNP Per Capita($)*	PQLI**	Literacy %	Life expectancy at birth (Years)
Europe				
Free Countries				
France	11,540	96	99	75
Greece	4,280	90	95	74
Ireland	5,050	93	99	73
Italy	6,790	94	98	74
Norway	14,270	97	99	76
Portugal	2,460	80	70	71
Spain	5,380	93	93	74
Sweden	13,840	98	99	77
Switzerland	16,960	96	99	79
United Kingdom	9,620	94	99	74
West Germany	12,300	94	99	73
Communist Countries				
Romania	2,560	91	98	71
USSR	2,600	92	99	69
Yugoslavia	3,100	84	85	71
Africa				
Algeria	2,350	45	46	57
Chad	80	23	15	44
Egypt	670	52	40	57
Nigeria	850	28	25	50
South Africa	2,650	60	50	63
Tanzania	270	50	60	52
Zaire	180	32	40	50
Asia				
Bangladesh	140	32	25	48
China	300	71	70	67
Hong Kong	6,150	--	--	75
India	260	43	36	55
Indonesia	580	55	64	53
Israel	5,320	91	88	74
Japan	10,050	97	99	77
Korea	1,910	83	92	67
Malaysia	1,870	73	60	67
Pakistan	380	38	23	50
Philippines	820	72	88	64
Singapore	5,980	86	76	72
Sri Lanka	320	81	81	69
Taiwan	2,570	87	89	72
Oceania				
Australia	11,140	95	99	74
New Zealand	7,910	94	98	73
South America				
Argentina	2,070	85	94	70
Brazil	2,170	69	75	64
Chile	2,190	79	90	70
Peru	1,260	65	72	58
Venezuela	4,140	79	86	68
North America				
Canada	11,330	95	99	75
Mexico	2,740	76	74	65
U.S.	13,160	95	99	75

*1982 estimates.
**PQLI—Physical Quality of Life Index: a composite index of infant mortality, life expectancy at age one, and literacy (each indexed on a scale from 0 to 100), calculated by averaging the 3 indexes, giving equal weight to each.

Sources: The World Almanac and Book of Facts, 1982 & 1984 editions, copyright © Newspaper Enterprise Association, 1981 and 1983, New York, N.Y. 10166. Also the World Development Report, 1984, copyright © 1984 by the International Bank for Reconstruction and Development/The World Bank. Reprinted by permission of Oxford University Press, Inc.

theless, the PQLI index is a useful indicator of a country's relative wealth.

Conclusion

Too often, financial economists look only at mathematical models of investment returns, while financial practitioners focus largely on daily transactions and events in financial markets. In this chapter, the economic, population, and production characteristics of countries are introduced to provide a familiar setting for both the practical and theoretical interpretations of investment markets.

The world's wealth is estimated to be over $200 trillion, or over $45,000 per capita. Eighty percent of this wealth is human capital. Physical capital, and more specifically financial or investment capital, comprises the remaining percentage, or over $9100 per person.

Since human capital is needed to build physical and financial capital, its distribution is significant and affects the location and activity of capital markets. Furthermore, investors themselves have most of their wealth in their human capital. In this book, various markets for physical and financial capital are considered in turn, but from here onward, human capital, the largest component of world wealth, is ignored.

More broadly, this chapter suggests the important effects of larger social and macroeconomic trends on investment returns. For example, much of the physical and financial capital of Japan and Western Europe was destroyed by World War II, yet their human capital was left largely intact. Those who foresaw the growth of Japan or the economic resurgence of Western Europe have had phenomenally high returns on investments in those countries. This again illustrates that human capital has the power to create physical and financial capital, and that such trends can dramatically affect the long-run returns of investors. Long-term predictions are difficult to make, but, because of its human resources, its technology, and its work ethic, Asia looks like a good bet over the next half century.

Suggested Reading

Kidron, M., and R. Segal: *The State of the World Atlas,* Simon & Schuster, Inc., New York, 1981. Portrays the world in dozens of maps, each indicating population, economic characteristics, military strength, social trends, etc.

Malthus, Thomas Robert: *An Essay on the Principle of Population.* Reprinted under the title *On Population,* Modern Library, Inc., New York, 1960. Seminal eighteenth-century treatise, now largely supplanted by modern economic knowledge.

Rostow, Walter W.: *The World Economy, History and Prospect,* University of Texas Press, Austin, 1978. A classic survey of the world economy.

Schultz, Theodore: "Investment in Human Capital," *American Economic Review,* vol. 51, 1961, pp. 1–17. Also, his *Economic Value of Education,* Columbia University Press, New York, 1963. Human capital theory, as presented by its originator.

Simon, Julian L.: *The Ultimate Resource,* Princeton University Press, Princeton, N.J., 1981. A popularization employing Schultz's ideas.

World Bank: *World Development Report,* Oxford University Press, New York, annual. The best overview of the world economy in a short format.

3
World Asset Returns

A global perspective on world asset returns can inform investors' judgments and improve their decisions. Yet the task of measuring the totality of assets in the world and then computing their returns is monumental. As astronomers are hampered in mapping the universe by the inadequacy of their equipment, so financial economists are only able to sketch the outlines of the world's investment horizons.

A Rationale for the Global Perspective

Practical Reasons

Knowing the magnitude of various markets can help investors improve their choices. Those who wish to buy gold, for example, will better understand its liquidity when they see the total value of gold relative to aggregate world investments. Those who wish to diversify will grasp the importance of investing abroad when they observe the size of foreign markets.

Even more important than the size of world investment markets, however, are the returns that world assets have provided. For example, investors might want to compare returns on stocks from the United States, Europe, and the Far East, to assess their relative riskiness, and to view them against the average for world equities. Through world-scale analysis, investors also gain hindsight on past profits from various investment markets.

Theoretical Reasons

Modern portfolio theory, and in particular the capital asset pricing model (CAPM), advances still another reason for studying world investments. With this model, the returns on an asset are judged relative to returns on the "market portfolio." Used in this sense, *portfolio* is defined as all assets in a given market, weighted by their market values. By definition, this market portfolio is perfectly diversified; in theory, all investors should try to match its composition to reduce risk and maximize returns.

Applying the CAPM on a world basis, the ideal portfolio should contain each class of world assets in proportion to its prevalence in the world market. In this chapter, equities, bonds, cash, real estate, and metals are referred to as *asset classes*. A group of different assets or asset classes from one section of the world is referred to as a *portfolio*—for example, we refer to the U.S. bond portfolio or the portfolio of all foreign assets. All world investments, then, are included in the world portfolio. No actual individual or institutional investor, of course, would hold this "ideal" world portfolio. Investors have individual risk preferences, tax considerations, information costs, and time horizons. Nevertheless, by examining the world portfolio, investors can upgrade their understanding of capital market returns and expand their investment horizons.

The World Portfolio

In the spirit of the CAPM, returns on various classes of world assets for the last quarter century were collected, and these returns were weighted according to each class's proportion of total world investments. This "world" analysis covers some but not all capital markets: the United States, 12 European countries, Japan, Hong Kong, Singapore, Canada, and Australia. These countries were chosen because they encompass most of the world's financial wealth and because consistent data on them are readily available.

The CAPM says that each asset's risk relative to the *entire* market is the only determinant of its return. The analysis herein goes beyond the CAPM to look at the relative returns and risks of various components and subcomponents of the world market. Specifically, portfolios of world assets, U.S. assets, and foreign assets, as well as numerous asset classes, have been constructed, and returns on these are computed and analyzed.

The World Asset Horse Race: Winners and Losers

If specific classes of world assets are thought of as horses in an international horse race, the first prize goes to Asian equities, with more than 15 percent compound annual return over a quarter of a century. Coming in second are U.S. over-the-counter (OTC) equities, and third, U.S. farm

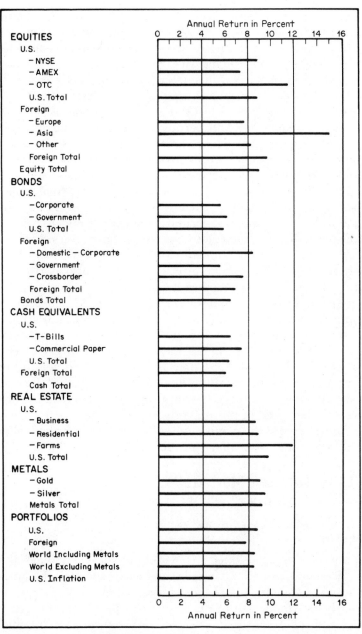

Figure 3.1. The world asset racing final—compound annual returns on world asset classes and portfolios, 1960–1984.

real estate, both with over 10 percent annual returns. Monetary metals, including both gold and silver, were the gambler's favorites in the 1970s because of their high, though volatile, returns. But metal prices fell sharply from 1981 to 1984, and, over the entire period, this horse had a mediocre record. The last horse to cross the finish line in the 25-year period was U.S. Treasury bonds. Despite the explosive 1982 bond rally, they earned a compound annual rate of return of only about 5 percent. Treasuries and long-term U.S. corporate bonds were the only entries to run slower than the pacesetting horse, U.S. inflation, which also ran at an annual rate of about 5 percent. Worse yet, both were riskier than the traditional safe bet, cash equivalents. The "racing finals" are illustrated in Figure 3.1. Of course, this race is never actually "final," since new results are always coming in, such as the dramatic stock and bond returns and the poor farm real estate returns of the mid-1980s.

Investors found it profitable to diversify over the period. Those who held a world portfolio had a better risk-return profile than those who limited themselves to a single asset class. The world portfolio had a compound return of over 8 percent.

"Race results" are presented statistically in Table 3.1. (All returns were computed by converting data in local currencies to U.S. dollars at year end, and then computing a U.S.-dollar-adjusted return.) Notice that both the arithmetic and geometric mean returns on various asset classes are shown for the 1960–1984 time period. When comparing returns over more than one period, the geometric mean, which is the same as a compound rate of return, is more appropriate then the arithmetic mean, for reasons described in the appendix to this chapter.

Let's now explore the composition of the world and regional portfolios, and the asset classes that they include.

World Investment Markets and Their Returns

Physical and Financial Capital of the World

Components of the developed free world's physical and financial capital are depicted in Figure 3.2. Using broad-brush estimates, this amounted to almost $28 trillion in 1984. Foreign real estate is the largest component of the portfolio, about $10 trillion or 37 percent of the total. Automobiles and other consumer durables also comprise a substantial portion of world investments, about 13 percent. Foreign assets make up a larger share of world investments than U.S. assets. Even so, only 17 of the most important industrial countries were used to make these foreign estimates. Other countries also have substantial physical and financial capital; were these to be included, the U.S. slices would become smaller.

Table 3.1. Total Annual Returns on World Asset Classes and Portfolios, 1960–1984

	Compound Return	Arithmetic Mean	Standard Deviation
Equities			
United States			
NYSE	8.71%	9.99%	16.30%
Amex	7.28	9.95	23.49
OTC	11.47	13.88	22.42
United States Total	8.81	10.20	16.89
Foreign			
Europe	7.83	8.94	15.58
Asia	15.14	18.42	30.74
Other	8.14	10.21	20.88
Foreign Total	9.84	11.02	16.07
Equities Total	9.08	10.21	15.28
Bonds			
United States			
Corporate			
Intermediate-term	6.37	6.80	7.15
Long-term	5.03	5.58	11.26
Corporate Total*	5.35	5.75	9.63
Government			
Treasury Notes	6.32	6.44	5.27
Treasury Bonds	4.70	5.11	9.70
U.S. Agencies	6.88	7.04	6.15
Government Total	5.91	6.10	6.43
United States Total	5.70	5.93	7.16
Foreign			
Corporate Domestic	8.35	8.58	7.26
Government Domestic	5.79	6.04	7.41
Crossborder	7.51	7.66	5.76
Foreign Total	6.80	7.01	6.88
Bonds Total	6.36	6.50	5.56

	Compound Return	Arithmetic Mean	Standard Deviation
Cash Equivalents			
United States			
U.S. Treasury Bills	6.25%	6.29%	3.10%
Commercial Paper	7.03	7.08	3.20
U.S. Cash Total	6.49	6.54	3.22
Foreign	6.00	6.23	7.10
Cash Total	6.38	6.42	2.92
Real Estate**			
Business	8.49	8.57	4.16
Residential	8.86	8.93	3.77
Farms	10.77	11.09	8.55
Real Estate Total	9.26	9.49	3.45
Metals			
Gold	9.08	12.62	29.87
Silver	9.14	20.51	75.34
Metals Total	9.11	12.63	29.69
U.S. Market Wealth Portfolio	8.53	8.65	5.08
Foreign Market Wealth Portfolio	7.76	8.09	8.48
World Market Wealth Portfolio			
Excluding metals	8.27	8.40	5.27
Including metals	8.32	8.48	5.84
U.S. Inflation Rate	5.24	5.30	3.60

* Including preferred stock.
** United States only.

Source: Roger G. Ibbotson, Laurence B. Siegel, and Kathryn S. Love, "World Wealth: Market Values and Returns," *Journal of Portfolio Management*, Fall 1985.

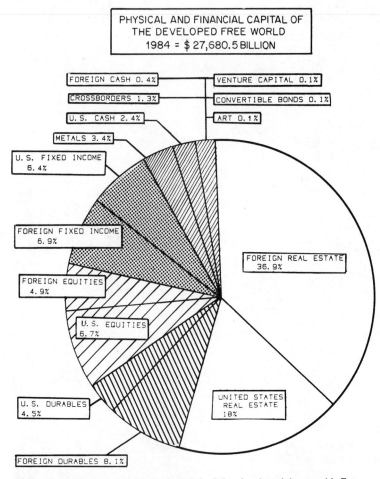

PHYSICAL AND FINANCIAL CAPITAL OF
THE DEVELOPED FREE WORLD
1984 = $ 27,680.5 BILLION

FOREIGN CASH 0. 4%

VENTURE CAPITAL 0.1%

CROSSBORDERS 1. 3%

CONVERTIBLE BONDS 0. 1%

U. S. CASH 2. 4%

ART 0.1%

METALS 3. 4%

U. S. FIXED INCOME
6. 4%

FOREIGN FIXED INCOME
6. 9%

FOREIGN REAL ESTATE
36. 9%

FOREIGN EQUITIES
4. 9%

U. S. EQUITIES
6. 7%

U. S. DURABLES
4. 5%

UNITED STATES
REAL ESTATE
18%

FOREIGN DURABLES 8. 1%

Figure 3.2. Physical and financial capital of the developed free world. Estimates are as of year-end 1984. (*Source: Roger G. Ibbotson, Laurence B. Siegel, and Kathryn S. Love, "World Wealth: Market Values and Returns,"* The Journal of Portfolio Management, *Fall 1985.*)

U.S. Investments

The U.S. portfolio of investment assets is the focus of Figure 3.3. Real estate represents a large portion, almost 54 percent of all U.S. investments. Next largest, over one-sixth of the pie, is the New York Stock Exchange; this generous slice indicates the importance of these equities in the U.S. economy. The prevalence of federal debt over corporate debt is also illustrated; debt of the federal government and its agencies makes up over three times as large a slice as corporate debt.

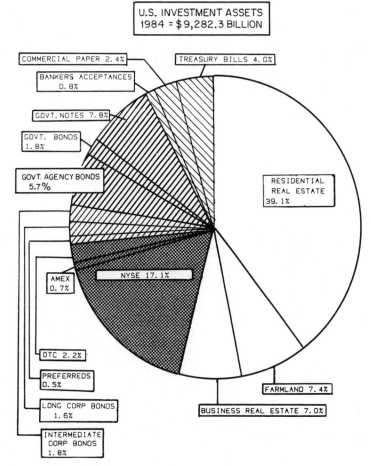

Figure 3.3. U.S. investment assets. (*Source: Roger G. Ibbotson, Laurence B. Siegel, and Kathryn S. Love, "World Wealth: Market Values and Returns," The Journal of Portfolio Management, Fall 1985.*)

Asset Returns

Total returns on five classes of world assets—cash, bonds, equities, metals, and U.S. real estate—are linked to form cumulative wealth indexes, which are graphed in Figure 3.4. The indexes are set to $1 at the beginning of 1960. Foreign real estate returns are not included because of measurement difficulties. Of these five large classes, U.S. real estate has the highest cumulative wealth index, $9.54 as of 1984. But real estate just barely beat world metals and world equities, which had indexes of

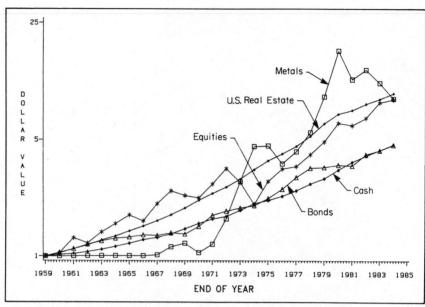

Figure 3.4. Cumulative wealth indexes of world asset classes. (Year-end 1959 = $1.) (*Source: Roger G. Ibbotson, Laurence B. Siegel, and Kathryn S. Love, "World Wealth: Market Values and Returns,"* The Journal of Portfolio Management, *Fall 1985.*)

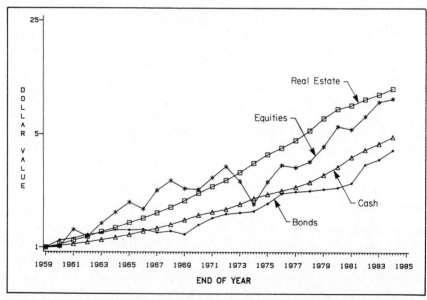

Figure 3.5. Cumulative wealth indexes of U.S. asset classes. (Year-end 1959 = $1.) (*Source: Roger G. Ibbotson, Laurence B. Siegel, and Kathryn S. Love, "World Wealth: Market Values and Returns,"* The Journal of Portfolio Management, *Fall 1985.*)

$8.85 and $8.77 respectively. Bringing up the rear are world cash and world bonds, both of which had cumulative wealth indexes of about $4.70.

In the U.S. market, shown in Figure 3.5, cumulative returns look about the same as in the world market. As before, real estate and equities head the list; cash and bonds show up at the bottom, although here bonds trail cash by almost a dollar due to rising interest rates over the period. Although inflation is not drawn on the graph, cash returns tracked the U.S. inflation rate closely.

The Relationships among the Classes

Correlation Measures

The interrelationships among the classes are as important as the average returns. Such interrelationships suggest how various classes of assets are affected by risk, and how the investor can minimize these risks. Here again, the five major classes of assets—stocks, bonds, cash, real estate, and metals—and regional portfolios are examined. (Statistical terms used in this section are defined in the appendix to this chapter.) Looking at the results in Table 3.2, the highest correlations are with other assets of the same class. For example, U.S. Treasury bonds have a 0.912 correlation with U.S. long-term corporate bonds, presumably because both types of bonds are affected in a similar way by interest rate changes. Like bonds, the classes of equities, cash, real estate, and metals exhibit high correlations within their components.

Some classes of world assets are also significantly correlated with other classes. World equities and world bonds have a correlation coefficient of approximately 0.155. Gold, which is sometimes considered a form of cash, is substantially correlated with world cash. Real estate is uncorrelated with equities and almost uncorrelated with bonds, but highly correlated with cash and metals. The higher correlations probably reflect inflation's influence on real estate returns and the tendency of tangible assets to follow similar trends.

Betas on Other Asset Classes

The *CAPM beta* describes the risk of an asset or security relative to the market, usually meaning the stock market. However, this is only one way of measuring expected return for a given level of risk. A more neutral procedure is to compute the beta of an asset class or component relative to a more comprehensive class or portfolio, as was done in Table 3.3. Such betas are preferable to a CAPM beta because they estimate the

Table 3.2. World Asset Returns: A Correlation Matrix

	NYSE	AMEX	OTC	U.S. TOTAL EQUITIES	EUROPE EQUITIES	ASIA EQUITIES	OTHER EQUITIES	FOREIGN TOTAL EQUITIES	WORLD EQUITIES	U.S. TREASURY NOTES	U.S. TREASURY BONDS	U.S. AGENCIES	U.S. TOTAL GOVT BONDS
NYSE	1.000												
AMEX	0.851	1.000											
OTC	0.900	0.897	1.000										
U.S. EQUITIES	0.997	0.883	0.629	1.000									
EUROPE EQUITIES	0.618	0.689	0.631	0.640	1.000								
ASIA EQUITIES	0.237	0.123	0.244	0.237	0.391	1.000							
OTHER EQUITIES	0.792	0.848	0.766	0.807	0.731	0.320	1.000						
FOREIGN EQUITIES	0.656	0.657	0.666	0.672	0.908	0.695	0.765	1.000					
WORLD TOTAL EQUITIES	0.955	0.879	0.914	0.964	0.787	0.409	0.853	0.841	1.000				
U.S. TREASURY NOTES	0.105	-0.102	-0.117	0.068	-0.159	-0.108	-0.252	-0.192	-0.037	1.000			
U.S. TREASURY BONDS	0.091	-0.153	-0.094	-0.030	-0.130	-0.005	-0.266	-0.165	-0.041	0.904	1.000		
U.S. AGENCIES	0.007	-0.201	-0.187	-0.006	-0.280	-0.178	-0.342	-0.327	-0.156	0.962	0.904	1.000	
U.S. TOTAL GOVT BONDS	-0.033	-0.183	-0.189		-0.201	-0.067	-0.296	-0.226	-0.105	0.972	0.950	0.964	1.000
U.S. INTERMEDIATE TERM CORP BONDS	0.361	0.058	0.110	0.302	0.095	0.045	-0.028	0.072	0.242	0.900	0.865	0.848	0.887
U.S. LONG TERM CORP BONDS	0.361	0.083	0.132	0.323	0.117	0.033	-0.033	0.052	0.219	0.858	0.912	0.808	0.859
U.S. TOTAL CORP BONDS	0.206	-0.047	-0.031	0.166	-0.045	-0.007	-0.019	-0.019	0.043	0.864	0.902	0.809	0.863
U.S. TOTAL BONDS	0.044	-0.025	0.107	0.050	0.315	0.269	-0.160	-0.074	0.015		0.256	0.915	0.967
FOREIGN DOMESTIC CORP BONDS	0.010	0.078	0.097	0.024	0.345	0.084	-0.028	0.314	0.156	0.035	0.172	-0.008	0.085
FOREIGN DOMESTIC GOVT BONDS	0.270	0.116	0.172	0.255	0.253	0.154	0.058	0.255	0.172	0.061	0.190	0.044	0.117
FOREIGN CROSSBORDER BONDS	0.042	0.067	0.112	0.052	0.343	0.153	0.017	0.215	0.249	0.560	0.716	0.552	0.607
FOREIGN TOTAL BONDS	0.136	0.035	0.069	0.124	0.248	0.122	0.028	0.281	0.144	0.097	0.239	0.072	0.153
WORLD TOTAL BONDS							-0.041	0.194	0.155	0.511	0.619	0.473	0.561
U.S. BUSINESS REAL ESTATE	0.159	0.227	0.138	0.164	0.268	0.218	0.243	0.332	0.233	0.262	0.036	0.179	0.206
U.S. RESIDENTIAL REAL ESTATE	0.123	0.213	0.090	0.125	0.207	-0.080	0.356	0.141	-0.133	0.068	-0.039	0.095	0.066
U.S. FARM REAL ESTATE	-0.164	-0.093	-0.223	-0.171	-0.097	-0.003	-0.063	-0.065	-0.139	-0.315	-0.256	-0.273	-0.267
U.S. REAL ESTATE TOTAL	0.054	0.166	0.006	0.054	0.156	-0.033	0.288	0.129	0.083	-0.051	-0.138	-0.024	-0.040
U.S. TREASURY BILLS	-0.055	-0.063	-0.160	-0.070	-0.169	-0.157	-0.101	-0.153	-0.114	0.395	0.111	0.328	0.325
U.S. COMMERCIAL PAPER	-0.112	-0.130	-0.210	-0.127	-0.211	-0.159	-0.150	-0.199	-0.174	0.394	0.115	0.348	0.330
U.S. TOTAL CASH	-0.064	-0.080	-0.170	-0.079	-0.178	0.009	-0.112	-0.162	-0.125	0.400	0.119	0.340	0.332
FOREIGN TOTAL CASH	-0.393	-0.355	-0.289	-0.386	-0.127	-0.115	-0.270	-0.107	-0.311	-0.203	-0.183	-0.154	-0.143
WORLD TOTAL CASH	-0.225	-0.240	-0.284	-0.238	-0.212		-0.225	-0.180	-0.242	0.270	0.032	0.237	0.236
GOLD	-0.094	-0.024	-0.067	-0.088	0.032	0.046	0.140	0.044	-0.058	-0.277	-0.252	-0.178	-0.206
SILVER	-0.093	0.374	0.142	0.116	0.052	0.181	0.410	-0.020	0.070	-0.131	-0.140	-0.064	-0.109
WORLD TOTAL METALS	-0.093	-0.011	-0.064	-0.086	0.032	0.036	0.152	0.039	-0.058	-0.279	-0.253	-0.177	-0.207
U.S. MARKET WEALTH PORTFOLIO	0.915	0.837	0.831	0.917	0.605	0.209	0.754	0.626	0.886	0.214	0.162	0.139	0.152
FOREIGN MARKET WEALTH PORTFOLIO	0.493	0.498	0.544	0.510	0.823	0.602	0.556	0.865	0.678	-0.086	0.021	-0.201	-0.083
WORLD MARKET WEALTH PORTFOLIO													
WORLD MARKET WEALTH PORT (W/O METALS)	0.853	0.799	0.814	0.861	0.782	0.406	0.765	0.815	0.914	0.109	0.119	-0.007	0.066
WORLD MARKET WEALTH PORT (W/ METALS)	0.747	0.723	0.727	0.757	0.706	0.351	0.753	0.732	0.805	-0.010	0.016	-0.059	-0.023

Table 1

	U.S. INTERMED. CORP BONDS	U.S. LONG CORP BONDS	U.S. TOTAL CORP BONDS	U.S. TOTAL BONDS	FOREIGN CORP BONDS	FOREIGN GOVT BONDS	CROSS-BORDER BONDS	FOREIGN TOTAL BONDS	WORLD TOTAL BONDS	BUS. REAL ESTATE	RESIDENTIAL STRUCTURES	FARM REAL ESTATE	TOTAL U.S. REAL ESTATE
U.S. INTERMEDIATE TERM CORP BONDS	1.000												
U.S. LONG TERM CORP BONDS	0.941	1.000											
U.S. TOTAL CORP BONDS	0.960	0.996	1.000										
U.S. TOTAL BONDS	0.956	0.962	0.962	1.000									
FOREIGN DOMESTIC CORP BONDS	0.211	0.263	0.264	0.180	1.000								
FOREIGN DOMESTIC GOVT BONDS	0.203	0.269	0.266	0.192	0.890	1.000							
FOREIGN CROSSBORDER BONDS	0.741	0.814	0.807	0.721	0.626	0.628	1.000						
FOREIGN TOTAL BONDS	0.260	0.326	0.323	0.242	0.950	0.985	0.689	1.000					
WORLD TOTAL BONDS	0.635	0.693	0.692	0.646	0.829	0.860	0.866	0.895	1.000				
U.S. BUSINESS REAL ESTATE	0.335	0.107	0.152	0.192	0.165	0.249	0.203	0.228	0.256	1.000			
U.S. RESIDENTIAL REAL ESTATE	0.085	-0.039	-0.030	0.017	0.091	0.293	0.108	0.225	0.191	0.493	1.000		
U.S. FARM REAL ESTATE	-0.252	-0.255	-0.273	-0.274	0.176	0.103	0.049	0.125	-0.013	0.016	0.214	1.000	
U.S. REAL ESTATE TOTAL	-0.004	-0.129	-0.123	-0.082	0.164	0.303	0.123	0.256	0.172	0.518	0.916	0.570	1.000
U.S. TREASURY BILLS	0.336	0.094	0.135	0.244	-0.269	-0.224	-0.060	-0.240	-0.091	0.685	0.428	-0.053	0.389
U.S. COMMERCIAL PAPER	0.313	0.070	0.108	0.230	-0.289	-0.232	-0.078	-0.234	-0.108	0.655	0.462	-0.040	0.415
U.S. TOTAL CASH	-0.139	-0.206	-0.236	-0.277	-0.225	-0.217	-0.054	-0.217	-0.085	0.681	0.447	-0.046	0.405
FOREIGN TOTAL CASH	-0.191	-0.225	-0.225	-0.192	0.616	0.617	0.101	0.608	0.393	0.231	0.317	-0.306	0.399
WORLD TOTAL CASH	0.122	-0.005	0.029	0.141	0.048	0.080	0.007	0.065	0.106	0.705	0.528	0.096	0.529
GOLD	-0.235	-0.316	-0.323	-0.280	0.001	0.107	-0.046	0.062	-0.079	0.219	0.586	0.517	0.684
SILVER	-0.150	-0.177	-0.187	-0.153	-0.286	-0.054	-0.076	-0.136	-0.177	0.188	0.532	0.351	0.580
WORLD TOTAL METALS	-0.239	-0.318	-0.326	-0.282	-0.011	-0.104	-0.047	-0.056	-0.085	0.220	0.596	0.526	0.696
U.S. MARKET WEALTH PORTFOLIO	0.446	0.367	0.393	0.284	0.153	0.171	0.395	0.191	0.288	0.394	0.422	-0.019	0.371
FOREIGN MARKET WEALTH PORTFOLIO	0.192	0.221	0.236	0.080	0.723	0.687	0.517	0.718	0.603	0.329	0.174	-0.008	0.177
WORLD MARKET WEALTH PORT (W/O METALS)	0.390	0.354	0.377	0.231	0.431	0.428	0.504	0.455	0.471	0.407	0.365	-0.014	0.332
WORLD MARKET WEALTH PORT (W/ METALS)	0.238	0.193	0.207	0.093	0.380	0.426	0.404	0.429	0.389	0.390	0.552	0.133	0.531

Table 2

	U.S. TREASURY BILLS	U.S. COMMERCIAL PAPER	U.S. TOTAL CASH	FOREIGN TOTAL CASH	WORLD TOTAL CASH	GOLD	SILVER	WORLD TOTAL METALS	U.S. MARKET WEALTH PORTFOLIO	FOREIGN MARKET WEALTH PORTFOLIO	WORLD MARKET EXCL. METALS	WORLD MARKET INCL. METALS
U.S. TREASURY BILLS	1.000											
U.S. COMMERCIAL PAPER	0.990	1.000										
U.S. TOTAL CASH	0.999	0.995	1.000									
FOREIGN TOTAL CASH	-0.008	0.033	0.010	1.000								
WORLD TOTAL CASH	0.881	0.895	0.891	0.460	1.000							
GOLD	0.179	0.256	0.210	0.419	0.366	1.000						
SILVER	0.125	0.127	0.123	-0.203	-0.014	0.438	1.000					
WORLD TOTAL METALS	0.177	0.253	0.207	0.401	0.355	0.999	0.477	1.000				
U.S. MARKET WEALTH PORTFOLIO	0.133	0.088	0.130	-0.233	0.013	0.104	0.291	0.111	1.000			
FOREIGN MARKET WEALTH PORTFOLIO	-0.254	-0.298	-0.258	0.218	-0.122	0.025	-0.110	0.018	0.533	1.000		
WORLD MARKET WEALTH PORT (W/O METALS)	-0.033	-0.083	-0.037	-0.059	-0.053	0.075	0.142	0.077	0.925	0.812	1.000	
WORLD MARKET WEALTH PORT (W/ METALS)	-0.014	-0.027	-0.004	0.105	0.046	0.427	0.283	0.427	0.873	0.727	0.924	1.000

Source: Roger G. Ibbotson, Laurence B. Siegel, and Kathryn S. Love, "World Wealth: Market Values and Returns," Journal of Portfolio Management, Fall 1985.

sensitivity of one class or portfolio relative to another, not to a prespeci-
fied market, such as the stock market. In other words, while CAPM betas
typically measure risk relative to one benchmark—the stock market—
betas computed here measure how a subclass relates to an overall class.

To compute such a beta, the excess return of an asset (i.e., its return in
excess of the U.S. risk-free rate) is compared to the excess return of the
broader asset class, using the statistical technique called regression. For
example, the excess return of U.S. equities is regressed on the excess
return of world equities. Likewise, each class's excess return is regressed
on the excess return of the world portfolio. Thus, world equities are also
regressed on the world portfolio. The results are shown in Table 3.3,
with the beta column giving each asset's risk relative to major asset
classes and various regional portfolios, or to the world portfolio itself.

The statistical analysis permits a number of conclusions. (The statistical terms used as column headings are defined in the appendix to this
chapter.) As measured by beta, U.S. equities, with a beta of 1.05, are
slightly more risky than foreign equities. Also by that measure, world
equities are the most risky component of the capital market relative to
world wealth excluding metals, with a beta of 2.32. Turning to bonds,
world bonds had low risk, with a beta of 0.67 relative to the world
portfolio excluding metals. This was about one-third as large as world
equities, also compared to the world portfolio excluding metals.

As measured by their R squareds, the various equity markets had
reasonably high correlations with their overall classes. The sole exception was Asian equities, with its R squared of 0.484. Metals correlated on
world wealth had a positive beta of 1.53, although metals are usually
thought to be countercyclical.

Composition of the World's Physical and Financial Capital

Inclusions and Exclusions

As defined in this chapter, the world portfolio includes equities, bonds,
cash, metals, and U.S. real estate. Yet these do not represent all assets in
the world "market." Huge wealth categories have been left out, while at
the same time other categories that are not properly considered wealth
have been included.

Even if the analysis is restricted to physical and financial capital, there
are still other omissions. Except for the rough estimate in Figure 3.2, the
value of foreign real estate is ignored due to measurement difficulties.
Municipal bonds are dropped because their tax-exempt status affects
their returns. Proprietorships, partnerships, and many small corpora-

Table 3.3. Regression Results for Asset Class Returns in Excess of U.S. Treasury Bill Rates, 1960–1984

Dependent Variable	Independent Variable	Alpha ($)	Alpha T Statistic	Beta	Standard Error of Beta	Adjusted R²	Standard Deviation of Residuals	1st Order Autocorr. of Residuals
U.S. Equities-NYSE	U.S. Equities	-0.06	-0.22	0.96	0.02	0.99	1.32%	0.04
AMEX	U.S. Equities	-1.10	-0.47	1.24	0.13	0.78	11.54	0.13
OTC	U.S. Equities	-2.73	-1.56	1.24	0.10	0.87	8.51	-0.05
U.S. Total Equities	World Equities	-0.22	-0.23	1.05	0.06	0.93	4.72	-0.05
Europe Equities	Foreign Equities	-1.57	-1.10	0.89	0.08	0.83	6.85	-0.48
Asia Equities	Foreign Equities	5.85	1.22	1.32	0.27	0.48	23.00	-0.15
Other Equities	Foreign Equities	-0.76	-0.26	0.99	0.17	0.59	14.02	-0.06
Foreign Equities	World Equities	1.19	0.64	0.90	0.11	0.72	9.10	-0.00
World Equities	World Wealth excl. metals	-1.14	-0.74	2.32	0.23	0.80	7.19	0.26
U.S. Corporate Bonds	U.S. Total Bonds	-0.05	-0.10	1.33	0.07	0.93	2.56	-0.28
U.S. Government Bonds	U.S. Total Bonds	0.12	0.36	0.84	0.05	0.94	1.60	-0.28
U.S. Total Bonds	World Total Bonds	-0.52	-0.47	0.72	0.17	0.43	5.46	0.20
Foreign Corporate Bonds	Foreign Total Bonds	1.56	3.31	1.02	0.06	0.93	2.35	-0.08
Foreign Government Bonds	Foreign Total Bonds	-1.00	-3.66	1.04	0.03	0.98	1.36	0.08
Crossborder Bonds	Foreign Total Bonds	0.91	1.04	0.64	0.11	0.60	4.33	0.12
Foreign Total Bonds	World Total Bonds	0.47	0.77	1.16	0.09	0.87	3.08	0.10
World Total Bonds	World Wealth excl. metals	-1.24	-1.08	0.67	0.18	0.36	5.39	0.17
U.S. Cash	World Cash	0.25	6.22	0.02	0.03	-0.02	0.20	0.26
Foreign Cash	World Cash	-0.73	-2.94	5.20	0.17	0.98	1.23	-0.26
World Cash	World Wealth excl. metals	0.05	0.16	0.04	0.06	-0.02	1.52	0.03
U.S. Business Real Estate	U.S. Real Estate	1.30	1.65	0.31	0.16	0.10	2.95	0.20
U.S. Residential Real Estate	U.S. Real Estate	-0.36	-0.87	0.94	0.09	0.83	1.55	0.11
U.S. Farm Real Estate	U.S. Real Estate	0.44	0.26	1.68	0.35	0.48	6.33	0.18
U.S. Real Estate	World Wealth excl. metals	2.52	3.71	0.31	0.10	0.25	3.20	0.57
U.S. Equities	U.S. Market Wealth	-3.17	-2.10	2.88	0.25	0.85	6.91	0.35
U.S. Bonds	U.S. Market Wealth	-1.34	-0.88	0.40	0.25	0.06	7.00	0.12
U.S. Cash	U.S. Market Wealth	0.28	6.58	-0.01	0.01	0.05	0.19	0.00
U.S. Real Estate	U.S. Market Wealth	2.42	3.35	0.32	0.12	0.20	3.31	0.62
U.S. Market Wealth	World Wealth excl. metals	0.60	1.51	0.85	0.06	0.89	1.86	-0.06
Foreign Equities	Foreign Market Wealth	2.05	1.14	1.50	0.18	0.74	8.80	0.06
Foreign Total Bonds	Foreign Market Wealth	-0.48	-0.46	0.67	0.11	0.61	5.21	0.09
Foreign Cash	Foreign Market Wealth	-0.62	-0.41	0.31	0.15	0.12	7.45	0.05
Foreign Market Wealth	World Wealth excl. metals	-1.22	-1.19	1.38	0.16	0.76	4.83	-0.08
World Wealth excl. metals	World Wealth incl. metals	0.19	0.43	0.88	0.07	0.88	2.16	0.14
Gold	Metals	-0.04	-0.14	1.00	0.01	0.10	1.43	-0.42
Silver	Metals	6.61	0.47	1.20	0.47	0.19	69.07	-0.37
Metals	World Wealth incl. metals	2.89	0.48	1.53	0.86	0.08	28.66	0.39

Source: Roger G. Ibbotson, Laurence B. Siegel, and Kathryn S. Love, "World Wealth: Market Values and Returns," Journal of Portfolio Management, Fall 1985.

tions are excluded. Personal holdings such as automobiles, cash balances, and the capital goods of consumers are omitted in all but the description of physical and financial capital in Figure 3.2. Not only has a large proportion of the world's investments been ignored, but it is also unclear how large the excluded portion is.

Yet the inclusions may misrepresent the world portfolio even more than the omissions. U.S. and foreign government debts are included, although not backed dollar for dollar by government-owned assets such as parks and bridges, but rather by claims on future taxes. Also, some corporations own parts of other corporations, causing double counting in the equity sector. Thus, the portfolio's inclusions also distort this picture of world investment.

While the calculations only provide a rough indication of the world's physical and financial capital, they nevertheless present market values and returns for asset classes that make up a large and important part of it. Moreover, these assets are the most marketable and the most widely held by investors.

Construction of the U.S., Foreign, and World Portfolios

The general classes of world assets—cash, bonds, equities, metals, and real estate—are constructed using published indexes from various sources. The class of U.S. equities is comprised of three principal equity markets—the New York Stock Exchange and the American Stock Exchange (AMEX), along with the OTC market, each measured separately and then aggregated using market-value weighting. Foreign stocks are a value-weighted aggregate of returns in the countries, with subportfolios representing Europe, Asia, and other non-U.S. markets.

United States bonds include corporate issues (intermediate- and long-term bonds plus preferred stocks) and government issues (Treasury notes, Treasury bonds, and agency issues). Foreign bonds are all bonds issued by foreign corporations and governments; this category includes bonds traded within a country's capital markets, as well as crossborder bonds outside any one country's markets. Cash includes U.S. issues (Treasury bills, commercial paper, and bankers' acceptances) and those of 10 foreign countries. United States real estate is composed of three indexes that represent the business, residential, and farm sectors. Monetary metals include the world's supply of gold and the noncommunist world's supply of silver.

The aggregate market values of the classes serve as weights for the purpose of constructing value-weighted portfolios, including those for the United States, foreign countries, and the world. Returns on these portfolios are then measured and used to form cumulative wealth indexes for various parts of the world.

Conclusion

This concludes the overview of world assets and the world portfolio. U.S. investors who want to diversify can see from the size of international markets that foreign assets are far too significant to be ignored. Furthermore, because there have been spectacular returns on some assets abroad, these investors may miss major profit opportunities if they do not maintain a global perspective.

A global view is consistent with the way the world economy is evolving. National boundaries become less important as, for example, securities are traded in round-the-clock markets comprised of the New York, London, Tokyo, and Singapore stock exchanges. Furthermore, the volume of international trade is growing, and nations are becoming more specialized. Consequently, each country's domestic portfolio, including that of the United States, is becoming less diversified. To achieve full diversification, investors must now cross international borders.

This chapter provides a snapshot of the developed free world's physical and financial capital. Like all photos, the snapshot represents only one point on the continuum of time. In the twentieth century, change and innovation have revolutionized the world's capital markets. Formerly nontraditional assets, such as real estate, are becoming "securitized" and, consequently, a more important part of the world's investment smorgasbord. As new asset classes grow in importance, investors would do well to learn more about them.

The rest of this book covers investment markets for many assets, both in the United States and abroad. A historical look at returns on various assets shows how each performs in different economic circumstances, and how each does relative to other investment choices. That information, along with a description of the asset's market characteristics, is the basis for investment advice that a financial economist can provide.

Suggested Reading

Brinson, Gary P., Jeffrey J. Diermeier, and L. Randolph Hood, Jr.: "The Multiple Markets Index," First Chicago Investment Advisors White Paper, Chicago, 1983. The Multiple Markets Index is updated periodically. Tracks the world market from the pension manager's point of view.

Ibbotson, Roger G., Laurence B. Siegel, and Kathryn S. Love: "World Wealth: Market Values and Returns," *Journal of Portfolio Management*, Fall 1985, pp. 4–23. The article upon which this chapter is largely based.

Appendix: Definitions of Basic Statistical Terms

The *arithmetic mean* of a number of annual returns is simply an average of the various return numbers. For example, if returns were +50 percent and −10 percent, the arithmetic mean is the sum of the two numbers divided by 2, or +20 percent. The *geometric mean,* or *compound annual return,* on the other hand, is computed by multiplying 1 plus each of the annual returns together successively and then taking the "n^{th}" root of this product, where n is the number of years, and then subtracting 1. For example, the geometric mean of +50 percent and −10 percent equals $\sqrt{1.5 \times 0.9} - 1 = 0.162$, i.e., 16.2 percent.

When comparing returns over more than one period, the geometric mean is more appropriate than the arithmetic mean. A simple example illustrates why this is so. Suppose $1 were invested in a common stock portfolio that experiences successive annual returns of +50 percent and −50 percent. At the end of the first year, the portfolio is worth $1.50. At the end of the second year, however, the portfolio's value drops to $0.75. The annual arithmetic mean is 0 percent (the average of +50 and −50), whereas the annual geometric mean is −13.4 percent (the annual rate of return required for a dollar to fall to $0.75 in 2 years). Naturally, it is the geometric mean that more directly measures the change in wealth over more than one period. On the other hand, the arithmetic mean serves as a better representation of typical performance over a single period. Note that the arithmetic mean is always greater than the geometric mean; in Table 3.1, for example, the arithmetic mean for gold is 12.62 percent, whereas the geometric mean (compound return) is only 9.08 percent.

The *standard deviation* of an asset's returns is a measure of the asset's risk. It is calculated as the square root of the average squared deviation around the arithmetic mean return. The standard deviation may be understood as the dispersion of actual returns around the mean return. Since the standard deviation measures how much an asset's return fluctuates, it is often used as a measure of risk. For example, in Table 3.1, OTC U.S. equities had a higher standard deviation than NYSE-listed equities: 22.4 percent versus 16.3 percent. Thus, OTC equities were riskier.

The *correlation coefficient* of two assets indicates the sensitivity of returns on one class or portfolio to those of another. Perfect comovement is indicated by a correlation of 1.0. A high correlation between two assets, say above 0.3, indicates that returns on the assets tend to move closely together. A zero correlation indicates no relationship, while a negative correlation indicates movement in opposite directions. In Table 3.2, returns on the NYSE are highly correlated with those on the AMEX, at a level of 0.851; however, NYSE returns move in the opposite direction from U.S. farm real estate, with a correlation of -0.164.

The *beta* of an asset is its level of risk relative to that of the class or portfolio on which it is regressed. An asset with a beta of 1 has the same level of economy risk as the class or portfolio to which the asset is compared; assets with betas above 1 have more of this risk. (Economy risk is the risk of stock price fluctuation due to changes in the profitability of the corporate sector of the economy.) All the examples on this page refer to Table 3.3. Asian equities, with a beta of 1.32 on foreign equities, have an economy risk greater than the total of foreign equities. Those with a beta below 1, such as NYSE-listed U.S. equities, with a beta of 0.96 on total U.S. equities, are less risky than this latter, more general, class.

The *standard error of a beta* is the square root of the variance of the estimation error of the beta. If the number of observations is large, the estimated standard error can be viewed as normally distributed; as such, two-thirds of the true value will be within one standard error of the beta.

The *alpha* of an asset expresses its superior or inferior performance after adjusting for its beta on the relevant market class. Assets that beat the market or broader asset class on a beta-adjusted basis have positive alphas, and those that were beaten by the market or class have negative alphas. For example, returns on OTC equities exceed the beta-adjusted return on world equities, with an alpha of 2.73 percent per year.

The *alpha t statistic* is the estimated alpha divided by the standard error, defined above. *T* statistics greater than 1.96 are significant at the 5 percent level under standard assumptions. For example, the alpha *t* of foreign corporate bonds on foreign total bonds is 3.31.

The *R squared* is a measure of the percent of the variance in one variable that is explained by another. For example, while 93 percent of the variance of returns on U.S. equities is explained by world equity returns, foreign equity returns explain only 48 percent of the variance of returns on Asian equities. The *R* squared in a simple regression is merely the squared correlation coefficient of the two variables.

The *standard deviation of the residuals* is the estimate of the square root of the variance of the residuals. That estimate for silver is 69.07%.

The *first-order autocorrelation* is the correlation between the return in one period and the return in the prior period. Autocorrelation is also known as *serial correlation*. For example, the residuals from the regression of U.S. real estate returns on the U.S. market wealth portfolio are highly autocorrelated, at a level of 0.62.

4
Theories of Capital Market Returns

When the Duke of Wellington met Napoleon at the battle of Waterloo, the British financial markets were in a state of suspense. If the British were defeated, securities would plummet; if they won, securities would soar. Nathan Rothschild, the great international financier, cautiously began buying. By the time official news of British victory arrived, Rothschild had accumulated a mass of securities at bargain prices. They rocketed in value on arrival of the battle information, and Rothschild's fortune was many times multiplied. The wily Rothschild had beaten the market because his information source—carrier pigeons—had beaten the government couriers.

Investors today can still profit from access to information, skill in selecting and timing transactions, and careful analysis of market behavior. Even in the highly efficient U.S. stock market, financial economists are continually discovering anomalies, or angles, in which returns are substantially higher or lower than one would expect by looking at risk. One possible reason for the existence of anomalies is that there are hidden risks, or nonrisk costs such as information costs, that affect the equilibrium return on a stock. It is also possible that the market for various stocks, or the whole market, is in a state of disequilibrium, in which market prices differ from underlying value.

To explain how capital markets function, economists often assume that such markets are in equilibrium, i.e., that prices cause demand to equal supply. Many financial economists also believe that markets are efficient, which means that the market prices of capital assets reflect their true, underlying values. If markets are efficient, then active management of investments is unnecessary and one stock is much like another. In this chapter, this startling concept is explained, and then two major theories of capital market returns based on this hypothesis, the *capital asset pricing model* (CAPM) and *arbitrage pricing theory* (APT), are considered. In addition, a third framework, referred to as *new equilibrium theory* (NET), is discussed, and arguments are presented as to why markets might not actually be efficient.

Capital Market Theories

The Random Walk Hypothesis

Beginning in the late nineteenth century with Charles Dow, formulator of the *Dow theory,* many market analysts thought they could predict future stock prices by examining past transactions. Gradually they developed various systems, generally called technical analysis or charting, to foretell price trends. As early as 1900, academic researchers such as the French statistician Louis Bachelier began to suspect that past price movements did not greatly affect future movements. By the 1960s, numerous empirical tests of various technical procedures largely discredited such methods. In fact, results suggested that price movements were nearly random. One academic, Harry Roberts, even produced fake stock charts from random numbers. Chartists thought they could see all sorts of patterns in them, as well as buy and sell signals. Roberts demonstrated that random numbers do not look random, but they are nevertheless unpredictable.

The new theory proposed by academic researchers became known as the *random walk hypothesis.* Market analysts began to pay attention to these results when academics such as Eugene Fama proclaimed them widely in the investment community.

The Efficient Markets Hypothesis

During the 1960s, academics broadened the random walk hypothesis into a theory of capital market equilibrium, called the *efficient markets hypothesis.* According to this theory, if market prices do not follow patterns, then perhaps current prices already reflect whatever is knowable about the future. Thus, market prices would always be fair ex ante. Not only would investors be unable to use past price information to predict future trends, but even with access to inside information, they could not expect to beat the market.

If investors believed that returns were unpredictable and prices captured all information, they should behave very differently from typical investors. Even if investors felt that the efficient markets hypothesis were only partly true, they should change their investment behavior dramatically. In the stock market, they should minimize risk by diversifying; for example, they could match the market merely by holding the entire market portfolio. The prescription for the investor who believes the market is efficient is simple; the investor should buy, hold, and diversify.

Arguments for Efficiency of Capital Markets

The efficient markets hypothesis states that the price of an asset reflects all available information. In other words, prices reflect the true, underlying value of assets. This hypothesis is suggested by assuming that the capital market is perfectly competitive. Such a market is comprised of rational investors who all have the same information, who incur no transactions costs or taxes when trading, and who trade in a central, continuous auction market.

Investors in perfectly competitive markets immediately recognize mispricing of an asset or portfolio of assets and instantaneously take advantage of the profit opportunity. By such activities, they bring the market price back to the fair price. If unfair prices persisted, even for an instant, active investors could realize profits costlessly by selling any overpriced securities and using the proceeds to buy underpriced securities. This activity is called *arbitrage* and those who pursue it, *arbitrageurs*. Of course, in this setting, mispricing cannot occur even for an instant, since arbitrageurs, by standing ready to act as described, prevent arbitrage opportunities from arising.

Although real capital markets are not perfectly competitive, many financial economists believe that the efficient markets hypothesis may hold to some extent. Thus even if investors have different information, incur transaction costs, and do not trade exclusively in central markets, assets such as stocks may still be fairly priced on average.

Modeling Capital Markets

Using the idea of efficient markets, mathematical models of capital markets have been formulated which emphasize different pricing factors. The CAPM and APT are both equilibrium models in which investors obtain different returns according to the risks that they bear. With the CAPM, expected returns vary exclusively with *market risk*, or beta—the extent to which an asset's return responds to the return on the overall market. In APT, expected returns are a result of multiple factors. Both models are more specific than, but consistent with, the efficient markets hypothesis.

In tests of the random walk theories over the past 40 years, and of the efficient markets hypothesis over the past 20 years, researchers generally have been unable to reject the null hypothesis that capital markets are efficient. The null hypothesis, of course, has an inherent advantage over competing hypotheses because it is not rejected without statistically significant evidence to the contrary.

While academics have not yet disproved the efficient markets hypothesis, markets do not always behave as the theory predicts. For example, the theory suggests that since assets should be fairly priced, investors should receive higher returns only by taking commensurately greater risk. Yet empirical evidence suggests that some assets are priced inefficiently. When equity markets are analyzed using the CAPM, small-capitalization stocks and new equity issues earn excess returns, that is, higher returns than their risk indicates. These anomalies may be profit opportunities caused by the institutional environment or may indicate that the CAPM does not include all the factors that determine asset prices. Although there may be isolated price inefficiencies, most economists believe that the efficient markets hypothesis describes the world relatively well.

Now let's look more closely at the CAPM and APT and then consider returns in a broader framework that includes investor-specific costs.

The Capital Asset Pricing Model

Capital markets are *in equilibrium* when the quantity of each asset demanded equals the quantity of each asset supplied by the market. The price at which the supply of an asset equals the demand is that asset's *equilibrium price*.

Assumptions of the Model

The CAPM, first proposed by William Sharpe and John Lintner, describes such a market equilibrium. Like the efficient market hypothesis, the CAPM is usually explained in the context of a perfectly competitive, frictionless capital market. In this market, risk-averse investors incur no transaction costs or taxes. Also, the market is composed of many small investors; no one investor has the power to control prices. Further, investors trade in a single period, basing their decisions on identical expectations of the future. Finally, such investors can hold a riskless asset such as a U.S. Treasury bill, which pays the "riskless rate," or buy any asset on margin and pay the riskless rate as interest. While these assumptions are unrealistic, the model has provided substantial insights into the pricing of assets and their returns.

The CAPM and Portfolio Choices

In this perfect, frictionless market, investors choose among alternative portfolios on the basis of expected returns and the standard deviation of those returns. But because all investors have identical beliefs, each chooses the same assets in identical proportions.

The sum of all investors' portfolios is the market portfolio. Because all investors choose the same portfolio, the market portfolio is composed of all of the assets in the market. Each asset's weight in the market portfolio is the aggregate market value of the asset as a proportion of the market value of all assets. For example, if the aggregate value of a major stock is 2 percent of the aggregate value of the market, its weight is 2 percent of this market portfolio. In the context of the CAPM, the market portfolio is the optimal portfolio of risky assets for every investor.

The expected return on this market portfolio is higher than the expected return on riskless assets such as U.S. Treasury bills by an amount called the *market risk premium.* This premium may be thought of as the compensation that investors require for investing in risky assets such as stocks rather than in riskless Treasury bills.

Beta as a Risk Measure

Beta measures the amount of nondiversifiable, or market, risk in a particular stock. Returns on a share of stock reflect both diversifiable and nondiversifiable risk. *Diversifiable risk* is risk that can be eliminated by holding a portfolio of various securities in the market. *Nondiversifiable risk*, however, is inherent in the market and cannot be diversified away. Investors are thus not compensated for taking diversifiable risk, but they are compensated for taking nondiversifiable risk, the intrinsic risk of equities.

The beta of a stock reflects the magnitude of the comovement of the stock's returns with those of the market. A stock with a beta of 1 moves with the market; a stock with a beta of 2 rises twice as far as the market during a rising market, and falls twice as much during a falling market. Stocks with betas between 0 and 1 move less than the market, but in the same direction.

According to the CAPM, the beta of a stock, multiplied by the market risk premium, gives the expected excess return of the stock over the risk-free rate. Adding the risk-free rate, which can be represented by the Treasury bill rate, to that expected excess return gives the expected return on the stock.

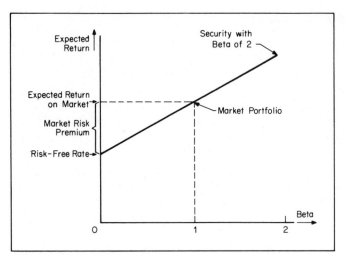

Figure 4.1. The capital market line.

Expected Return and Risk

The capital market line in Figure 4.1 expresses the relation between expected return, shown on the Y axis, and risk, or beta, shown on the X axis. The beta of the market portfolio is defined as 1. The market risk premium is the difference between the risk-free rate and the expected return on the market.

In equation form, the CAPM can be expressed as follows:

Expected return = risk-free rate + (beta × market risk premium)

where the market risk premium equals expected market return minus risk-free rate. In the CAPM, the relevant measure of risk is the risk of the individual security, or its beta. The larger the beta for a security, the greater its equilibrium expected return. When weighted by their market values (although not when equally weighted), the beta of the average asset is 1. The model predicts returns per period of time.

In the 1960s and 1970s, the CAPM provided a new understanding of how asset returns were priced. However, the model has been criticized because its assumptions are highly unrealistic and because there is some empirical evidence that the market does not perform as the theory predicts. Nevertheless, the model has helped investors to understand expected returns and their relationship to risk.

Arbitrage Pricing Theory

In economics, the *law of one price* states that two equal goods in a competitive market must have the same price. If two bushels of apples in

Benton Harbor, Michigan, are perfect substitutes, they should sell at the same price per bushel. Likewise, two capital assets, such as two shares of IBM's common stock, should be priced identically in a central market such as the NYSE.

Assumptions of the Model

Using the law of one price, Stephen Ross developed a theory, called *arbitrage pricing theory* (APT), which predicts that all equivalent portfolios ought to offer the same expected returns. If they were different, investors could buy one and sell the other, making a profit with no risk, that is, an arbitrage profit. Thus, prices adjust until portfolios cannot be formed to achieve further arbitrage profits. In this way, APT identifies equilibrium asset prices, or expected returns and risks. APT is derived by showing that, in equilibrium, any portfolio with no systematic risk, no net investment, and no unsystematic, or residual, risk must offer no return. If it did, investors would rush to hold it, proving that the initial price was not an equilibrium price.

Like the CAPM, APT was developed under the assumption that markets are perfectly competitive. Unlike the CAPM, however, APT is based on the belief that asset prices are determined by more than just one type of market risk.

Pricing Factors

According to APT, asset returns are influenced by several independent factors. For example, the expected return on a share of IBM's stock is determined by adding the risk-free rate to figures representing the compensation for several risk factors. One factor might be unexpected inflation, and another might be the unexpected return on the stock market. As in the CAPM, any diversifiable risk, or residual risk after accounting for the various risk factors, is unrewarded because investors can avoid this risk by diversifying.

The market rewards for taking various risks affecting asset returns can be derived using APT. Asset returns vary according to each asset's sensitivity to each risk factor. The CAPM, on the other hand, is concerned with only one factor—the security's one beta—and only one market risk premium. The CAPM thus may be thought of as the APT with only one risk factor.

Example of APT

A simplified version of the APT model with two pricing factors, the risk of the stock market and of unanticipated inflation, can be expressed as follows. The expected return on an asset is the riskless rate, plus the first risk factor—the equity beta times the equity risk premium—plus the second factor—the inflation beta times the inflation risk premium. As an equation, this is expressed as

Expected return = risk-free rate + (equity beta × equity risk premium)
                  + (inflation beta × inflation risk premium)

In this two-factor version of APT, unanticipated movements of the stock market and unanticipated inflation changes are assumed to be independent of one another. Also, the return of any asset, security, or portfolio is assumed to be a linear combination of the two factors, plus an idiosyncratic risk term that averages zero and is unique to each asset.

Each risk factor has a different risk premium, which is the compensation for assuming one unit of that risk. In theory, a specific asset has some number of units of each risk; those units are each multiplied by the appropriate risk premium. Thus, APT shows that the equilibrium expected return is the risk-free rate plus the sum of a series of risk premiums.

APT and Its Extensions

Researchers Nai-Fu Chen, Richard Roll, and Stephen Ross have identified at least five specific risk factors in the APT framework. These are:

- Changes in industrial production
- Changes in anticipated inflation
- Changes in unanticipated inflation
- The default premium on corporate bond returns
- The return differential between long- and short-term bonds

Work is currently being done to identify different or additional factors and to measure risk premiums and factor sensitivities of various assets.

APT is more realistic than CAPM because investors can consider other characteristics besides the beta of assets as they select their investment portfolios. While neither the CAPM nor APT is a perfectly realistic model, each is beginning to be widely employed to test and predict the relationship between expected return and various risk factors.

The NET Framework

In January 1986, Detroit Edison had 10-year corporate bonds with a yield to maturity of almost 11 percent, while at the same time their tax-exempt industrial revenue bonds had a yield to maturity of 9 percent. While these two bonds had similar maturities and a similar risk of default, their expected returns are very different. Traditional asset pricing models do not explain why this occurs, because they ignore the price effects of the bonds' tax status.

CAPM, APT, and NET

Formal demand-side theories such as the CAPM and APT are useful mathematical formulations for deriving assets' expected returns. Both these theories, however, assume that all costs borne by investors are due specifically to risk. The CAPM specifies the payoff demanded by investors for bearing one cost—beta, or market, risk; APT treats multiple risk factors. Other research has addressed nonrisk factors, but each in isolation.

The NET framework considers the nonrisk factors in asset pricing. It is called NET both because prices are determined *net* of investor-specific costs and because it calls for a *new equilibrium theory*. This framework integrates the costs arising from all sources—including various risks, as well as taxability, marketability, and information costs—and affecting all assets in an investor's opportunity set—stocks, bonds, real estate, human capital, venture capital, tangibles, and intangibles. Like CAPM and APT, the NET framework is best understood where markets are efficient. Market participants in the NET framework have investor-specific costs; their choices are not solely motivated by general calculations of risk and return. While it does not provide a detailed analysis of each particular cost or a mathematical pricing equation, the NET framework, developed by Roger Ibbotson, Jeffrey Diermeier, and Laurence Siegel, is useful in explaining observed investor behavior.

NET and the Cost of Capital

The objective of the NET framework is to determine the cost of capital for each asset in the market, given the characteristics of the asset and the demand functions of investors. The cost of capital for an asset is the aggregation of all investors' capital costs to acquire and hold the asset. It is typically expressed as a percentage of the asset's value in each year.

This cost of capital can also be interpreted as an expected return to investors or as a discount rate used in valuation. The higher the discount rate, the lower the present value of any given set of expected cash flows. Hence, higher expected returns are associated with lower values or prices.

The demand for capital market returns can be explained in a few sentences. Investors regard each asset as a bundle of characteristics for which they have various preferences and aversions. Investors then translate each characteristic into a cost, and they require compensation in the form of expected returns for bearing these costs. Thus, although all investors perceive the same expected return for any given asset, each also has individually determined costs to hold that asset. On the basis of perceived expected returns *net* of these individually determined costs, investors choose to hold differing amounts of each asset. Thus, in the NET framework, investors evaluate capital asset returns after, or net of, specific costs to hold an asset.

The NET framework assumes an instantaneous supply and demand setting. Here, uncertainties, investment horizons, taxes, entry and exit costs, and other perceived costs decrease the present value of an asset. The instantaneous setting is suitable as long as all costs can be expressed as present values.

Pricing Characteristics of Assets

Investors view assets as bundles of characteristics that they then translate into their own heterogeneous costs. The effects of these risk, tax, and marketability characteristics on the expected returns of various assets are summarized in Table 4.1. The terms *positive* and *high* refer to expected returns that must be increased to compensate for this relatively undesirable attribute, raising the discount rate used in estimating the present value of the asset and thereby lowering the asset's price. In contrast, the terms *negative* and *low* refer to expected returns that are lower and prices, higher.

For example, corporate bonds contain a great deal of inflation risk, that is, they are very sensitive to changes in inflation. An increase in inflation raises the expected return on bonds and lowers bond prices relative to other assets. Also, because bonds are highly taxed, the pretax expected returns earned in the market must be higher to compensate for this characteristic, and the corresponding present value of a given set of coupon and principal cash flows is less. On the other hand, gold's expected return is negatively related to inflation risk, so that the expected return on gold is lower, raising gold's price.

Table 4.1. Effects of Characteristics on Expected Returns on Assets

| | Characteristics | | | | | | Marketability | | |
| | Risks | | | | | | | | |
Asset	Stock Market Beta	Inflation	Real Interest Rate	Residual Risk Cost*	Tax-ability*	Informa-tion Costs*	Search Transac-tions Costs	Divisibility Costs	Miscellaneous Factors
Large company stocks	Near one	Low posi-tive	Positive?	Near zero	Low	Low	Low	Very low	Probably efficiently priced
Small company stocks	Varies	Low posi-tive	Positive?	Low	Low	High	Medium*	Very low	
Treasury bonds	Near zero	Positive	Low	Near zero	High	Low	Low	Medium*	Efficiently priced
Corporate bonds	Low	Positive	Low	Near zero	High	Low	Low	Medium*	
Municipal bonds	Near zero	Positive	Low	Low	Zero	Low	Low	Medium*	
Treasury bills	Zero	Zero	High	Near zero	High	Low	Low	High*	
Houses, condos	Low	?	?	High	Negative	High	High*	Very high*	High management costs
Gold	Zero or negative	Negative?	?	Low	Low	Low	Low	Very low	No income; portable
Art	Low	Negative?	?	High	Low	Very high	Very high	Very high	Nonpecuniary benefits; no income
Foreign securities	Varies	Varies	?	Varies	Low	High	Varies	Low	
Human capital	High	?	?	Very high	Very high	High	High*	Very high*	Cannot sell, only rent or borrow against

Note: Low, medium, high, etc. refer to positive coefficients unless indicated to be negative.
Effects of Characteristics on Expected Returns on Assets:
High or Positive = raises expected return, lowering price
Low or Negative = decreases expected return, raising price
*Financial intermediaries are likely to be important in reducing these costs.

Source: Reprinted from the article by Roger G. Ibbotson, Jeffrey J. Diermeier, and Laurence B. Siegel. "The Demand for Capital Market Returns: A New Equilibrium Theory," *Financial Analysts Journal*, January/February 1984.

Risk. Risk characteristics, used in both the CAPM and APT, need only a brief mention. The primary types of risk are beta (or market risk), inflation risk, real interest rate risk, and residual risk, or the risk resulting from lack of diversification in a portfolio. In the NET framework, unlike those of the CAPM and APT, residual risk may be rewarded in the market when it is costly to diversify. Real estate and human capital are especially difficult for most investors to diversify, and thereby must offer investors a higher expected return and have a correspondingly lower value.

Taxability. Taxability also has a substantial impact on an asset's expected return. An asset may generate positive or negative taxes on income, expenses, or capital appreciation, and thus investors include tax costs in their prices. As shown in Table 4.1, returns from human capital, or labor income, are highly taxed, while returns from municipal bonds are free from federal taxes. The taxability characteristic is inherently complex because of the intricacies of the U.S. and foreign tax systems. Individual taxes vary because each investor may pay different taxes on the same asset. The general principle is that highly taxed assets are lower priced—i.e., have higher pretax expected returns—than lower-taxed assets having otherwise similar characteristics. It is the pretax return that is observed directly in the marketplace, with each investor applying his or her own appropriate tax rate in order to calculate the after-tax return.

Marketability Costs. All the entry and exit costs associated with buying and selling an asset are grouped into the category of *marketability costs.* Since the NET framework is instantaneous, it provides no description of how investors came to hold their particular portfolios, or when or how they may rebalance them. Marketability costs include information, divisibility, and search and transaction costs. Again referring to Table 4.1, houses and condos have high marketability costs, raising expected returns and lowering real estate's price; large-company stocks are very low on these dimensions, decreasing expected returns and raising their value.

Miscellaneous Pricing Factors. Other miscellaneous factors may affect the price of a capital asset. These include certain expenses such as management, maintenance, and storage costs. Such costs are sometimes treated as costs of capital, rather than as decrements to cash flow, because they may differ across investors. They also include benefits (negative costs) of holding certain assets. The aesthetic benefits of holding artwork increase its value and lower its expected financial return, since part of the return is realized in nonpecuniary form.

The Aggregate Supply of Capital Market Returns

Prices in capital markets are set by the interaction of demand and supply. This relationship is commonly expressed as the "supply of and demand for capital." But turning this relationship around and viewing it as the demand for and supply of capital market *returns* has the advantage of focusing attention on returns as the goods being priced in the marketplace. As used here, *capital market returns* are the compensation each investor requires for holding assets with various characteristics. While modern portfolio theory traditionally focuses on the demand side, the supply aspects of this equilibrium are important too.

From a macroeconomic perspective, Diermeier, Ibbotson, and Siegel observe that the supply of total investment returns equals income returns for all assets, plus growth in aggregate market value of investable assets, less new issues. This observation makes possible a forecast of the total returns on aggregate financial assets, if this aggregate value of investable assets is assumed to be a fixed proportion of total social wealth. The gross national product (GNP) is considered the "return" on social wealth, and the return on investor wealth is consequently related to GNP growth. Based on the real GNP growth rate over the two decades ending in 1982, 2.6 percent, a forecast of expected capital market returns can be made using the supply model. The GNP growth rate of 2.6 percent may be projected forward and combined with current yield and new-issue data to produce a forecast of 5.4 percent per year *real* return on the aggregate of investable assets.

The supply model is intended to place in perspective the various demand-driven models, such as CAPM and APT, which dominate thinking about investors' expected returns. Investors cannot expect a much greater—or fear a much lesser—return than that provided by businesses in the real economy, so that investors' expectations should be guided at least in part by the supply of market returns.

Are Capital Markets Efficient?

Both modern portfolio theory and the more realistic but less precisely specified NET framework are usually explained in the context of efficient markets. Three arguments are presented below which demonstrate why markets may *not* actually be efficient.

The Costly Information Argument

When inquisitive students first hear about the efficient markets hypothesis, they often remark: "If every investor believed that markets were efficient, then the market could not be efficient since no one would analyze securities." Even upon first hearing the efficient markets hypothesis, students recognize the obvious justification for inefficient markets. Market prices reflect what is knowable about publicly traded companies only if investors try to earn superior returns by analyzing all relevant information about these companies quickly and perceptively. If investors abandoned such efforts, the efficiency of the market would diminish to nought.

Sanford Grossman and Joseph Stiglitz have shown that *costless* information is not only a sufficient but also a necessary condition for the existence of efficient markets. If information has a cost, and if investors buy information, then information must have value. Marginal buyers of the information have to believe they can at least break even after paying to obtain it. Thus stock prices, for example, must differ from their "fair" prices by at least the cost of the information, divided by the number of shares that informed investors can buy.

In fact, investors seldom have access to the same information and, in addition, bear different costs to obtain it. If valuable information about a particular security is costly, investors either buy it or not. If some buy the information but not others, the former will recognize any mispricing of the security. If no investors buy the information, it does not get reflected in the security's price. In either case, the security's price does not always reflect all information of all investors in the market. Hence, security markets must be inefficient.

The Costly Arbitrage Argument

Inefficiencies may also arise because arbitrage is costly. In practice, arbitrageurs must concentrate their holdings into undiversified portfolios, incur transactions costs, and often take short positions. An investor would only be willing to behave this way if the expected returns were very large. Investors find that the borrowing and short selling needed for efficient arbitrage are especially costly, since these financing techniques involve monitoring of collateral as well as credit-granting costs. Consequently, investors may not take advantage of all mispricing and may not arbitrage away all price discrepancies. Because investors may not always be willing to bear arbitrage costs, the market as a whole may inefficiently price various assets and their returns.

To clarify this argument, consider an extreme example. The person best able to arbitrage would be someone with *certain* information about the future. Suppose you are given an advance copy of *The Wall Street Journal* one full year before the prices are actually transacted and reported to everyone else. Clearly, you could make a lot of money by correctly anticipating all of the price changes.

Yet even in this case, the infinite arbitrage needed to bring prices completely in line with those a year from now is next to impossible. Often institutional constraints like bank lending limits and exchange margin requirements, along with limitations in your collateral and creditworthiness (assuming you cannot show the *Journal* to anyone else), would severely restrict your impact on today's security prices. Thus, even if you could know the future with certainty (which of course is not possible), your arbitrage activities would not be likely to bring today's (or the intervening year's) security prices into line, reflecting the known information. One investor, no matter who, can only have a limited impact on the market.

The Socratic Argument

The ancient Greek philosopher Socrates claimed to have special knowledge. Other Athenians were so threatened by his claim that they brought him to trial to ask just what special knowledge he had. He replied: "I know what I do not know."

If investors have differing abilities to analyze and act on information, markets may be inefficient since the smart will exploit the less smart. However, some academics argue that even if market participants have differing abilities, markets can still be efficient. Unskilled investors might see that they lose money relative to talented investors. As a result, unskilled investors would drop out of active security selection, either by following a "buy and hold" strategy or by hiring the talented ones to manage their portfolios. Thus, talented investors would remain in the market and arbitrage away any mispricing. Hence, even with investors of differing abilities, markets can still be efficient.

However, if market participants are not knowledgeable in the Socratic sense, the unskilled will remain as active participants. They do not know their relative knowledge, and consequently do not behave according to the advice academics would give them, as explained above. Thus the unskilled investor (without Socratic knowledge) would still be exploited by the skilled investors, and markets may be inefficient.

The volume of trading suggests that unskilled as well as talented investors remain in the market. Not all unskilled investors drop out or else the market would dry up. The argument that markets are efficient despite differing abilities can also be refuted by carrying it to its logical conclusion. Suppose all investors knew what they did and did not know, thus perceiving their relative ranking. Investors in the lower half of the hierarchy would know that they are below average and drop out of the market. Once that group dropped out, the second quartile would become below average. Each successive group would drop out until only the top-ranked investor would be left—without trading partners.

Although investors are generally rational, they probably have inexact and unrealistically high perceptions of their relative rankings. Most if not all active investors believe themselves to be above average, although obviously not all can be. If investors have differing abilities and do not perceive these differences, then markets are inefficient. This argument is based upon investors having bounded rationality, giving them biased perceptions of their relative rankings.

Conclusion

Modern portfolio theory is developed from the efficient markets hypothesis, which states that the price of an asset reflects its true, underlying value. Two principal models for pricing the returns on capital assets are the CAPM and APT. CAPM assumes prices to be determined solely by market risk, while APT allows additional factors to influence returns. Within the frameworks of the CAPM and APT, the "fair" prices for assets can be calculated; thus, these models can be applied in real capital markets to identify mispriced assets.

Asset characteristics other than price include both risk and nonrisk characteristics. The CAPM and APT have described the risk characteristics, but the nonrisk characteristics are not as well understood. They include taxation, marketability, and information costs.

For many assets, these nonrisk characteristics may affect price even more than the risk characteristics. In its broadest sense, the price of an asset is determined by its benefits, or expected returns, net of investor-specific costs. The more "bad" characteristics or the higher investor-specific costs an asset has, the higher the investor's expected return must be. Because of these individually determined costs, investors must use judgment when employing the CAPM or APT to identify the cost of capital or the rate at which to discount the expected cash flows when valuing assets.

Investors regard asset characteristics as having varying costs, and they evaluate expected returns net of these costs. While not a mathematical pricing equation, the NET framework applies to all assets—including stocks and bonds, real estate, venture capital, durables, and even intangibles such as human capital—and incorporates all asset characteristics.

Widely accepted academic theories incorporate efficient markets. Based on those theories, a "buy, hold, and diversify" strategy becomes the optimal one. Yet asset markets may be inefficient for three primary reasons:

1. Some investors are willing to pay for information, so it must have value.

2. Arbitrage is costly or constrained, so that it cannot remove all mispricing.

3. Investors have different abilities, which they misperceive, so that the less smart investors remain in the market to be exploited by the smarter investors.

Thus, markets cannot literally be efficient, and extraordinary opportunities exist for some of the best investors. Still, concepts of capital market equilibrium and efficient capital markets help to focus on the nature of value and expected returns.

Suggested Reading

Diermeier, Jeffrey J., Roger G. Ibbotson, and Laurence B. Siegel: "The Supply of Capital Market Returns," *Financial Analysts Journal*, March–April 1984, pp. 74–80. Considers that returns to investors must parallel output of return-generating businesses in the macroeconomy.

Grossman, Sanford J., and Joseph E. Stiglitz: "On the Impossibility of Informationally Efficient Markets," *American Economic Review*, June 1980, pp. 393–408. A more rigorous treatment of the argument against efficient markets, based on costly information. (The other two arguments in the text are those of the authors.)

Ibbotson, Roger G., Jeffrey J. Diermeier, and Laurence B. Siegel: "The Demand for Capital Market Returns: A New Equilibrium Theory," *Financial Analysts Journal*, January–February 1984, pp. 22–33. Presents the NET theory, portraying investor costs as the determinant of an asset's expected returns.

Ross, Stephen A: "The Arbitrage Theory of Capital Asset Pricing," *Journal of Economic Theory*, December 1976, pp. 341–360. The best-known academic paper on arbitrage pricing theory, by its principal proponent.

Schwed, Fred: *Where Are the Customer's Yachts? Or A Good Hard Look at Wall Street*, Simon & Schuster, Inc., New York, 1940. Insider's look at the old-fashioned ways of money management, many of which persist today.

Sharpe, William F.: *Investments*, 3d ed., Prentice-Hall, Inc., Englewood Cliffs, N.J., 1985. A widely respected textbook on the investment side of finance.

PART 2
Equity Markets

5

U.S. Equity Returns from Colonial Times to the Present

If George Washington had put just $1 from his first Presidential salary check into U.S. equities, his heirs would have been millionaires about five times over by the mid-1980s. U.S. stocks have provided a phenomenal return to investors over the long run. Partly because of this past success, the American equity market is the largest and most closely studied market in the world. Currently, in the mid-1980s, well over 100 million shares are traded each day on the New York Stock Exchange (NYSE), with more than 100 million additional shares traded in the over-the-counter (OTC) market and on other stock exchanges. The value of outstanding equities exceeds $2 trillion.

From price appreciation alone, equities yielded a return, called a *capital appreciation return,* of 2.9 percent, compounded annually, between the 1780s and the 1980s. Without dividends reinvested, a nominal dollar invested in 1789 would have grown to almost $450 in the 1980s. This capital appreciation return is shown graphically in Figure 5.1.

Total returns, in contrast to capital appreciation returns, include dividend reinvestment as well as price appreciation. Assuming dividends were paid from the 1790s to the 1870s at the same rate as from the 1870s to the 1980s, the compound total return was 8.2 percent per year, resulting in a value of almost $5 million by year-end 1985.

Nonetheless, this spectacular return came at a substantial risk to investors. Total returns were negative in about 29 percent of the years. These returns have a standard deviation of over 19 percent, another indication of their relatively wide variability. The distribution of annual total returns since 1790 is displayed as a histogram in Figure 5.2.

Before returns on individual stock exchanges are examined in detail, it is important to understand just how returns on stocks are measured. Let's turn, then, to the construction of market indexes for stock returns.

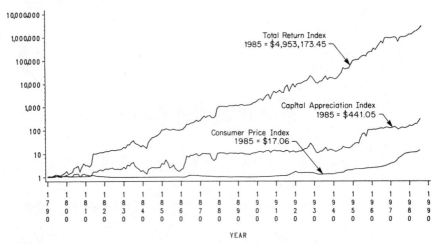

Figure 5.1. U.S. equities: Growth of a dollar in nominal terms, 1789–1985. (If $1 had been invested in the U.S. stock market in 1789, it would have grown to over $441 by 1985 solely from capital appreciation, and to almost $5 million if dividends were also reinvested when earned. The inflation index would be about $17 by that time. Dividends are assumed to be 5.0 percent annually over 1790–1871.)   (*Source: For stock market returns, Tables 5.2, 5.3, and 5.4; Table 11.3 for inflation.*)

Indexes of Stock Returns

To measure returns from the stock market, an index in which each stock is weighted according to the market value of its outstanding shares is used in subsequent tables. Such an index, called a *market-value-weighted index* or simply a *market index,* provides the best measure because it represents the performance of the market as a whole. A market index of aggregate stock returns captures what would happen to a sum of money invested at a particular time, presuming that the investment was divided between all of the market's securities in proportion to each security's total value.

The Market Index Explained

Let's see how a market index is constructed for a small, hypothetical market with just two firms. Assume, for simplicity's sake, that one firm, Cheap Inc., has 10 shares outstanding, each with a market value of $50. A second company, Dear, Ltd., also has 10 shares outstanding, each worth $100. To construct the index, determine the total market value of each firm, which in this case is $500 and $1000, respectively. The market's total value is, then, $1500. At the beginning of the next period,

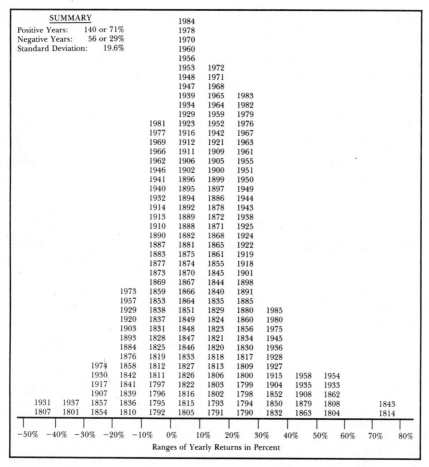

Figure 5.2. Frequency distribution of U.S. equity total returns, 1790–1985. (Returns on U.S. equities are roughly independent from one period to another and are approximately lognormally distributed.) (*Source: Tables 5.2, 5.3, and 5.4.*)

assume that Cheap Inc.'s stock appreciates to $75 and Dear, Ltd.'s stock stays at $100. The market's total value at this point is $1750. The capital appreciation over the first period is $250 for the market as a whole, or a 16.7 percent return ($250 divided by the starting value of $1500 is 0.167 or 16.7 percent). Equivalently, the ratio of each stock's total value to the market's total value is multiplied by its percentage return, and the results are summed. If $1 were invested initially in this market, it would grow to $1.167 by the period's end. Likewise, an index initialized at 1.00 in the first period grows to 1.167.

Now let's add dividends to our two-company market. Assume that Dear, Ltd. paid a $10 dividend per share, or a total dividend for all shares of $100. In a market index, dividends are invested proportionally in all segments of the market. Since the firms' market values are now $750 and $1000, respectively, 43 percent, or $43, is invested in Cheap Inc. and 57 percent, or $57, in Dear, Ltd. The values of each company are $793 and $1057, for a total of $1850. The market index now stands at 1.23. Its 23.3 percent rise from the initial index value of 1.00 consists of about 16.7 percent from capital appreciation and about 6.7 percent from dividend (income) reinvestment. Larger markets are more complicated, but the market index is constructed in the same way.

Compounding the Market Index

When compounded through the reinvestment of dividends, the market index grows geometrically. That is, the initial investment is multiplied by the quantity 1 plus the rate of return. For example $1 + 0.1 = 1.1$, where 0.1, or 10 percent, is the rate of return. That sum is taken to a power equal to the number of periods. For example, the value of $100 invested at 10 percent is $100 times 1.1^1, or $110, after 1 year; $100 times 1.1^2, or $121, after 2 years; etc. At first, the index grows slowly, but then it picks up speed and zooms into the stratosphere. Such a sum grows to $259 in 10 years, to $673 in 20 years, and to $1745, $4526, and $11,739 in 30, 40, and 50 years, respectively. Using an index of 1 in the first period, the index stands at 2.59 in 10 years, at 6.73 in 20, etc. Such is the magic of compounding.

A Well-Constructed Market Index

A well-constructed market index has five important attributes. First, it is broad, reflecting all of the securities in a particular market. Second, each security's return is weighted according to its market value at the beginning of the period over which the return is measured. (As before, the market value is defined as the price times the number of shares outstanding.) Third, total returns, consisting of capital appreciation and dividend income, rather than capital appreciation alone, are measured. Fourth, dividend income is recorded in the period received and is reinvested quickly in the market.

Finally, stocks which are delisted, go bankrupt, or become worthless have their last return included in the index. This procedure eliminates a selection bias favoring companies which succeed. If, for example, a stock is delisted from the NYSE and becomes listed elsewhere, the first stock quote off the NYSE (even if it is zero) should be used as if it were the last NYSE quote.

Popular Indexes Evaluated

In the 1930s, Alfred Cowles developed a stock index that partially satisfies these broad criteria. His index for NYSE stocks was the first to measure total returns and to weight these returns correctly. Unfortunately, his index uses the average value of the market in each month, rather than its end-of-month value, so that returns *over* a given period can only be approximated. Nevertheless, Cowles provides valuable data, which are used in a later table.

In the 1960s, University of Chicago professors James Lorie and Lawrence Fisher contributed significantly to information on equities when they compiled data on security returns for the University of Chicago's Center for Research on Security Prices (CRSP). The CRSP index, the best-constructed index of the stock market's performance now available, satisfies all five criteria. Investors can study not only the aggregate index, but all information that went into constructing it, including returns on individual stocks, industrial sectors, and other groupings of securities. The Cowles and CRSP indexes are the primary basis for subsequent analyses of returns on the NYSE.

While not used for tables in this chapter, two popular indexes of stock performance that should be evaluated against the above criteria are the Standard & Poor's (S&P) 500 Stock Index and the Dow Jones Industrial Average. The S&P 500 is broad enough to capture most of the value in the U.S. equity market, but it has two limitations. First, the index does not contain all of the stocks listed on the NYSE or any other market. Second, the S&P measures only capital appreciation returns, not total returns. The latter shortcoming can easily be overcome, however, because dividends and hence total returns are made available on a timely basis by a number of sources, including Ibbotson Associates' *Stocks, Bonds, Bills, and Inflation* services.

Perhaps the best known market "barometer" is the Dow Jones Industrial Average. Although widely quoted, the Dow satisfies none of the five criteria for a good index and is not even called an index. The Dow consists of 30 stocks of large corporations. It is price-weighted, which means that it is a simple average of prices per share, adjusted over the years to reflect past splits and other capital changes. Furthermore, the Dow measures only capital appreciation returns. On the other hand, even a narrow average of major stocks such as the Dow will track the market to a large extent; as such, the Dow has provided investors with an indication of short-term market trends since before the turn of the cen-

tury. Over the long term, however, the Dow has consistently underper-
formed the market as a whole because it covers only large companies
and ignores dividend payments.

Returns on the New York
Stock Exchange

When the United States was emerging as a nation, centralized markets
for stocks and bonds already existed in Europe. London, Paris, Brussels,
Amsterdam, and other cities had functioning stock exchanges. While the
American Colonies did not have a central stock exchange, brokers and
traders often gathered in specified locations, particularly outdoors on
Wall Street in New York, to do business.

The NYSE's Background

In May of 1792, a group of security brokers met under a buttonwood
tree at 68 Wall Street and pledged "not to buy or sell from this day for
any person whatsoever, any kind of public stock at a less than one quarter percent commission on the specie value, and that we will give preference to each other in our negotiations." The NYSE officially began with
this agreement. (This and other key dates in the history of U.S. stock
exchanges are summarized in Table 5.1.) Since its founding, the NYSE
has been the primary market for securities trading in the United States.

The Buttonwood Agreement set the precedent for fixing commissions
and excluding competition by limiting the number of "seats" (member-
ships) on the Exchange. Thus from 1792 until 1975, the NYSE was
legally regarded as a private club and was permitted monopoly power
over security trades. However, in April 1975, the Securities and Exchange Commission (SEC) abolished the fixed commission system and
permitted competition in commission rates.

In 1975, the SEC also required that ticker tapes reporting the prices of
stock trades be consolidated. Thus, all trades of NYSE-listed issues, including trades not executed on the NYSE, were reported together and
available nationwide. As a result, regional exchanges became important
second markets for companies listed on the NYSE and AMEX. Traditionally, regional exchanges like the Midwest Stock Exchange or the
Pacific Coast Exchange provided a primary market for securities of regional rather than national interest. The Denver Exchange, for example, was the principal market for mining stocks, while the Minneapolis–

Table 5.1. Key Dates in the History of Stock Exchanges in the United States

May 17, 1792	NYSE formed with Buttonwood Agreement
Mar. 16, 1830	NYSE's slowest day -- 31 shares traded
Nov. 15, 1867	NYSE introduced first stock tickers
Oct. 23, 1868	NYSE membership made salable
July 3, 1884	Dow Jones average started
Dec. 15, 1886	NYSE's first one million share day -- 1,200,000 shares
June 27, 1921	New York Curb Exchange moved to indoor location and ticker service was initiated
Sept. 3, 1929- July 8, 1932	The Great Crash: Dow fell from 381.17 to 41.22
June 6, 1934	Securities Exchange Act of 1934 enacted
Jan. 5, 1953	New York Curb Exchange is renamed American Stock Exchange
July 14, 1966	NYSE Stock Price Index started
Feb. 5, 1971	NASD's quotation system (NASDAQ) for OTC markets began
April 11, 1973	Chicago Board Options Exchange began options trading
Apr. 30, 1975	SEC abolished fixed commissions
Aug. 7, 1980	New York Futures Exchange started trading
Aug. 18, 1982	NYSE's first 100 million share day -- 132,681,000 shares
April 1, 1982	NASD's National Market system began

Source: 1982 NYSE Fact Book, "Significant Historical Dates " (selected items), p. 62; other items noted by the authors.

St. Paul Exchange had a large concentration of agricultural firms. Since the mid-1970s, however, the regional exchanges have become more important as alternative markets for nationally traded stocks.

The NYSE's Returns

Since its founding, the NYSE has expanded in all dimensions. The dollar value of listed shares, size of trading volume, and number of listed companies have all steadily increased. But the Exchange's greatest expansion has been in the dimension of return. Annual returns over different periods are presented in Tables 5.2, 5.3, and 5.4; together they form a continuous series from 1789 to the 1980s.

Returns up to 1871, shown in Table 5.2, are based on linking of various indexes with undocumented characteristics. Because dividends were not recorded for those issues, the average annual dividend from 1872 to date was assumed. By these calculations, a dollar invested in 1789 would have grown to $569.60 by 1871; this growth represents an 8.0 percent compound return per year.

More reliable data on NYSE returns are available for the period 1871–1925 and are presented in Table 5.3. A dollar invested in this NYSE index at the end of 1871 would have grown to $36.56 in 54 years, representing a compound total return of 6.9 percent per year. It is noteworthy that only about one-quarter of this return, or 1.8 percent per year, is due to capital appreciation. Three-quarters comes from the reinvestment of dividends.

Annual return data for a value-weighted portfolio of all NYSE stocks from 1926 to the 1980s are shown in Table 5.4. A dollar invested in a market portfolio of NYSE stocks at the end of 1925 would have grown to $233.89 in just under 60 years, for a compound total return of 9.5 percent per year, about half from dividend reinvestment and half from capital appreciation.

The compound returns plotted in Figure 5.2 appear to be almost normally distributed. The distribution is actually lognormal.

In a lognormal distribution (assuming a median of 0), a stock would have an equal probability of rising 100 percent or falling 50 percent. This is in contrast to a normal distribution, in which the stock would have an equal probability of rising 50 percent or falling 50 percent. Also, in a lognormal distribution, as in the stock market, the price cannot fall below zero. A lognormal distribution of returns is characterized by a longer right tail than left tail, and thus is somewhat asymmetrical. Over time, equity returns are not symmetrical, since investors cannot lose more than they invest, but they can gain many times their investments.

NYSE Returns by Fifty-Year Periods and Decades

NYSE returns and their associated risks both have been astonishingly stable over the past 200 years. To examine the market's performance over subperiods, the years between the 1790s and the 1980s are divided into four periods of roughly 50 years each. Statistics for these subperiods

Table 5.2. U.S. Stock Market Returns, 1790–1871 (Composite Portfolio, Annual Returns in Percent) (Index Values: December 31, 1789 = 1.00)

Year	Total Return %	Year End Total Return Index	Year End Capital Appr. Index	Year	Total Return %	Year End Total Return Index	Year End Capital Appr. Index
1789		1.00	1.00				
1790	27.82	1.27	1.22	1835	10.86	61.15	6.80
1791	12.96	1.44	1.32	1836	-17.20	50.63	5.29
1792	-7.56	1.33	1.15	1837	-7.52	46.82	4.63
1793	15.62	1.54	1.28	1838	-7.20	43.44	4.06
1794	27.88	1.97	1.57	1839	-13.62	37.52	3.30
1795	-0.51	1.96	1.48	1840	13.54	42.60	3.59
1796	-8.62	1.79	1.28	1841	-13.36	36.91	2.93
1797	-3.45	1.73	1.17	1842	-14.40	31.59	2.36
1798	27.76	2.21	1.44	1843	77.08	55.95	4.06
1799	21.04	2.67	1.67	1844	16.58	65.23	4.53
1800	26.59	3.39	2.03	1845	11.30	72.61	4.82
1801	-33.36	2.25	1.25	1846	2.97	74.76	4.72
1802	17.10	2.64	1.40	1847	5.00	78.50	4.72
1803	13.48	3.00	1.52	1848	5.00	82.43	4.72
1804	53.34	4.60	2.26	1849	9.06	89.90	4.91
1805	6.91	4.92	2.31	1850	33.81	120.30	6.33
1806	10.17	5.42	2.43	1851	0.53	120.94	6.05
1807	-41.34	3.18	1.30	1852	31.52	159.08	7.65
1808	59.16	5.06	2.01	1853	-9.81	143.47	6.52
1809	25.54	6.35	2.42	1854	-23.50	109.75	4.66
1810	-11.14	5.64	2.03	1855	12.22	123.17	5.00
1811	-0.34	5.62	1.92	1856	20.50	148.43	5.77
1812	-8.55	5.14	1.66	1857	-20.21	118.42	4.31
1813	15.23	5.93	1.83	1858	-11.94	104.27	3.58
1814	73.57	10.29	3.09	1859	-3.78	100.32	3.27
1815	8.51	11.17	3.19	1860	22.94	123.33	3.85
1816	3.30	11.54	3.14	1861	17.86	145.37	4.35
1817	21.70	14.04	3.67	1862	53.91	223.75	6.48
1818	13.88	15.99	3.99	1863	46.56	327.94	9.18
1819	-5.06	15.18	3.59	1864	0.18	328.55	8.73
1820	19.41	18.13	4.11	1865	13.08	371.54	9.44
1821	10.90	20.11	4.35	1866	4.46	388.12	9.39
1822	1.50	20.41	4.20	1867	9.01	423.09	9.77
1823	10.60	22.58	4.43	1868	14.15	482.99	10.66
1824	11.44	25.16	4.72	1869	-8.89	440.04	9.18
1825	-6.73	23.47	4.17	1870	8.90	479.23	9.54
1826	3.78	24.35	4.11	1871	18.85	569.60	10.86
1827	7.99	26.30	4.24				
1828	-0.46	26.18	4.01				
1829	12.22	29.38	4.30				
1830	20.92	35.53	4.98				
1831	-7.79	32.76	4.34				
1832	37.58	45.07	5.76				
1833	0.09	45.12	5.48				
1834	22.25	55.16	6.42				

SUMMARY STATISTICS:

	Total Return (%)
Compound Annual Return	8.04%
Arithmetic Mean Return	9.93%
Standard Deviation of Returns	20.67%

Note: Indices are generally narrow, representing a limited number of prominent stocks. Although these indices, like the Dow Jones Industrial Average, are constructed using a small number of the market's stocks, they probably track market trends reasonably well and thus provide useful information for this analysis. While the stocks may have traded on the NYSE, the indices before 1871 do not represent the NYSE as a whole, and are reported only to capture early period returns.

Source: "Historical Record: Stock Prices 1789–Present (Data Bulletin 1975-1)," pp. 8-12, Foundation for the Study of Cycles, Pittsburgh. The Foundation uses its internal index for 1789 to June 1831; the Cleveland Trust Company railroad stock index from July 1831 to February 1854; the Clement-Burgess Index from March 1854 to July 1871; and the Cowles Index for August to December 1871. These indices, except for the Cowles Index, may suffer from survivorship bias, which means that firms that fail are not considered, biasing returns upward, and from other inde-terminate biases. We used these indices to construct returns and a cumulative wealth index initialized to 1.000 at 12/31/1789. Dividend income in each year is assumed to be the average over 1872-1985.

Table 5.3. New York Stock Exchange, 1872–1925: Value-Weighted Annual Returns (in Percent) (Index Values: December 31, 1871 = 1.0000)

Year	Total Return %	Income %	Capital Appr. Return %	Year-End Total Return Index	Year-End Capital Appr. Index
1871				1.0000	1.0000
1872	12.07	5.26	6.81	1.1207	1.0681
1873	-7.05	5.70	-12.75	1.0417	0.9319
1874	9.35	6.54	2.81	1.1391	0.9581
1875	2.79	6.89	-4.10	1.1709	0.9188
1876	-11.44	6.51	-17.95	1.0370	0.7539
1877	-2.35	7.02	-9.38	1.0125	0.6832
1878	11.91	5.78	6.13	1.1331	0.7251
1879	48.08	5.12	42.96	1.6780	1.0366
1880	23.39	4.70	18.69	2.0704	1.2304
1881	7.76	4.78	2.98	2.2310	1.2670
1882	1.95	4.84	-2.89	2.2745	1.2304
1883	-3.33	5.18	-8.51	2.1987	1.1257
1884	-13.15	5.69	-18.84	1.9096	0.9136
1885	26.37	6.31	20.06	2.4132	1.0969
1886	13.44	5.09	8.35	2.7376	1.1885
1887	-2.76	3.85	-6.61	2.6621	1.1099
1888	1.88	4.24	-2.36	2.7122	1.0838
1889	7.56	4.18	3.38	2.9172	1.1204
1890	-9.67	3.88	-13.55	2.6351	0.9686
1891	21.85	4.01	17.84	3.2108	1.1414
1892	5.89	4.28	1.61	3.3998	1.1597
1893	-15.70	4.16	-19.86	2.8659	0.9293
1894	2.49	5.03	-2.54	2.9374	0.9058
1895	5.20	4.62	0.58	3.0900	0.9110
1896	1.67	3.97	-2.30	3.1417	0.8901
1897	16.80	4.15	12.65	3.6694	1.0026
1898	22.70	3.90	18.80	4.5023	1.1911
1899	10.31	3.72	6.59	4.9666	1.2696
1900	17.23	3.21	14.02	5.8224	1.4476
1901	20.23	4.50	15.73	7.0004	1.6754
1902	5.10	3.85	1.25	7.3575	1.6963
1903	-14.81	3.71	-18.52	6.2679	1.3822
1904	30.41	4.65	25.76	8.1739	1.7382
1905	19.84	4.18	15.66	9.7958	2.0105
1906	6.66	3.53	3.13	10.4477	2.0733
1907	-29.37	3.96	-33.33	7.3789	1.3822
1908	42.88	5.38	37.50	10.5429	1.9005
1909	19.12	4.93	14.19	12.5584	2.1702
1910	-7.87	4.31	-12.18	11.5697	1.9058
1911	5.53	4.84	0.69	12.2091	1.9188
1912	7.92	4.92	3.00	13.1762	1.9764
1913	-9.45	4.85	-14.30	11.9305	1.6937
1914	-3.13	5.37	-8.50	11.5569	1.5497
1915	33.90	5.01	28.89	15.4742	1.9974
1916	8.39	4.98	3.41	16.7721	2.0654
1917	-25.05	5.62	-30.67	12.5704	1.4319
1918	23.91	7.82	16.09	15.5757	1.6623
1919	20.31	7.24	13.07	18.7392	1.8796
1920	-17.93	5.75	-23.68	15.3799	1.4346
1921	13.43	6.13	7.30	17.4453	1.5393
1922	26.56	6.49	20.07	22.0784	1.8482
1923	3.39	5.80	-2.41	22.8273	1.8037
1924	24.52	5.94	18.58	28.4241	2.1387
1925	28.64	5.87	22.77	36.5636	2.6257

SUMMARY STATISTICS:

	Total Return (%)	Income (%)	Capital Appr. Return (%)
Compound Annual Return	6.89%	5.04%	1.80%
Arithmetic Mean Return	8.12%	5.04%	3.08%
Standard Deviation of Returns	16.08%	1.03%	15.97%

Note: The Cowles index is generally considered to be the first high-quality, broad-based index of U.S. stock market returns. Cowles collected both monthly value-weighted capital appreciation returns and monthly dividend yields on all NYSE-listed stocks. The authors combined these, using the assumption that dividend returns equalled promised yields, to construct the total returns and cumulative wealth index (initialized to 1.000 at 12/31/1871) shown here. Survivorship bias is corrected for, by including the last return after delisting or failure of a stock. Unfortunately, Cowles's capital appreciation returns are based on each stock's average price over a month, not the month-end closing price, so that the yearly returns measure price changes from (on average) mid-December to mid-December. In other words, they lag a year-end index by about one-half month.

Source: Alfred Cowles, *Common Stock Indexes,* 1871-1937, Bloomington, Ind.: Principia Press, 1938. Reprinted with permission of Trinity University Press.

Table 5.4. New York Stock Exchange, 1926–1985: Value-Weighted Annual Returns (in Percent) (Index Values: December 31, 1925 = 1.0000)

Year	Total Return %	Income %	Capital Appr. Return %	Year End Total Return Index	Year End Capital Appr. Index	Aggregate Value ($ Billions)
1925				1.0000	1.0000	27.35
1926	9.59	5.84	3.75	1.0959	1.0375	30.95
1927	33.23	6.26	26.97	1.4601	1.3173	42.49
1928	38.91	5.34	33.56	2.0281	1.7595	58.96
1929	-14.78	3.13	-17.91	1.7283	1.4443	55.22
1930	-28.40	3.24	-31.64	1.2375	0.9873	41.31
1931	-44.42	3.23	-47.65	0.6878	0.5168	21.57
1932	-8.93	6.08	-15.01	0.6264	0.4393	18.52
1933	58.31	6.52	51.79	0.9916	0.6668	28.16
1934	4.16	4.16	0.00	1.0329	0.6668	28.92
1935	44.40	5.83	38.57	1.4915	0.9240	40.46
1936	32.80	5.67	27.13	1.9806	1.1746	52.45
1937	-34.48	3.48	-37.95	1.2978	0.7288	32.98
1938	27.65	5.41	22.24	1.6566	0.8909	40.83
1939	1.83	4.76	-2.94	1.6868	0.8647	39.83
1940	-7.81	5.18	-12.99	1.5551	0.7524	35.00
1941	-9.57	6.10	-15.67	1.4064	0.6345	29.86
1942	16.28	7.62	8.66	1.6353	0.6895	32.51
1943	27.97	6.35	21.62	2.0927	0.8385	40.30
1944	21.38	5.88	15.50	2.5402	0.9684	46.91
1945	38.41	5.50	32.91	3.5159	1.2872	63.16
1946	-6.11	3.80	-9.91	3.3011	1.1596	60.20
1947	3.31	5.59	-2.28	3.4103	1.1332	60.67
1948	2.31	6.24	-3.93	3.4892	1.0887	59.15
1949	20.21	8.00	12.21	4.1943	1.2215	68.32
1950	29.94	8.72	21.22	5.4500	1.4807	85.70
1951	20.96	6.68	14.27	6.5920	1.6921	101.73
1952	13.32	5.95	7.37	7.4701	1.8168	112.24
1953	0.38	5.44	-5.06	7.4983	1.7249	109.26
1954	50.52	7.08	43.45	11.2866	2.4743	162.54
1955	25.27	5.02	20.25	14.1383	2.9753	200.79
1956	8.62	4.21	4.41	15.3566	3.1065	217.31
1957	-10.69	3.71	-14.40	13.7142	2.6591	194.27
1958	44.27	5.48	38.79	19.7850	3.6906	276.48
1959	12.87	3.59	9.27	22.3312	4.0329	309.25
1960	0.60	3.41	-2.81	22.4660	3.9196	307.71
1961	27.17	3.75	23.42	28.5695	4.8376	388.05
1962	-9.40	3.03	-12.43	25.8849	4.2365	337.15
1963	21.41	3.80	17.61	31.4264	4.9827	401.64
1964	16.36	3.44	12.91	36.5672	5.6262	462.92
1965	13.99	3.37	10.62	41.6827	6.2235	523.84
1966	-8.87	2.99	-11.86	37.9838	5.4853	469.07
1967	26.88	3.82	23.06	48.1955	6.7503	585.17
1968	12.82	3.29	9.54	54.3758	7.3941	662.42
1969	-9.82	2.78	-12.60	49.0342	6.4623	598.70
1970	1.31	3.60	-2.29	49.6763	6.3142	605.26
1971	15.81	3.43	12.37	57.5279	7.0953	705.06
1972	17.77	3.17	14.60	67.7493	8.1312	836.13
1973	-16.92	2.59	-19.52	56.2851	6.5443	681.10
1974	-26.80	3.26	-30.06	41.2025	4.5773	480.24
1975	37.72	5.71	32.01	56.7451	6.0426	650.57
1976	26.26	4.96	21.30	71.6488	7.3298	816.15
1977	-4.81	4.40	-9.21	68.2003	6.6545	765.45
1978	7.39	5.46	1.93	73.2395	6.7830	793.49
1979	21.82	6.34	15.47	89.2170	7.8326	923.14
1980	32.70	6.67	26.02	118.3876	9.8709	1204.96
1981	-4.22	4.70	-8.92	113.3911	8.9908	1112.97
1982	20.72	6.58	14.14	136.8858	10.2617	1273.60
1983	23.00	5.28	17.72	168.3696	12.0801	1538.96
1984	5.11	4.77	0.35	176.9765	12.1220	1549.37
1985	32.16	5.82	26.34	233.8921	15.3149	1950.33

SUMMARY STATISTICS:

	Total Return (%)	Income (%)	Capital Appr. Return (%)
Compound Annual Return	9.52%	4.92%	4.63%
Arithmetic Mean Return	11.70%	4.93%	6.77%
Standard Deviation of Returns	21.12%	1.43%	20.34%

Source: Center for Research in Security Prices, Graduate School of Business, University of Chicago. 1985 data represent the S&P 500 (not all NYSE stocks) and are from the *Stocks, Bonds, Bills, and Inflation 1986 Yearbook*. Ibbotson Associates, 1986.

Table 5.5. Summary Data on Equity Total Returns by Subperiod, 1790–1985

Period	Compound Annual Return	Arithmetic Mean Return	Standard Deviation	Serial Correlation	Best Year	Worst Year
1790-1985	8.2%	10.0%	19.7%	-0.01	1843 (+77.1%)	1931 (-44.4%)
1790-1839	7.5	9.4	20.4	-0.11	1814 (+73.6%)	1807 (-41.3%)
1840-1889	7.9	9.4	19.0	0.12	1843 (+77.1%)	1854 (-23.5%)
1890-1939	6.3	8.6	21.6	-0.01	1933 (+58.3%)	1931 (-44.4%)
1940-1985	11.4	12.7	17.1	-0.05	1954 (+50.5%)	1974 (-26.8%)

Source: Tables 5.2, 5.3, and 5.4.

are shown in Table 5.5. Interestingly, average returns are similar for all four subperiods. But most remarkable is the consistency of the market's standard deviation, or variability of returns, over almost 2 centuries.

The serial correlation (or first-order autocorrelation) of returns over the 50-year intervals is also reported in Table 5.5. Serial correlation of returns measures the relation of the return in one period to the return in the next period. Directly related series have a correlation of 1, unrelated series a correlation of 0, and negatively related series a correlation of −1. Since the serial correlations in Table 5.5 are below 0.15, the returns from one period show little relation to returns in the subsequent period. This suggests that investors cannot forecast returns (except as a probability distribution) by knowing past returns.

Decade by decade returns for about 2 centuries are displayed in Table 5.6. Here both nominal returns and inflation-adjusted (real) returns are presented for each decade. A nominal return is a return computed without adjustment for inflation. For example, if $100 is invested at 12 percent per year, the return is $12, or 12 percent. But if inflation during the period were 4 percent, approximately $4 of the return would be from inflation and the real return would be about 8 percent, or $8. (To be precise, the inflation-adjusted index equals the return index divided by the inflation index.) As the right-hand column of Table 5.6 shows, nearly all the real return over the period comes from reinvestment of dividends. The real *capital appreciation* index has increased less than twelvefold in 196 years.

Table 5.6. Compound Total and Capital Appreciation Returns on U.S. Equities by Decade in Nominal and Real Terms, 1790–1985 (All Index Values: December 31, 1789 = 1.00)

| | Nominal | | | | Inflation | | Real | | | |
| | Capital Appreciation Returns | | Total Returns | | | | Capital Appreciation Returns | | Total Returns | |
Period	Decade Mean Stock Return	End of Decade Index Value	Decade Mean Stock Return	End of Decade Index Value	Decade Mean	End of Decade Index	Decade Mean Stock Return	End of Decade Index Value	Decade Mean Stock Return	End of Decade Index Value
1789		1.00		1.00		1.00		1.00		1.00
1790–1799	5.3%	1.68	10.4%	2.68	3.9%	1.47	0.1%	1.01	5.1%	1.65
1800–1809	3.7	2.42	9.0	6.36	-0.6	1.38	4.9	1.62	10.1	4.34
1810–1819	4.0	3.59	9.1	15.19	-0.2	1.35	4.0	2.39	9.0	10.32
1820–1829	1.8	4.30	6.8	29.38	-3.6	0.94	5.0	3.89	10.0	26.78
1830–1839	-2.6	3.31	2.5	37.53	0.0	0.94	-3.0	2.88	2.1	33.03
1840–1849	4.0	4.92	9.1	89.90	0.6	1.00	3.3	3.98	8.3	73.77
1850–1859	-4.0	3.27	1.1	100.32	0.4	1.04	-5.4	2.27	-0.3	71.60
1860–1869	10.9	9.18	15.9	440.05	4.4	1.60	5.5	3.87	10.5	195.46
1870–1879	2.1	11.26	8.1	955.77	-3.5	1.12	5.5	6.58	11.4	578.41
1880–1889	0.8	12.17	5.7	1,661.67	-0.1	1.11	3.7	7.27	5.9	1,025.55
1890–1899	1.3	13.80	5.5	2,829.03	-0.3	1.08	1.9	8.44	5.7	1,785.86
1900–1909	5.5	23.58	9.7	7,153.35	3.0	1.45	1.4	10.66	6.6	3,379.21
1910–1919	-1.4	20.42	4.1	10,673.98	6.6	2.76	-8.3	4.16	-3.4	2,397.75
1920–1929	7.3	41.20	12.9	35,995.72	-0.3	2.68	5.9	7.65	12.0	7,457.71
1930–1939	-5.0	24.67	-0.2	35,130.81	-2.0	2.18	-2.2	6.10	2.5	9,543.17
1940–1949	3.5	34.85	9.5	87,354.70	5.4	3.69	-2.7	4.64	3.3	13,227.72
1950–1959	12.7	115.06	18.2	465,087.61	2.2	4.59	10.4	12.46	15.9	57,895.64
1960–1969	4.5	184.37	8.2	1,021,227.78	2.5	5.88	2.2	15.43	5.5	99,070.50
1970–1979	1.9	223.46	6.2	1,958,108.58	7.4	11.98	-6.0	8.29	-1.8	82,860.36
1980–1985	12.0	441.05	16.7	4,953,173.45	6.1	17.06	5.8	11.60	11.5	159,336.77
Whole Period*										
1790–1985	3.2%		8.2%		1.5%		1.3%		6.3%	

*Compound annual return over whole period (1790–1985). All decade mean returns are compound annual returns.

Source: Equity returns from Tables 5.2, 5.3, and 5.4; inflation rates from Table 11.3.

Table 5.7. Great Bear Markets

Period	Percent Decline During Bear Market		Percent Advance in First Year After Bear Market	
	Nominal	Real	Nominal	Real
1836–1842	–48.32 %	–47.80 %	77.06 %	76.92 %
1853–1859	–36.94	–50.88	22.95	24.04
1929 (Sept)–1932 (June)	–83.41	–78.74	162.91	181.62
1973 (Jan)–1974 (Sept)	–42.63	–52.24	38.13	28.22

Note: All returns are total returns. A bear market is defined as a period in which a year-end investor over 1789-1925, or month-end investor over 1926-1985, would have suffered at least a 45% total return loss in real terms.

Source: Tables 5.2 and 5.4.

NYSE Returns in Bear and Bull Markets

Bear markets, defined here as periods in which investors lost at least 45 percent of their wealth in real terms, occurred in four periods, identified in Table 5.7. Year-end investors watched their wealth erode most in the bear market of 1929 to 1932, during which stocks declined by 83 percent on a year-end basis. Precedents to the Great Crash were the bear market of 1836 to 1842, associated with a 48 percent decline, and the decline between 1853 and 1859, when losses amounted to 37 percent. In recent times, the contraction of 1973 to 1974, sometimes called the Second Great Crash, resulted in a loss of 43 percent, a decline exacerbated by the high inflation rate of those years. There have been four major reductions in stock prices during two centuries, but not in any regular pattern such as the 40- or 50-year Kondratieff wave sometimes thought to exist.

Bull markets are defined here as periods when stock prices at least doubled without a major interruption. Such markets have occurred 10 times since 1790 as shown in Table 5.8. Unusually rapid advances occurred in the late 1920s, during the 1932 to 1937 recovery from the Great Crash, in the explosive postwar period of 1949 to 1966, and in the 1980s.

Bear and bull markets reflect major changes in the general level of stock prices. Yet these labels are after-the-fact characterizations; they do not imply that stock returns follow trends. As the French statistician Louis Bachelier first showed in 1900, the serial correlation of asset returns is practically zero. Thus excess returns, or stock returns in excess of the riskless rate, follow close to a random walk. This means that no one can predict next year's excess returns by knowing this year's. A random walk process, however, produces results which visually resemble a trend and which, over these "trendy" periods, greatly affect investors' wealth.

War and NYSE returns

Whether war is good or bad for stock markets is an unsettled question. Because wars mandate high productivity, they might benefit the economy and thus the stock market. On the other hand, the goods produced are generally destroyed and detract from both consumption and investment. When one blows up one's capital, it makes sense that this would affect wealth negatively and have disastrous effects on the market.

U.S. equity returns during wartime do not support either hypothesis. Total returns during war years appear in Table 5.9. In nominal terms, wartime markets appear quite healthy, with an average return of 15

Table 5.8. Great Bull Markets

Period	Percent Advance during Bull Market		Compound Annual Return during Bull Market	
	Nominal	Real	Nominal	Real
1790-1800	239.00%	105.00%	11.74%	6.74%
1813-1818	210.68	237.58	20.80	22.48
1843-1845	129.78	119.64	31.96	29.99
1860-1863	226.89	174.19	34.46	25.39
1897-1905	212.10	163.05	13.48	11.35
1924-1929 (Aug)	369.69	375.00	31.39	31.65
1932 (July)-1937 (Feb)	414.58	395.19	42.05	40.89
1942 (May)-1946 (May)	210.02	171.29	31.93	27.69
1949 (July)-1966 (Jan)	1260.93	921.66	17.05	15.04
1982 (Aug)-1985 (Dec)	131.55	113.20	27.86	24.80

Note: All returns are total returns. A bull market is defined as a period in which a year-end investor over 1790 to 1925, or a month-end investor over 1926 to 1985, would have earned a 100 percent or greater total return in real terms without major interruption. A major interruption is (arbitrarily) considered to be a year with a large negative return or a series of years with low (positive or negative) returns.

Sources: For 1790-1925, Tables 5.2 and 5.3 for equity returns and Table 11.3 for inflation rates. For 1926-1985, *Stocks, Bonds, Bills, and Inflation: 1986 Yearbook*, Ibbotson Associates, Chicago, 1986.

Table 5.9. Stock Market Total Returns during Wartime
in the United States

War	Years	Arithmetic Mean Return	
		Nominal	Real
War of 1812	1812-1814	26.75%	18.64%
Mexican War	1846-1848	4.32	0.40
Civil War	1861-1865	26.32	14.26
Spanish-American War	1898	22.70	19.57
World War I	1917-1918	− 0.57	−18.01
World War II	1942-1945	26.01	21.81
Korean War	1950-1953	16.15	12.86
Vietnam War	1966-1973	4.87	0.08
ALL WAR YEARS		15.13%	8.38%
ALL PEACETIME YEARS		9.05%	8.32%
ALL YEARS		9.98%	8.33%

Source: Tables 5.2, 5.3, and 5.4.

percent, compared to 9 percent during peace time. However, after adjusting for high inflation associated with wars, American investors on
average did not earn unusually high returns during these periods.

Investors on the winning side of wars, of course, fare differently from
those backing the losers. The United States has won every major war in
its history. Hence, it is not surprising that U.S. returns are generally
positive. On the other hand, war, along with hyperinflation, has often
destroyed the wealth and capital markets of defeated countries.

Presidential Elections
and NYSE Returns

Because politicians affect a country's business and economic climate,
political changes affect the stock market. Total returns for Presidential
election years, reported in Table 5.10, have been substantially better
than in nonelection years. Perhaps investors are optimistic when a new
or reelected president begins a new term with a fresh agenda. But more

likely, the election-year returns are superior because political campaigns provide information about the future business climate and thus some uncertainty is resolved.

Detailed analysis of the results suggests no "November effect," or jump in returns immediately after the election. And contrary to popular opinion, the first half of a presidential term is no better for the market than the second half. Furthermore, second-term presidents do not necessarily have a salutary effect on stock prices. Finally, returns seem unrelated to the party of the winner; the market favors neither Republicans nor Democrats.

Table 5.10. U.S. Stock Market Presidential Election Year Returns in the Twentieth Century

Year	Total Return	Inflation Adjusted Total Return
1900	17.23%	14.81%
1904	30.41	28.67
1908	42.88	39.95
1912	7.92	4.35
1916	8.39	0.82
1920	−17.93	−33.76
1924	24.52	24.32
1928	38.91	39.87
1932	−8.93	1.37
1936	32.80	31.59
1940	−6.01	−6.96
1944	21.51	19.41
1948	1.82	−0.89
1952	12.76	11.88
1956	9.16	6.30
1960	0.90	−0.58
1964	16.83	15.64
1968	14.60	9.88
1972	17.37	13.96
1976	26.58	21.77
1980	32.95	20.55
1984	5.11	1.16
Arithmetic Mean Total Return in Election Years*	14.99%	12.00%
Arithmetic Mean Total Return in All Other Years (through 1985)*	8.43%	5.36%

* The standard error of the mean for election years was 3.4%, and for nonelection years 2.8%. Thus the means (both nominal and real) are separated by approximately two standard errors, suggesting that the difference of means is significant near the 95% level, assuming normally distributed, stationary returns for both series.

Returns in Other American Markets

The OTC Market

Throughout U.S. history, shares of stock have traded "over the counter." In such trading, a seller informally offers to sell shares to potential buyers at a price negotiated between them. Until fairly recently, most shares in small and new firms were traded over the counter, while the NYSE and AMEX handled almost all trading of large and medium-sized company stocks.

The OTC market has grown faster than any exchange since 1971, when the National Association of Securities Dealers (NASD) automatic quotation system, NASDAQ, was introduced. Its market share expanded from over 6 percent in the 1960s to over 12 percent in the 1980s, while the NYSE lost 4, and AMEX 2, percentage points. From the mid-1970s to the mid-1980s, the number of companies traded on

Table 5.11. Total Returns and Total Return Indexes of the U.S. Stock Exchanges, 1959–1984

YEAR	Total Returns				Year-End Total Return Indices			
	NYSE	AMEX	OTC	TOTAL	NYSE	AMEX	OTC	TOTAL
1959					1.0000	1.0000	1.0000	1.0000
1960	0.60 %	4.16 %	1.93 %	0.90 %	1.0060	1.0416	1.0193	1.0090
1961	27.17	25.76	35.35	27.63	1.2794	1.3099	1.3796	1.2877
1962	−9.40	−5.11	−12.44	−9.35	1.1591	1.2430	1.2080	1.1673
1963	21.41	10.93	23.94	20.90	1.4073	1.3788	1.4972	1.4112
1964	16.36	13.20	26.02	16.84	1.6375	1.5609	1.8868	1.6488
1965	13.99	15.50	32.90	15.45	1.8666	1.8028	2.5075	1.9036
1966	−8.87	−7.70	−12.29	−9.10	1.7009	1.6640	2.1993	1.7304
1967	26.88	51.40	57.37	30.57	2.1582	2.5192	3.4611	2.2594
1968	12.82	25.94	22.70	14.60	2.4350	3.1726	4.2468	2.5894
1969	−9.82	−27.04	−5.80	−10.67	2.1958	2.3149	4.0004	2.3130
1970	1.31	−18.14	−12.23	−1.26	2.2245	1.8949	3.5112	2.2838
1971	15.81	17.86	37.19	17.83	2.5761	2.2333	4.8170	2.6909
1972	17.77	5.18	20.35	17.36	3.0338	2.3491	5.7972	3.1582
1973	−16.92	−30.09	−28.47	−18.81	2.5205	1.6422	4.1470	2.5642
1974	−26.80	−37.61	−32.71	−27.82	1.8451	1.0246	2.7905	1.8509
1975	37.72	38.77	33.76	37.44	2.5411	1.4218	3.7326	2.5439
1976	26.26	28.25	29.20	26.57	3.2085	1.8235	4.8225	3.2199
1977	−4.81	9.80	10.53	−3.18	3.0540	2.0021	5.3303	3.1176
1978	7.39	16.95	15.81	8.46	3.2797	2.3414	6.1730	3.3814
1979	21.82	58.47	31.91	24.07	3.9952	3.7106	8.1428	4.1952
1980	32.70	30.61	37.38	32.99	5.3015	4.8465	11.1866	5.5794
1981	−4.22	−6.10	−0.01	−3.95	5.0777	4.5511	11.1855	5.3592
1982	20.72	4.93	21.07	19.98	6.1298	4.7753	13.5423	6.4299
1983	23.00	28.27	21.77	23.09	7.5397	6.1251	16.4904	7.9147
1984	5.11	−5.83	−9.13	3.06	7.9250	5.7680	14.9849	8.1569

Source of NYSE data: 1959-1984 from the Center for Research in Security Prices, University of Chicago, using value-weighted returns; AMEX 1960-1962 computed using an equally-weighted sample of twenty stocks; AMEX 1962-1984 from the Center for Research in Security Prices, University of Chicago, using value-weighted returns.

Source of OTC data: National Quotation Bureau, through 1971, for capital appreciation and dividends. The authors summed the components to form total returns. Starting 1972, capital appreciation returns are from the NASDAQ OTC Composite Index, published by the National Association of Securities Dealers. Dividend yields are from Media General, Inc., for 1974-1984; the authors estimated dividends for 1972 and 1973.

Table 5.12. Returns in U.S. Equity Markets, 1960–1984

Market	Nominal			Real		
	Compound Annual Return	Arithmetic Mean Return	Standard Deviation	Compound Annual Return	Arithmetic Mean Return	Standard Deviation
TOTAL RETURNS						
NYSE	8.6 %	9.9 %	16.3 %	3.0 %	4.6 %	17.3 %
AMEX	7.3	9.9	23.5	1.5	4.6	23.9
OTC	11.5	13.9	22.4	5.7	8.6	23.4
U.S. Equity Composite*	8.8	10.1	16.9	3.1	4.8	17.9
CAPITAL APPRECIATION RETURNS						
NYSE	4.5	5.8	15.7	-1.1	0.5	16.8
AMEX	4.7	7.3	23.0	-1.1	2.0	23.4
OTC	8.6	11.0	22.1	2.8	5.7	23.1
U.S. Equity Composite*	4.9	6.2	16.3	-0.8	0.9	17.4

* U.S. equity composite is the value-weighted combination of NYSE, AMEX, and OTC.
Source: Table 5.11

NASDAQ climbed more than 50 percent, while the number of NYSE listings has remained stable and AMEX listings have fallen substantially. Because the OTC has more small companies, the overall number of OTC stocks is much greater than the number on the NYSE or AMEX.

Likewise, OTC returns, displayed in Table 5.11 and summarized in Table 5.12, have far exceeded returns on the other exchanges. A dollar invested at year-end 1959 grew to almost $15 by the mid-1980s, with all income reinvested. This total return represents a compound return of 11.5 percent per year, compared with an NYSE total return of 8.6 percent over the same period.

While OTC returns have been superior to those on the NYSE and AMEX, the OTC's risk is only slightly higher. The standard deviation of the OTC's total returns, 22.4 percent, was only modestly greater than the standard deviation of NYSE returns, 16.3 percent, and actually less than that of the AMEX, with 23.5 percent.

The AMEX

For many years, AMEX was second only to the NYSE as a security market. However, AMEX has not grown in number of securities like the NYSE and OTC markets. The market value of all outstanding AMEX shares grew from approximately $21 billion in the late 1950s to over $80 billion in the 1980s, but this was a result of capital appreciation, not new listings.

Due to the smaller size and more speculative nature of its stocks, AMEX returns differ appreciably from those of the NYSE. In Table 5.11, total returns on the AMEX are contrasted with total returns on the NYSE and in OTC markets over the past several decades. A dollar

Table 5.13. Stock Exchange Statistics, 1985

	NYSE	AMEX	OTC (NASDAQ)
Number of Listed Issues	2,298	1,290	N/A
Number of Listed Common Issues	1,503	825	4,136
Number of Listed Shares (Billions)	52.3	6.4	20.7
Market Capitalization (Billions)			
1920	30.95	N/A	
1930	41.31	N/A	
1940	35.00	N/A	4.80
1950	85.70	N/A	9.40
1960	307.71	21.00	23.30
1970	605.26	35.90	63.20
1980	1194.54	72.30	122.40
1985	1950.33	87.30	287.30
Trading Volume (Billions of Shares)			
1960	0.77	0.29	N/A
1970	2.94	0.84	N/A
1980	11.35	1.63	6.69
1985	27.51	2.10	15.0
Seat Price	$ 460,000	$ 260,000	N/A

Source: NYSE market capitalization and AMEX market capitalization after 1960 from the Center For Research in Security Prices, University of Chicago; 1960 AMEX market capitalization was estimated by the authors. OTC market capitalization after 1980 from annual NASDAQ factbooks; earlier figures were estimated by the authors. Other data from NYSE, AMEX, and NASDAQ factbooks.

invested at year-end 1959 in AMEX stocks would have grown to about $6, with dividends reinvested, by the 1980s. Such a portfolio provided a compound total return of 7.3 percent per year, in contrast to a compound total return of 8.6 percent from NYSE stocks. In particular, dividend income over the term was below that of NYSE stocks, since many AMEX-listed firms seek growth, or capital appreciation, by reinvesting earnings rather than distributing them as dividends.

The NYSE, AMEX, and OTC markets are compared for vital statistics, such as market capitalization and trading volume, in Table 5.13. In the 1980s, the NYSE has over six and a half times the capitalization of the OTC market and does about twice as much trading, while the AMEX ranks a distant third. Among markets, the NYSE clearly dominates in capitalization and trading volume, but the OTC is growing the most quickly.

Conclusion

In the last 2 centuries, the U.S. economy has grown tremendously. During that time, investors in U.S. equities earned returns that are unparalleled in world history. Because returns averaging about 8 percent per year were compounded, investors earned big money in the long run, partly from capital appreciation but mostly from dividend reinvestment. Nevertheless, over short periods, investors faced the risk of losing a large chunk of their capital.

As indexes of the stock market's performance improved, better analysis of equity returns was possible. Early attempts, like the Dow Jones Industrial Average, measured only capital appreciation and were price-weighted, not market-weighted. Alfred Cowles and CRSP constructed better indexes covering later periods. Now indexes for any number of equity markets are available instantaneously on computer.

Careful analysis now confirms that equity returns follow close to a random walk. That is, returns in one year are independent of returns in the previous year. Moreover, returns are roughly normally distributed. In addition, the reward and risk of equity investments has been extremely stable over two centuries. While stocks have a higher level of risk than other investments, equities' risk has paid off handsomely with higher returns.

In the last several decades, returns on the OTC have surpassed those of the NYSE and AMEX. With only slight differences in standard deviation, nominal and real returns on the OTC exceed the NYSE's real returns, which in turn are often greater than those on AMEX. Although the risk of OTC stocks is higher, investors have been rewarded with much higher returns. Consequently, the OTC market, along with regional exchanges, is becoming increasingly important over time.

Suggested Reading

Brealey, Richard A: *An Introduction to Risk and Return from Common Stocks,* 2d ed., MIT Press, Cambridge, Mass., 1983. Very readable exposition of modern portfolio theory, often used as a supplementary textbook.

Ibbotson Associates: *Stocks, Bonds, Bills, and Inflation: 1987 Yearbook: Market Results for 1926–1986,* Ibbotson Associates, Chicago, annual. A basic reference work, giving monthly and annual data on the principal asset classes in the U.S. economy.

Ibbotson, Roger G., and Rex Sinquefield: *Stocks, Bonds, Bills, and Inflation: The Past and the Future.* Financial Analysts Research Foundation, Charlottesville, Va., 1982. Uses historical data to derive "market consensus forecasts" of future asset returns. The original (1977) edition of this work prefigured computer-based asset allocation models.

Lorie, James H., Peter Dodd, and Mary Hamilton Kimpton: *The Stock Market: Theories and Evidence,* 2d ed., Dow Jones-Irwin, Homewood, Ill., 1985. Often used by professors as a supplementary textbook.

6
Analyzing the U.S. Stock Market

In the past, most investors have tried to achieve high returns by selecting stocks having the greatest return potential. Investors have traditionally performed an appraisal, or *fundamental analysis,* of a stock, using non-market information, to determine its value. Investors then buy stocks whose market price is below the fundamental value, hoping that the market will eventually recognize that value.

Other investors have used *technical analysis,* which forecasts the supply and demand for a given security, independent of its underlying value. The discovery that stock returns follow a generally random walk has made the search for high returns more difficult. If returns have no pattern, technical analysis cannot reveal a pattern to be exploited.

Finally, some investors try to make money by *timing the market.* If the stock market as a whole departs from fair value, such investors adjust the amount of stocks as a proportion of their portfolios. The more sensible systems require that investors acquire or process information faster than the market. The relationship between inflation and stock returns, for example, is so powerful that some investors find it intriguing to see if they can beat the market by forecasting inflation rate changes.

While these methods—fundamental and technical analysis and market timing—are not necessarily reliable, careful analysis of *groups* of stocks has revealed some patterns. One of the most striking is the superior record of small-capitalization stocks. (Capitalization is the aggregate value of the company's stock, i.e., its price per share times the number of shares outstanding.) Other stock characteristics are related to their returns with varying degrees of accuracy. Profit opportunities also appear to exist in certain specialized segments of the market. For example, venture capital and new issues are equity categories with very high but extraordinarily volatile returns. In the following sections, the U.S. stock market is analyzed to determine where to look for superior stock returns.

Inflation's Effect on Stock Prices

Years ago, it was generally believed that inflation is good news for the stock market. However, evidence from the inflationary years between the mid-1960s and the present belies this notion. The high-inflation years of 1973 and 1974 were disastrous for the stock market. Later in the 1970s, modest increases in equity prices were negated by extremely high inflation. In a subsequent period of moderate inflation in the 1980s, the stock and bond markets both rallied strongly.

Yearly equity returns are ranked by the year's inflation rate in the upper half of Table 6.1. Six rates of price change are identified. The categories are

- Extraordinary deflation
- Moderate deflation
- Price stability
- Moderate inflation
- High inflation
- Extraordinary inflation

For each group, the average inflation-adjusted total return of the stock market (specifically, the NYSE) is then calculated.

Price stability, moderate deflation, and extraordinary deflation all had salutary effects on stock prices, and consequently on total real equity returns. During the years of moderate inflation, the stock market's returns were unexceptional. Stocks performed worst—in fact, real returns were negative—in periods of extraordinary inflation, that is, inflation in excess of 8 percent per year. Returns were only a little better in periods of high inflation. These statistics all refute claims that inflation is good for the stock market.

Changes in the inflation rate also have very predictable effects on stock market returns. In the lower half of Table 6.1, inflation-adjusted total returns on the NYSE are grouped by inflation's rate of change in each year. The categories are

- Rapid deceleration
- Low deceleration
- Low acceleration
- Rapid acceleration

Table 6.1. Inflation, Inflation Rate Changes, and Real Total Returns on Stocks: The Long-Run Relationship (1790–1985) and the Postwar Experience (1946–1985)

Inflation Range	THE LONG RUN 1790–1985		POSTWAR 1946–1985	
	Number of Years	Average Real Total Stock Market Return*	Number of Years	Average Real Total Stock Market Return*
Extraordinary deflation -4% and below	32	11.27 %	0	n/a
Moderate deflation -3.99% to -1%	24	12.90	1	22.01 %
Price stability -0.99% to 0.99%	35	12.53	5	23.02
Moderate inflation 1% to 3.99%	55	10.23	18	10.32
High inflation 4% to 7.99%	26	3.65	8	8.47
Extraordinary inflation 8% and above	24	-5.65	8	-7.82
Inflation Rate Changes from Previous Year				
Rapid deceleration Down 5% or more	34	11.74 %	4	10.37 %
Low deceleration Down 0.01% to 4.99%	63	10.76	17	16.91
Low acceleration Up 0 to 4.99%	68	6.87	16	0.39
Rapid acceleration Up 5% or more	31	2.69	3	-8.61
ALL YEARS	196		40	
Arithmetic mean		8.31 %		7.74 %
Geometric mean (compound return)		6.28		6.02

*Arithmetic mean except where noted.

Source: Tables 5.2, 5.3, 5.4, and 11.3.

The highest returns over the past 2 centuries occurred in the years of rapid deceleration, when the inflation rate was 5 or more percentage points below the previous year. Average real returns were 11.74 percent per year in these years. Real returns were lowest in periods when inflation accelerated rapidly; real returns averaged only 2.69 percent per year under those conditions.

In the postwar period, the results are similar. The best returns, 16.91 percent on average, occurred when inflation rates fell by a moderate amount, and the worst real returns, a miserable −8.61 percent on average, showed up when the inflation rate rose rapidly. Thus, reductions in the rate of inflation are good for the stock market, and increases in inflation are bad.

Beta: Comovement with the Market

Beginning in the late 1960s, financial economists emphasized the importance of a stock's beta. Beta, as defined in the CAPM, provides a simple and theoretically elegant view of risk and return. During the period studied, the CAPM would not predict much of a relationship between beta and return, primarily because the return on the stock market during the period was similar to the riskless return. During 1967–1984, the compound annual return on the value-weighted NYSE was 8.6 percent, compared to 7.4 percent on U.S. Treasury bills.

The upper portion of Table 6.2 displays compound annual returns and standard deviations for decile portfolios of NYSE stocks, ranked each year by their betas. (A decile makes up one-tenth of the stocks listed on the NYSE.) Each year, all NYSE stocks' betas are estimated and ranked from lowest to highest. The stocks having the lowest betas are considered to be in the first decile, and those with the highest betas are in the tenth decile. The data indicate that beta explains little about stock performance over the aggregate period 1967–1984. Low-beta stocks had higher returns than high-beta stocks by a considerable margin over the period. This result is somewhat surprising since the CAPM suggests that high- and low-beta stocks should have roughly equivalent returns during a time period in which stock market returns in excess of the riskless rate were essentially zero.

Since the failure of the data to confirm the CAPM was surprising, further analysis was done. By breaking the period into "up" and "down" years (measured as S&P total returns in excess of riskless Treasury bill rates) beta does have a substantial predictive effect on returns and the CAPM theory is supported. In results not shown in Table 6.2, for the 10

Table 6.2. Summary Statistics of NYSE Stocks, 1967–1984, Sorted into Deciles along Various Dimensions

BETA

Decile	Compound Annual Return	Standard Deviation of Annual Returns	Ending (12/31/84) Value of a Dollar Invested on 12/31/66
1 (lowest)	11.17 %	17.88 %	$ 7.48
2	10.26	19.02	6.39
3	8.67	19.56	4.85
4	5.05	17.51	2.55
5	7.49	16.70	3.95
6	6.51	18.71	3.31
7	5.49	19.89	2.76
8	3.97	21.78	2.10
9	4.40	25.98	2.27
10 (highest)	2.56	28.74	1.62

MARKET CAPITALIZATION (SIZE)

Decile	Compound Annual Return	Standard Deviation of Annual Returns	Ending (12/31/84) Value of a Dollar Invested on 12/31/66
1 (largest)	6.49 %	16.58 %	$ 3.30
2	8.19	18.77	4.46
3	10.00	20.52	6.11
4	10.35	24.54	6.50
5	10.93	24.32	7.18
6	12.69	26.02	9.67
7	13.52	29.19	11.12
8	13.12	30.78	10.41
9	14.84	32.32	13.86
10 (smallest)	16.52	35.85	18.26

DIVIDEND YIELD

Decile	Compound Annual Return	Standard Deviation of Annual Returns	Ending (12/31/84) Value of a Dollar Invested on 12/31/66
1 (lowest)	5.40 %	24.73 %	$ 2.72
2	8.96	22.35	5.10
3	6.34	25.48	3.21
4	5.57	20.45	2.80
5	7.69	20.13	4.09
6	6.23	18.88	3.15
7	7.46	17.12	3.92
8	11.76	17.97	8.26
9	10.99	19.83	7.25
10 (highest)	9.28	22.79	5.40

PRICE-EARNINGS RATIO

Decile	Compound Annual Return	Standard Deviation of Annual Returns	Ending (12/31/84) Value of a Dollar Invested on 12/31/66
1 (lowest)	14.08 %	24.07 %	$12.22
2	13.81	21.51	11.67
3	10.95	23.72	7.21
4	10.29	20.65	6.43
5	9.20	16.68	5.32
6	6.43	19.82	3.27
7	7.00	18.28	3.62
8	5.57	18.44	2.80
9	5.50	20.18	2.77
10 (highest, incl. negative earnings stocks)	5.58	25.31	2.81

MARKET-BOOK RATIO

Decile	Compound Annual Return	Standard Deviation of Annual Returns	Ending (12/31/84) Value of a Dollar Invested on 12/31/66
1 (lowest)	14.36 %	26.94 %	$12.80
2	14.40	23.15	12.88
3	14.39	22.68	12.87
4	12.43	20.80	9.26
5	8.82	18.81	4.98
6	8.36	18.46	4.60
7	7.69	20.94	4.09
8	5.63	20.30	2.83
9	5.26	18.69	2.65
10 (highest)	6.06	20.68	3.06

Source: Roger G. Ibbotson "Decile Portfolios of the New York Stock Exchange, 1967-1984" working paper, Yale School of Management, 1986.

"up" years, the highest-beta decile had an average return of 26 percent, while the lowest-beta decile had an average return of 22 percent in the same years. In the 9 "down" years, the highest-beta decile had an average return of −15 percent, while the lowest-beta decile had an average return of 2 percent.

Market Capitalization

The Size Effect: Large Returns for Small Stocks

Much of a stock's return can be explained statistically by firm size, or, more specifically, market capitalization. Rolf Banz first observed the "small-stock effect" when he sorted NYSE stocks into quintiles based on their market capitalization and calculated total returns for a value-weighted portfolio of stocks in each quintile. His results, summarized in Table 6.3, indicate that returns from the smallest quintile surpassed all the other quintiles', as well as the Standard & Poor's Composite Index (S&P 500) and other indexes of large stocks. A dollar invested in the largest quintile grew to only about $109 after 55 years, while the same dollar invested in the smallest quintile grew to $524. The second section of Table 6.2 shows results for capitalization deciles over 1966–1984; here, too, the superior performance of small stocks is dramatically evident.

Table 6.3. Total Annual Returns on NYSE Stocks, 1926–1980, Sorted into Quintiles According to Market Capitalization (Portfolios Are Value-Weighted)

	QUINTILE				
	(largest) First	Second	Third	Fourth	(smallest) Fifth
Compound Annual Return	8.9%	10.1%	11.1%	11.7%	12.1%
Arithmetic Mean Return	10.9%	13.5%	15.3%	17.0%	18.2%
Standard Deviation of Returns	20.2%	26.9%	30.1%	33.4%	37.3%
First-Order Autocorrelation of Returns	0.06	0.05	0.06	0.08	0.11
End of 1980 Value of $1.00 Invested in 12/31/25	$108.67	$200.22	$333.76	$443.69	$524.00

Source: Professor Rolf W. Banz, Dimensional Asset Management, Ltd., Albemarle House, One Albemarle Street, London W1X 3HF England, provided monthly total returns by quintile; the authors calculated the summary statistics presented here.

Table 6.4. A Comparison of Total Returns on Small and Large Stocks, 1926–1985

Year	Large Stock (S&P) Total Return	Small Stock Total Return	Small Stock Premium (Small minus Large)	Year	Large Stock (S&P) Total Return	Small Stock Total Return	Small Stock Premium (Small minus Large)
				1955	31.56%	20.44%	-9.52%
1926	11.62%	0.28%	-10.12%	1956	6.56	4.28	-3.12
1927	37.49	22.10	-11.62	1957	-10.78	-14.57	-4.71
1928	43.61	39.69	-3.22	1958	43.36	64.89	15.50
1929	-8.42	-51.36	-46.60	1959	11.95	16.40	3.84
1930	-24.90	-38.15	-15.47	1960	0.47	-3.29	-3.95
1931	-43.34	-49.75	-5.42	1961	26.89	32.09	4.53
1932	-8.19	-5.39	8.61	1962	-8.73	-11.90	-3.14
1933	53.99	142.87	69.64	1963	22.80	23.57	0.49
1934	-1.44	24.22	31.58	1964	16.48	23.52	6.14
1935	47.67	40.19	-4.64	1965	12.45	41.75	26.75
1936	33.92	64.80	25.56	1966	-10.06	-7.01	3.66
1937	-35.03	-58.01	-31.77	1967	23.98	83.57	49.78
1938	31.12	32.80	11.07	1968	11.06	35.97	23.03
1939	-0.41	0.35	9.84	1969	-8.50	-25.05	-16.94
1940	-9.78	-5.16	10.40	1970	4.01	-17.43	-19.48
1941	-11.59	-9.00	4.11	1971	14.31	16.50	2.89
1942	20.34	44.51	20.21	1972	18.98	4.43	-12.26
1943	25.90	88.37	54.46	1973	-14.66	-30.90	-17.29
1944	19.75	53.72	29.66	1974	-26.47	-19.95	6.79
1945	36.44	73.61	28.82	1975	37.20	52.82	12.31
1946	-8.07	-11.63	-2.37	1976	23.84	57.38	29.04
1947	5.71	0.92	-4.08	1977	-7.18	25.38	34.81
1948	5.50	-2.11	-6.75	1978	6.56	23.46	18.25
1949	18.79	19.75	1.26	1979	18.44	43.46	22.72
1950	31.71	38.75	5.65	1980	32.42	39.88	7.22
1951	24.02	7.80	-13.22	1981	-4.91	13.88	19.70
1952	18.37	3.03	-13.37	1982	21.41	28.01	4.89
1953	-0.99	-6.49	-5.71	1983	22.51	39.67	14.23
1954	52.62	60.58	4.89	1984	6.27	-6.67	-12.16
				1985	32.16	24.66	-5.73

SUMMARY STATISTICS, 1926 - 1985

COMPOUND ANNUAL RETURN	9.84%	12.61%	3.83%
ARITHMETIC MEAN RETURN	12.01%	18.34%	5.66%
STANDARD DEVIATION OF RETURNS	21.19%	36.00%	19.82%
SERIAL CORRELATION OF RETURNS	0.01	0.10	0.37

Source: *Stocks, Bonds, Bills, and Inflation: 1986 Yearbook,* Chicago: Ibbotson Associates, 1986.

In Table 6.4, year by year returns on small stocks (the fifth quintile) are compared with the S&P 500 for the last 60 years. The small-stock return minus the S&P return is labeled the *small-stock premium*. The premium on small stocks is highly autocorrelated, at a level of 0.37 over 1926 to 1985. That is, the series has lengthy predictable "runs" of winning and losing years relative to large stocks. Furthermore, much of the excess return came in relatively short periods, notably the early 1940s and 1974–1983. During the stock market's crash in 1929–1932, small stocks had much poorer performance than S&P stocks, but their later high returns more than compensate for the large early losses.

The "January Effect" on Small Stocks

Much of the excess return on small stocks is earned in January of each year, and even more astonishingly, in the first few days of January. Donald B. Keim divided stocks on both the NYSE and AMEX into quintiles and showed that the quintile with the smallest companies had large positive premiums in January, compared with negative premiums for large stocks. After adjusting for risk, Keim concludes that in January, small stocks generally earn a 15 percent premium, defined as the average excess return per day, multiplied by the number of trading days in the month. Since this premium is larger than the average premium on small stocks for the whole year, Keim concludes that the entire small-stock effect is a "January effect."

According to Marc Reinganum, the January effect on small stocks may be limited to the first 5 trading days in January—a "turn of the year effect." He finds that the first trading day in January usually provides the holder of the smallest quintile of stocks a 4 percent premium, the second day a 2.5 percent premium, and the third day a 1.75 percent premium. These 1-day premiums are so high that they are almost unbelievable. Academics do not understand why small stocks behave this way at the beginning of the year, and some claim that the effect may be due to measurement error or a statistical artifact of some kind. Others argue that investors sell stocks at year end to realize tax losses and repurchase stocks in January, forcing prices up then. Recent research suggests that there is also a time of month, day of week, and time of day effect on stock returns. These effects appear to have an impact on both large and small stocks, although to different degrees.

The Relationship of Returns to Other Stock Characteristics

Dividend Yield

The average dividend yields of stocks included in the S&P Index are shown in Table 6.5. Dividend yields are highest during periods of low stock prices. Yields peak in the early 1940s and early 1950s, the highest being 8.3 percent in 1950. The lowest dividend yields occur in the boom periods of the late 1920s, the 1960s, and the early 1970s, with the lowest

Table 6.5. Statistics on the S&P Index through History
(1926–1985)

Year	Standard and Poor's Composite Index (Year-end)*	Dividend Yield (%)	Price-Earnings Ratio	Market-Book Ratio**
1926	13.49	5.62 %	10.88	
1927	17.66	5.20	15.91	
1928	24.35	4.32	17.64	
1929	21.45	3.82	13.32	
1930	15.34	4.88	15.81	
1931	8.12	6.59	13.31	
1932	6.89	7.97	16.80	
1933	10.10	5.25	22.95	
1934	9.50	4.79	19.39	
1935	13.43	4.58	17.67	
1936	17.18	4.78	16.84	
1937	10.55	5.47	9.34	
1938	13.21	4.76	20.64	
1939	12.49	5.32	13.88	
1940	10.58	6.18	10.08	
1941	8.69	7.51	7.49	
1942	9.77	7.13	9.49	
1943	11.67	5.45	12.41	
1944	13.28	5.31	14.28	
1945	17.36	4.50	18.08	
1946	15.30	4.22	14.43	
1947	15.30	5.65	9.50	1.37
1948	15.20	6.11	6.64	1.23
1949	16.76	7.72	7.22	1.05
1949				1.11
1950	20.41	8.30	7.19	1.22
1951	23.77	6.51	9.74	1.27
1952	26.57	5.95	11.07	1.32
1953	24.81	5.98	9.88	1.20
1954	35.98	5.39	12.99	1.63
1955	45.48	4.16	12.56	1.81
1956	46.67	3.81	13.69	1.77
1957	39.99	4.08	11.87	1.36
1958	55.21	3.91	19.10	1.80
1959	59.89	3.23	17.67	1.86
1960	58.11	3.59	17.77	1.72
1961	71.55	3.12	22.43	2.05
1962	63.10	3.51	17.19	1.74
1963	75.02	3.32	18.66	1.97
1964	84.75	3.13	18.63	2.11
1965	92.43	3.12	17.81	2.13
1966	80.33	3.41	14.47	1.76
1967	96.47	3.24	18.10	2.08
1968	103.86	3.18	18.03	2.07
1969	92.06	3.25	15.93	1.78
1970	92.15	3.87	17.96	1.75
1971	102.09	3.20	17.91	1.85
1972	118.05	2.95	18.39	2.02
1973	97.55	3.16	11.95	1.55
1974	68.56	4.44	7.71	1.01
1975	90.19	4.41	11.33	1.27
1976	107.46	3.95	10.84	1.41
1977	95.10	4.84	8.70	1.16
1978	96.11	5.45	7.79	1.08
1979	107.94	5.50	7.26	1.09
1980	135.76	5.42	9.16	1.25
1981	122.55	5.29	8.04	1.06
1982	140.64	5.85	11.10	1.19
1983	164.93	4.52	11.80	1.27
1984	167.24	4.81	10.76	1.51
1985	211.28	4.71	11.49	1.79

* S & P Composite consists of 500 stocks starting March, 1957, and 90 stocks previously.

** Market-book ratio is calculated for S & P Industrial Index only.

Sources: S & P Composite Index, price-earnings ratios, and book values for calculating market-book ratios are taken from Standard and Poor's Trade and Securities Statistics, various issues, with updates from the Wall Street Journal. The authors divided market values (S & P 400 Industrial Index levels) by book values to arrive at market-book ratios. Dividend yields are take from Stocks, Bonds, Bills, and Inflation: 1986 Yearbook, Chicago: Ibbotson Associates, 1986.

being 2.95 percent. Yields are high when prices are low because dividend payments are less volatile than stock prices. When stock prices drop, corporate officers often maintain dividends to sustain investor confidence, driving up the dividend yield.

Dividend yields are not good predictors of equity returns. The third section of Table 6.2 displays the returns on NYSE stocks sorted into deciles according to their dividend yields. Stocks with the lowest dividends are sorted into the first decile and stocks with the highest into the tenth decile, and all stocks are resorted at each year end. The value-weighted total return on each of these decile portfolios is then calculated.

Over 1966–1984, there is no clear, discernible relationship between dividend yield and total return. For certain periods, the results do suggest a relationship: high-dividend stocks have the highest returns over 1969–1977, for example. But the results over the whole period studied indicate that a stock's dividend yield has no direct relation to its return, and this finding is more compelling.

Price/Earnings Ratios

The price/earnings (P/E) ratio is a commonly used statistic for assessing stock value across business sectors and between companies. P/E ratios for the S&P Index over the last half century are also shown in Table 6.5. Although low P/E ratios typically prevail during periods of low stock prices, this was emphatically not true during the Great Depression. In the early 1930s, corporate profits fell so low that the extremely depressed stock prices of 1933 were, on average, 23 times earnings. This is the highest average P/E ratio on record, approached only once again, in the bull market of 1961.

In 15 of the past 60 years, the market's average P/E ratio fell below 10. After a period of low P/E ratios, the market has often rallied sharply. For example, the bull market of the 1950s, the period of greatest nominal increases in the history of the stock market, was preceded by a string of years in which the P/E ratio of the market remained below 10. The pattern was repeated at the end of 1981.

Over the last 2 decades, P/E ratios had a direct relationship to return. In the fourth section of Table 6.2, returns are displayed on deciles of NYSE stocks sorted according to their P/E ratios. Stocks with the lowest P/E ratios were placed in the first decile, while those with the highest P/E ratios, as well as those with undefined P/E ratios due to zero or negative earnings, were placed in the tenth decile. Stocks with low P/E ratios greatly outperformed the others during the period studied. In general, buying stocks with low P/E ratios has been a profitable strategy and may continue to be.

Market/Book Ratios

Fundamental stock analysts often compare a firm's market value to its true, or economic, value. If the accounting measure of book value is related to true value, then the market/book ratio may indicate which stocks are over- and undervalued. To test this, NYSE stocks are sorted into deciles according to their market/book ratios. As shown in the bottom section of Table 6.2, stocks with low market/book ratios had substantially higher returns than high market/book stocks over the decade.

Because past inflation and noneconomic depreciation have wreaked havoc with corporate book values, it is difficult to draw significant conclusions either from this section of Table 6.2 or from Table 6.5, which shows the S&P market/book ratios for the post-World War II period. The S&P Industrials' average market/book ratio appears to be related both to inflation and to the real level of stock prices. One of the lowest market/book ratios for the S&P Industrial Average, 1.06, occurred in 1981, following a period of prolonged inflation. The highest market/book ratio occurred in 1965, after a succession of years with very high stock returns. Market/book ratios may also be compared across firms at a point in time to help find bargains in individual stocks, but may be unreliable guides to true value because accounting book values differ from economic value.

Markets with Special Profit Opportunities

New Issues

When the owners of a privately held firm want to raise capital from the public, they retain an investment banker to issue the new security in a public offering; this security is called a *new issue,* or *initial public offering.* New issues are potentially profitable because there are periods in which these securities have predictable and high returns in the initial period (measured until the end of the first calendar month) after the stock "goes public." In Figure 6.1, the number of new issues and their average initial performance is shown graphically. New issues occur in giant waves lasting several years, interspersed with periods having almost no new issues. Three large waves are evident in the bottom portion of Figure 6.1. The first was from 1960 to 1962, the second from 1967 to 1972, and the third from 1980 to 1982. A fourth wave of activity was taking place during the mid-1980s.

When the number of new issues is large, initial performance is consistently high—and often remarkable, as in the case of the return of 104 percent in December 1967. Average initial performance was negative in only 54 out of 276 months, and when returns were negative, the nega-

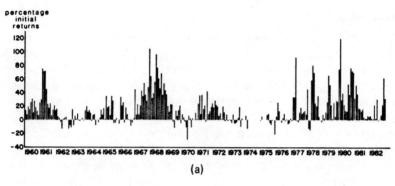

(a)

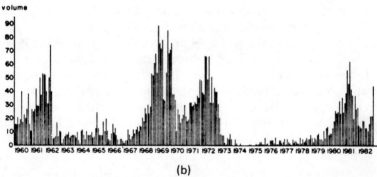

(b)

Figure 6.1. Initial public offerings: (a) Average initial returns by month for S.E.C.-registered initial public offerings; (b) number of S.E.C.-registered initial public offerings by month. (*Source: Jay D. Ritter, "The Hot Issues Market of 1980," Journal of Business, April 1984. Reprinted by permission of the University of Chicago Press, © 1984.*)

tive figure was usually very small. During the 1970s, average initial performance was 16.8 percent. Furthermore, because returns had a very high (0.74) serial correlation, the next month's initial performance is generally predictable given this month's. The average initial performance of new issues and the serial correlation of those returns were lower in the 1970s and 1980s than in the 1960s.

The monthly volume of new issues also has a very high serial correlation. Furthermore, a delayed relationship between initial performance and the number of new offerings exists. When the graphs in Figure 6.1 are viewed together, the volume of new issues peaks when their initial performance is at its highest or just afterwards. At other times, new-issue markets are dry. In several months during 1974 and 1975, for example, no new issues were reported. Nearly dry markets are associated with initial monthly performance that is unexceptional or poor.

Many persons have speculated on the reasons for the high returns on new issues. Kevin Rock suggests that insiders have a good idea of a new stock's true value and outsiders do not. Investment bankers, acting as underwriters, allocate the new issues among insiders and outsiders without knowing who is in what group. But insiders know to queue up for the relatively underpriced issues, leaving outsiders with the poorer ones.

Now, Rock's argument continues, suppose there are not enough insiders to go around. Underwriters must then count on outsiders to buy much of the total set of new issues. Outsiders demand a competitive return and get stuck with the relatively overpriced issues. These relatively bad issues must be at least fairly priced to induce outsiders to take their chances in the new-issue market. If the bad issues are fairly priced at issuance, then the good issues must be *underpriced*, making the whole market underpriced on average. This hypothesis may explain why average new issues are underpriced at the start, and therefore have high initial performance. It does not explain why firms would willingly issue such underpriced securities, although possibly they have a strong desire to bring their offerings to a successful completion.

Venture Capital

The term *venture capital* is used to cover a broad range of transactions, from the infusion of a few thousand dollars in a family enterprise to the placement of millions of dollars in a high-potential venture. Sometimes venture capital is used to start a new business, but often venture capital finances a business with good earning potential after operations have begun. Several types of firms make investments in venture capital:

- Small-business investment companies
- Venture capital subsidiaries of major financial institutions
- Independent venture capital companies
- Certain wealthy individuals

Since data on returns from venture capital placements are unavailable, the market price of companies that invest in venture capital is examined and results are displayed in Table 6.6. Returns from such stocks, and by analogy, to venture capital, are unusually high and spectacularly volatile. A total return index set at $1 at year-end 1959 rose to over $15 by 1968, with much of the gain occurring in the superboom year of 1967. The bear market of 1969–1970 was magnified in the venture capital market, with a decline of 75 percent in those 2 years combined. Further declines in 1974–1975 set the index back nearly to its 1960 level. Large gains in the late 1970s and early 1980s then carried the index above its 1968 level. Returns on the index were considerably above those of S&P stocks over the same period.

Table 6.6. Venture Capital Returns and Return
Indexes, 1959–1985

Year	Total Returns	Year-End Total Return Indices
1959		1.00
1960	-1.90 %	0.98
1961	89.41	1.86
1962	-21.52	1.46
1963	65.00	2.41
1964	13.36	2.73
1965	-9.44	2.47
1966	-42.30	1.43
1967	371.17	6.72
1968	128.05	15.31
1969	-58.82	6.31
1970	-40.40	3.76
1971	-0.31	3.75
1972	7.50	4.03
1973	-40.72	2.39
1974	-26.19	1.76
1975	26.29	2.23
1976	38.82	3.09
1977	19.96	3.71
1978	46.78	5.44
1979	36.54	7.43
1980	96.79	14.62
1981	-9.34	13.25
1982	25.61	16.65
1983	43.70	23.92
1984	8.59	21.87
1985	21.33	26.54

Source: First Chicago Investment Advisors constructed an index using
stock prices of independent venture capital investment companies, for
1969-1985; prior to 1969, a selected sample of newly listed issues, quoted
in the Bank and Quotation Record, was constructed by the authors.

The standard deviation of the returns, 86 percent, is higher than that
of any major stock market in the world. Since venture capital companies
invest in multiple projects, this standard deviation is already dampened
by grouping each company's profitable and unprofitable investments
into one stock price. Thus, investment in individual ventures contains a
tremendous amount of risk, with a significant probability of total loss of
capital.

Investment Strategies

1. Inflation—Watch for indications of changes in the inflation rate and buy equities as the rate goes down.

If you could forecast inflation accurately only 1 year in advance, you would make large profits over the long run. Unfortunately, even the best economists have remarkably poor track records with inflation forecasts. Nevertheless, the magnitude of the effect of inflation's acceleration and deceleration on stocks may motivate you to try a market-timing strategy, based on your expectations about changes in the rate of inflation.

2. Beta—Beta isn't everything, but it does help you to estimate risk and expected return.

A particular stock's beta is very useful in predicting how much the stock will go up or down, given that you know which way the stock market will go. Also, in general, there is a relationship between a stock's equilibrium expected return and its beta, as predicted by the CAPM.

3. Small stocks—If you have substantial tolerance for risk in part of your portfolio, buy small stocks, especially at year end.

Many explanations for the small-stock effect have been suggested. According to new equilibrium theory, investors' information, search, and transaction costs may force smaller companies to sell their stocks at lower prices, raising expected return on small stocks above that of large stocks. However, you can reduce your search costs substantially by forming a diversified, index-type portfolio of small stocks. For example, buy *all* of the stocks in the smallest decile of the NYSE rather than expending effort or costs to determine which ones to buy. Although small-stock returns are more volatile, they are also high. Small stocks have their highest returns in January, especially during the first week.

4. Dividend yields—Choose stocks that pay low dividends if you are in a high tax bracket.

The last chapter emphasized that most of the return from equities came from the reinvestment of dividends. But this is largely because corporations have traditionally paid dividends to satisfy shareholders' desires for cash flows. Economically, it does not really matter whether the corporation or the investor reinvests as long as dividends are reinvested by somebody. If the corporation retains earnings instead of paying them out as dividends, the investor can expect a capital gain. Capital gains are preferred to ordinary income (even when taxed at the same rate) because capital gains can be deferred and realized only when the investor chooses. Thus, you should hold stocks paying low dividends if you are in a high tax bracket. There is no clear recommendation in this regard if you are in a low tax bracket or manage tax-exempt money.

5. P/E ratios—Stocks with low P/E ratios may represent bargains.

Stocks with low P/E ratios have had superior returns when compared to stocks with higher P/E ratios. This P/E effect is not quite as powerful as the small-stock effect, but is nevertheless still important. Further, the P/E effect is incremental to the small-stock effect, since low-P/E stocks do not overlap small stocks very much.

6. Market/book ratio—Market/book ratios may also be useful in predicting stock returns.

Firms with low market/book ratios have had better returns than those with high market/book ratios. However, inflation makes this measure less reliable.

7. New issues—Buy new issues if you have favorable inside information. Also, if initial performance on new issues was high last month, buy new issues this month.

The data on new-issue performance suggest that:

1. On average, new-issue performance is positive.

2. High and low returns come in predictable waves.

3. There are "cold" and "hot" markets with few or many new issues.

4. Initial performance and the number of new offerings appear to be related.

What should you do about new issues? On first glance, it would appear that you should buy new issues since they are generally underpriced. But generally the more underpriced an issue is, the harder it is to get. If insiders know which ones are most underpriced, outsiders may suffer adverse selection.

Still, you can time your purchases of new issues. In hot, high-volume–high-performance markets, it is hard to lose money and easy to find new issues to buy. For example, you did not have to be an insider to make money in hot markets like those of 1961, 1968, and 1983. Thus, when the volume of new issues is high, the initial performance of a new issue will probably also be high when you buy in the next period.

8. Venture capital—If you are an aggressive risk taker, buy venture capital because the returns are very high. But be prepared to lose your shirt, because returns are also extremely volatile.

Since new businesses continually grow and displace old businesses, the expected return from investing in venture capital should be high enough to compensate investors for the very high risk. The successes must be sufficiently profitable to make up for failures to induce investors to commit funds to new ventures. Venture capital investing should be done at the margin of your portfolio, with funds that you can afford to lose. The potential returns on successful venture investments, however, are higher than on any other type of equity.

Suggested Reading

Banz, Rolf: "The Relationship Between Return and Market Value of Common Stocks," *Journal of Financial Economics,* vol. 9, 1981, pp. 3–18. The original work identifying the high returns from small stocks.

Brown, Stephen J., and Mark P. Kritzman (eds.): *Quantitative Methods in Financial Analysis,* Dow Jones-Irwin, Homewood, Ill., 1987. A book of readings of financial analysis.

Graham, Benjamin, David L. Dodd, and Sidney Cottle: *Security Analysis: Principles and Techniques,* 4th ed., McGraw-Hill Book Company, New York, 1962. Explains how to find bargains in the stock market. While some material is dated, this is the "bible" for fundamental analysis.

Ibbotson Associates: *Stocks, Bonds, Bills, and Inflation: 1987 Yearbook,* Ibbotson Associates, Chicago, annual. Basic reference work, giving monthly and annual data on the principal asset classes in the U.S. economy.

Keim, D.: "Size-Related Anomalies and Stock Return Seasonality: Further Empirical Evidence," *Journal of Financial Economics,* vol. 12, 1983, pp. 13–32. Describes the January effect, among others.

Leuthold, Steven C.: *The Myths of Inflation and Investing,* Crain Books, Chicago, Ill., 1980. Recommends investment strategies for high- and low-inflation periods.

Rock, K.: "Why New Issues Are Underpriced," *Journal of Financial Economics,* vol. 15, 1986, pp. 187–212. Provides an explanation of new-issue underpricing.

7

Foreign Equity Returns

The Japanese economy has captured the world's attention. Japanese cars outsell American- and European-made cars in many parts of the United States. Japanese consumer goods in many industries—ranging from electronic devices and microchips to motorcycles and musical instruments—dominate world markets. American workers lose jobs to workers in some Japanese plants whose efficiency—*not* wage-adjusted—is reportedly twice that of the Americans. These results are from a country which lost a world war and which in 1946 had one of the world's lowest per capita incomes: $29 a year.

Can this economic success be discerned in the stock market? The answer is an emphatic *yes*. From 1960 to the mid-1980s, $1 invested in Japanese equities would have grown to about $50, assuming reinvestment of dividends. This performance far outshone that of any other country. United States and European equities were practically tied, with a dollar growing to about $11 in the United States and Europe.

Foreign Stock Market Returns Since 1960

Foreign equities have provided healthy returns to U.S. investors in the past quarter century, primarily because of Japan's spectacular performance and the large size of the Japanese market. Figure 7.1 shows the results which would have been obtained if a dollar had been invested in portfolios of Asian, European, U.S., and other stocks at the beginning of 1960. Asia was clearly the big winner, while the other regions were tied for a poor second place. Over 1960–1969, the Asian index consists exclusively of Japan, but beginning in 1970, Hong Kong and Singapore are given a small weight in the index. Though small, these growing

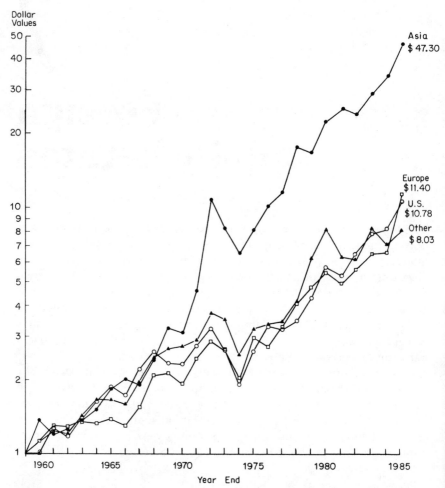

Figure 7.1. Growth of a dollar invested in world equities, 1960–1985. (Year-end 1959 = $1.) (*Source: Roger G. Ibbotson, Richard C. Carr, and Anthony W. Robinson, "International Equity and Bond Returns,"* Financial Analysts Journal, *July–August 1982, with updates by the authors of this book.*)

markets have also had spectacular returns. The portfolio of "other" countries in Figure 7.1 includes Canada and Australia.

Foreign returns in this chapter are converted to U.S. dollars. Since the U.S. investor consumes in dollars, dollar-adjusted returns are relevant from a U.S. perspective. In addition, they represent realizable returns after accounting for currency fluctuations but before transaction costs and taxes.

Total returns vary widely among countries of the world, and are annualized for 5-year periods in Table 7.1. The smallest and largest annual returns (not shown) occurred in the newly developed Asian countries: the highest was +211 percent in Singapore in 1972 and the lowest was −60 percent in Hong Kong in 1974. But annual returns (not shown) were volatile in the established industrial countries too, ranging from +183 percent in Norway in 1979 to −50 percent in the United Kingdom in 1974.

Summary statistics of foreign equity returns since 1960 are shown in Table 7.2. A country's standard deviation gives the variability of its returns and thus is a measure of risk. Two markets with the highest returns, Singapore and Hong Kong, were extremely risky, as was Norway, which had only average returns. Japan and the United Kingdom were riskier than average. Most other countries had a level of stock market risk comparable to that of the United States.

In Figure 7.2, the size of each major foreign equity market is shown as a percentage of the total. Japan dominates the foreign market. Other large markets include the United Kingdom, Canada, Germany, France, Switzerland, and Australia.

Table 7.1. Foreign Equities: U.S. Dollar-Adjusted Annual Returns for 5-Year Periods, 1960–1985 (For Summary Statistics, See Table 7.2)*

	EUROPE								
PERIOD	AUSTRIA	BELGIUM	DENMARK	FRANCE	GERMANY	ITALY	NETHER-LANDS	NORWAY	SPAIN
1960–64	13.3%	7.2%	8.9%	2.6%	6.5%	−0.7%	7.2%	4.40%	14.7%
1965–69	0.9	2.5	4.9	3.8	9.6	10.7	7.1	7.3	18.1
1970–74	19.5	13.7	15.5	−0.6	4.8	−9.4	−0.2	19.0	14.5
1975–79	8.3	18.9	7.7	22.2	16.3	−1.4	23.9	17.6	−10.2
1980–85	8.6	15.8	17.0	10.7	18.0	22.3	18.3	7.4	8.4

	EUROPE			ASIA			OTHER	
PERIOD	SWEDEN	SWITZERLAND	UNITED KINGDOM	HONG KONG	JAPAN	SINGAPORE	AUSTRALIA	CANADA
1960–64	11.8%	10.1%	6.6%		8.8%		8.8%	12.7%
1965–69	6.1	9.9	11.2		16.4		15.4	5.9
1970–74	8.2	3.7	−11.2	4.1%	15.9	11.2%	−10.7	4.6
1975–79	5.1	21.7	32.8	40.1	18.8	29.5	21.5	18.0
1980–85	24.7	11.0	16.4	8.7	20.7	2.2	5.4	7.7

* Sample includes one six-year period, 1980–1985. Returns are compound annual (geometric mean) returns over the period indicated.
Source: Constructed by the authors using capital appreciation returns and dividend yields from Morgan Stanley Capital International Perspective, New York.

Table 7.2. World Equities: Summary Statistics, 1960–1985

| Asset | Annual Returns in U.S. Dollars | | | Year-End Wealth Index 1959=$1.00 | 1985 Year-End Value in Billions U.S. $ |
	Compound Return (%)	Arithmetic Mean (%)	Standard Deviation (%)		
Europe					
Austria	9.9	13.6	35.9	11.63	4.0
Belgium	11.6	12.9	17.4	17.35	20.9
Denmark	10.9	13.8	27.8	14.90	13.1
France	7.6	10.1	25.2	6.66	78.5
Germany	11.2	14.3	29.9	15.62	179.0
Italy	4.4	8.8	34.6	3.06	64.7
Netherlands	11.2	12.8	19.4	15.79	51.6
Norway	10.8	18.1	48.1	14.48	9.8
Spain	8.6	10.9	21.7	8.52	18.7
Sweden	11.5	13.4	20.6	16.79	29.8
Switzerland	11.1	14.1	27.9	15.62	90.3
United Kingdom	10.5	14.5	31.2	13.27	328.3
Asia					
Hong Kong*	16.1	29.5	56.8	10.90	38.0
Japan	16.2	19.2	28.9	49.72	909.1
Singapore*	13.0	24.2	59.5	7.05	20.4
Other					
Australia	7.4	10.2	24.9	6.40	62.5
Canada	9.6	10.9	17.3	10.81	146.9
United States	9.6	11.2	16.9	10.78	1955.4

*1970-1985

Source: Returns, wealth indices, and year-end values from
Morgan Stanley Capital International Perspective, New York.

Markets That Move Together: Equity Return "Blocs"

Correlation of dollar-adjusted total returns shows which countries' stock markets move together (i.e., have high cross correlations) and which go their own ways. In Table 7.3, "blocs" of countries whose stock markets have had high cross correlations are displayed. Substantial comovement might be expected for countries related by such factors as geographical proximity, currency arrangements, trading partnerships, or cultural similarity.

In fact, several central European countries form a distinct equity return bloc: Germany, Switzerland, and the Netherlands are each correlated with the others at a level above 0.5. (Perfect comovement, or identical return, is represented by a correlation coefficient of 1.0; no relationship, 0.0; precise opposite movement, −1.0.) France and Belgium are less distinctly associated with this bloc, although the Netherlands and Belgium are highly correlated (not shown in Table 7.3), as might be expected due to their proximity and their past political ties.

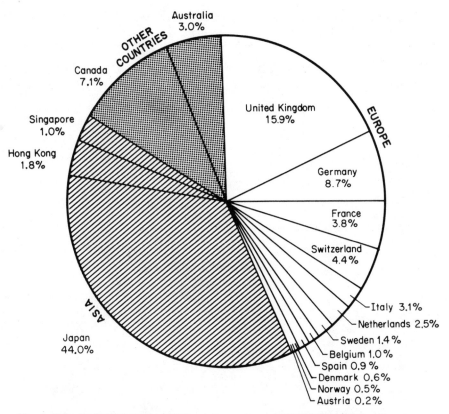

Figure 7.2. Market values of non-U.S. equities at the end of 1984. (Percentages of total non-U.S. market.) (*Source: Aggregate values from* Morgan Stanley Capital International Perspective.)

Proximity or cultural similarity, though, is not a sufficient determinant of an equity bloc. Germany and Austria share a language, a border, and many cultural traits but have a correlation below 0.3 (not shown). Sweden and Norway, which used to be one country, have an extraordinarily low correlation, −0.2 (not shown), perhaps because Norway's is largely a resource economy while Sweden is heavily industrial. Confirming this conjecture, the other two resource-dominated economies in the group, Canada and Australia, have correlations of 0.5 and 0.2 (not shown) with Norway, respectively.

The Asian equity bloc is remarkable for its high correlations across what are actually very dissimilar countries. Japan, Hong Kong, and Singapore comprise this bloc: each country is correlated with the other at a level above about 0.7. Note that these three countries are geographically very far apart. Tokyo and Singapore are about as far apart as

Table 7.3. Equity Return Blocs: Cross Correlations of
U.S. Dollar-Adjusted Total Returns, 1960–1985

Central Europe

	Germany	Netherlands	Switzerland
Germany	1.000		
Netherlands	0.654	1.000	
Switzerland	0.839	0.716	1.000

East Asia

	Japan	Hong Kong	Singapore
Japan	1.000		
Hong Kong	0.690	1.000	
Singapore	0.848	0.796	1.000

Anglo-Pacific

	U.S.	Canada	Australia
United States	1.000		
Canada	0.691	1.000	
Australia	0.627	0.656	1.000

	United Kingdom and United States	
	United Kingdom	United States
Australia	0.611	0.630
Belgium	0.352	0.431
Canada	0.374	0.701
France	0.475	0.268
Germany	0.331	0.264
Hong Kong	0.484	0.654
Japan	0.202	0.197
Netherlands	0.663	0.741
Singapore	0.297	0.521
Switzerland	0.485	0.467
United States	0.629	1.000

Source: Table 7.1 cross-correlated by the authors.

London and New York. The Asian bloc of countries all have heavily industrialized, export-oriented economies.

The United States, Canada, and Australia also form a bloc, with all cross correlations exceeding 0.6. These countries are all English-speaking, were once British colonies, cover very large land areas, have high per capita incomes, and are rich in natural resources. In addition, they are strong political allies. The United States, however, is a service economy first and a manufacturing economy second, while Canada and Australia are resource economies with large agricultural export sectors. The massive volume of U.S.-Canadian trade helps to explain the high correlation of these two countries. Australia, though, is far away; the point on the Earth's surface directly opposite Perth, Australia lies between Florida and Bermuda. Australia also trades heavily with east Asia as well as with the North American countries. While not studied due to the small size of its equity market, New Zealand has many similarities to Australia and western Canada, and can be included in this bloc, called the Anglo-Pacific group of countries.

The United Kingdom cuts across all regions and national boundaries to form a bloc of its own. The United Kingdom is correlated to some degree with every country of economic importance, including the United States (0.6), France (0.5), Germany (0.3), and even Japan (0.2). Correlations of the United Kingdom with its present and former Asian colonies are also high: 0.5 for Hong Kong, which is still a British colony, and 0.3 for Singapore. This extraordinary association of the United Kingdom with the rest of the world's equity markets indicates that extent to which the United Kingdom dominated world trade, politics, and culture for more than a century, affecting the capital markets as well as other institutions of diverse countries throughout the world.

Risk-Adjusted Returns

In Table 7.4, the alphas and betas for each country and regional portfolio, measured over approximately the last quarter century, are displayed. Alphas are risk-adjusted returns relative to the world stock market, and betas are a measure of risk, where the beta of a country having an average risk is equal to 1. The alpha of a country is expressed in percent per year and is positive for countries that beat the world market on a risk-adjusted basis. Countries that were beaten by the world market have negative alphas.

Asian countries had the highest alphas. Hong Kong, which was studied over 15 years, as compared with 25 years for most of the countries, had the highest alpha of any country, 13.2 percent. Of the countries studied for 25 years, Japan's very high alpha, 8.9 percent, was second only to Norway's. Hong Kong and Singapore were very risky as measured by their betas, which were 2.6 and 2.5 respectively. Japan was less risky than the world market, with a beta of 0.8.

The performance of the European countries was widely varied, with Norway (alpha of 9.6 percent) being the standout. Excepting Norway, alphas ranged from −4.1 percent in Italy to 3.5 percent in Sweden. Betas were low except for that of the United Kingdom, which had a beta of 1.43. The European portfolio had negative risk-adjusted performance, with an alpha of −0.6 percent and a beta of 0.8 on the world market.

Canada outperformed Australia, with alphas of 1.2 and −1.0 percent respectively. Canada also had a lower beta than Australia.

The non-U.S. portfolio, containing all 17 countries, outperformed the United States in risk-adjusted terms. The non-U.S. portfolio had an

Table 7.4. Dollar-Adjusted Equity Returns: Regressions on World Equities, 1960–1984

| Country or Region | Excess Return Regressions of Country Equities on World Equity Portfolio | | | |
	Alpha (%)	Alpha T-statistic	Beta	Unadjusted R²
Austria	0.34 %	0.08	0.17	0.02
Belgium	2.39	0.93	0.51	0.31
Denmark	3.02	0.56	0.69	0.16
France	−1.44	−0.34	0.65	0.22
Germany	1.20	0.31	0.54	0.18
Italy	−4.05	−0.77	0.46	0.08
Netherlands	1.13	0.50	0.96	0.67
Norway	9.62	5.06	0.08	1.05
Spain	3.17	0.68	0.01	0.00
Sweden	3.52	0.95	0.50	0.17
Switzerland	0.68	0.17	0.93	0.39
United Kingdom	1.36	0.28	1.43	0.51
Europe Total	−0.63	−0.30	0.84	0.65
Hong Kong*	13.21	1.22	2.60	0.58
Japan	8.93	1.54	0.78	0.17
Singapore*	12.60	1.03	2.46	0.49
Asia Total	8.65	1.43	0.89	0.20
Australia	−0.99	−0.26	1.20	0.54
Canada	1.21	0.47	0.87	0.56
Other Total	0.26	0.11	0.97	0.66
Non-U.S. Total	1.34	0.71	0.88	0.71
United States Total	−0.25	−0.25	1.07	0.93

*1970-1984
Note: All returns are excess returns, i.e., total returns in excess of the U.S. Treasury bill return.
Source: Table 7.1 for year-by-year returns by country; *Stocks, Bonds, Bills, and Inflation 1986 Yearbook*, Ibbotson Associates, Chicago, for Treasury bill returns; Roger G. Ibbotson, Laurence B. Siegel, and Kathryn S. Love, "World Wealth: Market Values and Returns," *Journal of Portfolio Management*, Fall 1985, for returns on portfolios (regional and world) of countries' equities.

alpha of 1.3 percent and a beta of 0.9, while the U.S. portfolio had an alpha of −0.3 percent and a beta of 1.1. As noted before, investors would have had both improved risk-adjusted performance and reduced economy risk by holding a global rather than a U.S.-only portfolio over the last 25 years.

Long-Run Returns on Foreign Stocks

The past quarter century of foreign stock returns is of great current interest. This modern period does not, however, tell a complete story.

First, it was a period of relative *political* stability, with no major wars, no large changes in borders, and no shifts in economic systems of the important economic powers. Second, by starting at 1960, the rapid growth phases of Europe, the United States, and Canada, and to some extent Asia, are missed. Finally, the emergence of equity markets is an interesting story in its own right.

Stocks in the Distant Past

The invention of the joint-stock company is usually credited to England or Holland in the 1600s. Surprisingly, though, French water-mill shares were traded 500 years before that, in the Middle Ages. The Bazacle water mill at Toulouse, France, was first built in the 800s, and price quotes on shares of its stock date back to the 1100s. Quotes on a more or less continuous basis start in the 1400s. From the 1600s to 1946, Bazacle shares were traded on the Paris Bourse. Apparently having little appreciation of the history of capital markets, the French government nationalized the mill, long since turned into an electrical generating station, and made it a part of the national electric company, Électricité de France.

The story of the British, Dutch, and French joint-stock companies is better known. The British and Dutch East India companies, which owned various rights to trade in Asia, thrived for long periods and became the effective rulers of the colonies in which they traded. Eventually, with the decline of the colonial empires, these companies were dissolved, but not before they had provided high returns to investors over certain periods.

The Hudson's Bay Company had the least promising endowment: the right to trade in Canada's arctic Hudson Bay region. This firm evolved into a dry-goods retailer and is now one of the leading Canadian department store chains. Its stock is actively traded on the Toronto exchange.

France's Mississippi Company was less successful. At the outset, the Mississippi Company seemed especially promising, since it held the rather enticing right to trade in the French-owned Mississippi Valley, about one-third of the present U.S. land area. Although its stock crashed around 1720, the share price was so high before the crash that the company's market capitalization exceeded the wealth of France. Long after Mississippi Company investors lost their rights to French America, the Mississippi Valley itself grew tremendously in value. This story indicates that the value of claims on an asset may diverge from the value of the asset itself, creating the investment risk that is not inherent in the asset.

Divergence of Asset and Claim Values: The Japanese Experience

Returns in prewar and postwar Japan exemplify the divergence of values of assets and claims. Earlier in this chapter, Japanese stocks were shown to be the unchallenged winner over the period starting in 1960. Now let's suppose an investor had bought Japanese stocks in the 1860s. What would have been the result?

Japan's Meiji Restoration in 1867 brought a procapitalist government into power and opened Japan to world trade. Japanese equity returns were high, similar to those in the other high-growth countries of that time, the United States and Britain. Foreign as well as Japanese investors would have fared well by buying Japanese stocks in the 1860s and holding them. But, during World War II, U.S. investors would have lost all claims to Japanese stocks, making their Japanese equity portfolios worthless. After the war, U.S. investors would have had to invest new capital in Japanese equities to reap the high postwar returns.

Even in economically "winning" countries having high long-term returns, foreign investors face the risk of losing their equity claims. Let's now turn to the risk of investing in "losing" countries.

Interrupted Markets and the Winner-Loser Country Phenomenon

Eighteenth- or nineteenth-century investors who bet on the United States, Canada, or Britain would have been prodigious forecasters of the world economy. Investors cannot ordinarily expect to have such foresight. In 1900, an international investor might well have bought Austro-Hungarian, Russian, and German stocks instead of U.S. and British issues. The Austro-Hungarian equities would have lost all their value by the end of World War I. The Russian equities would have been rendered worthless by the communist government, which nationalized firms not long after the Russian Revolution of 1917. And German equity claims were wiped out by World War II.

In Table 7.5, summary statistics of long-term equity returns are shown for a large number of countries. Many of these countries' returns were interrupted by war, or were terminated by communism or a country's loss of sovereignty. Long-term investors may expect growth in the overall world economy, yet if they do not diversify, international investors run a very substantial risk of choosing a country which will turn out to be a "loser."

Table 7.5. Summary Statistics on World Equities

US Dollar Adjusted Returns	Number of Years of Data	Compound Annual Return	Arithmetic Mean Return	Standard Deviation	1982 Cumulative Wealth Index Value	1982 Agg. Mkt. Capitalization in Billions $US
1926-1982 Total Returns						
United Kingdom	57	8.1 %	11.2 %	28.0 %	113.53	$ 181.6
United States (NYSE)	57	9.2	11.4	21.6	136.89	1294.7
1926-1982 Capital Appreciation						
Uninterrupted Series						
Canada	57	4.2	6.7	22.5	14.28	105.0
Sweden	57	4.7	7.0	20.9	17.02	17.1
Switzerland	57	5.8	7.7	21.1	25.40	41.4
United Kingdom	57	3.1	6.6	28.0	10.73	181.6
United States (NYSE)	57	4.4	6.6	20.8	10.26	1294.7
1929-1982 Capital Appreciation						
Interrupted Series						
Australia	54	2.9	—	—	4.75	41.4
Belgium	54	1.2	—	—	1.94	8.1
Denmark	54	2.8	—	—	4.52	6.0
Finland	54	2.5	—	—	3.77	N/A
Italy	54	-0.6	—	—	0.71	19.7
Japan	54	-1.3	—	—	0.49	410.2
Mexico	54	-3.0	—	—	0.19	1.1
Norway	54	3.0	—	—	4.87	1.6

Sources: Morgan Stanley Capital International Perspective, New York, for all countries for 1960-1982 except Finland and Mexico; various government, United Nations, and private sources collected by the authors for the other years and for Finland and Mexico for all years.

**Diversification: The Key to
Intelligent International Investing**

While investors cannot avoid the risk of picking losing countries or being
separated from their claims, diversification minimizes this risk. If a hypothetical investor of 1900 had held U.S. and British equities as well as
those of the fallen European powers, much of the risk would have been
diversified away, and the investor would have substantial capital today.
Diversification across countries is analogous to diversification across
stocks within one country. While investors may not be able to predict
which stock, or which country, will be the winner and which the loser, by
holding a diversified portfolio they are virtually guaranteed some winners over the long run. This diversification argument is the primary
argument for investing internationally. Let's now examine the logic of
international equity investing in greater conceptual detail.

Why Invest Internationally?

As the economies of nations gradually meld themselves into an interde-
pendent world economy, investing across national borders has become a
strategy of great interest. The Europeans, living in small, specialized
countries, have been investing in each others' capital markets—as well as
others around the world—for decades or longer. Today, investors in the
United States are beginning to realize that their country, too, is becoming a specialist in the world economy; that self-sufficiency is a path to
inefficiency, while specialization leads to economic success; and that international investing to achieve diversification therefore makes sense.

Americans have generally shied away from international equity investing until the last decade or so. Earlier, a few maverick investors and
money managers, such as John Templeton, made great fortunes in foreign stocks. Yet Americans have traditionally viewed other countries as
less reliable than the United States in many dimensions—political stability, economic growth, and the accuracy of business information. Moreover, Americans have tended to doubt their own savvy in international
affairs, compared with that of sophisticated foreign financiers. This
aversion to foreign stocks is fading fast.

Investing in foreign equities is justified for three reasons:

- The size of foreign markets
- The performance and diversification available in foreign markets
- The increasing integration or interdependence of the world economy

Each will now be treated in turn.

Size and Opportunity

For many years, foreign markets have constituted a large share of world equity value. Furthermore, these markets have been increasing in relative importance. U.S. stocks made up roughly two-thirds of the world's equity value in 1960, and foreign countries' stocks the other third. By 1984, although the U.S. market had grown considerably, its share of the world market had fallen to 58 percent.

This observation alone makes a case for international investing. By holding only U.S. equities, an investor eliminates two-fifths of the world's equity markets. Of course, accounting and other inputs to stock analysis differ among countries both in form and accuracy, putting the U.S. analyst of foreign companies at a relative disadvantage.

Performance and Diversification

As noted earlier, high returns in foreign countries—especially Japan—and low correlations with U.S. equity returns have provided investors with an opportunity both to make money and to diversify their portfolios. The need for diversification is made clearer by considering once-promising foreign markets where investors lost all their capital to war, communism, or conquest. Investors run the same risk today, and they can only minimize it by diversifying across the equity markets of the world.

An Interdependent World

The final reason for investing internationally is the interdependence of national economies. The world is in a state of transition from being a set of nation-states, each striving for self-sufficiency, to a community of trading nations which specialize according to their comparative advantages. Japan has become the consumer goods manufacturer of the world, Switzerland the world's banker, Germany the purveyor of luxury automobiles. The United States too is losing its highly diversified character and is becoming a specialist in service and information technologies; these include banking, brokerage, and money management, as well as computers, telecommunications, education, medicine, and agriculture. To find the successful companies in these diverse fields, therefore, investors must search across national borders.

How to Invest Internationally

The world's stock exchanges are compared in Table 7.6. A country may have numerous stock exchanges (e.g., Germany) or no active exchange

Table 7.6. Stock Exchanges around the World

Country	Exchange(s)	1982 Trading Volume (Bil US $)	1982 Number of Issues Listed Domestic	Foreign	12/31/1982 Market Capitalization (Bil US$)	Principal Share Price Indices
Argentina	Buenos Aires	0.2	247	1	1.0	Buenos Aires Stk. Exch. Index – 248 issues
Australia	Total of 6	5.1	931	20	41.5	Australian Share Price Index – 260 issues
Austria	Vienna	0.1	62	35	1.5	Wiener Borsehammer Index – 43 issues
Belgium	Brussels	1.9	212	139	8.6	Indice General du Comptant – 67 issues
Brazil	Rio de Janiero	3.7	607	0	N/A	IBV Index – 30 issues
	Sao Paulo	2.2	478	0	10.3	BOVESPA Index – 109 issues
Canada	Montreal	2.2	387	18	167.9	General Index – 85 issues
	Toronto	14.3	759	60	103.5	TSE 300 Composite Index – 300 issues
Denmark	Copenhagen	0.1	206	4	5.5	Copenhagen Stock Exchange Index – 38 issues
France	Paris	9.6	535	164	38.1[3]	CAC Index – 262 issues
Germany	Total of 8	16.6	450	177	69.0	Frankfurter Allgemeine Zeitung – 100 issues
Hong Kong	Total of 4	N/A	N/A	N/A	24.0	Hang Seng Index
Israel	Tel Aviv	6.7	212	1	15.9	General Share Index – all listed issues
Italy	Milan	2.8	138	0	19.9	MIB Historical Index – 129 issues
Japan	Osaka	18.4	1009	0	370.6	300 Common Stock Index
	Tokyo	146.9	1427	12	417.4	Tokyo Stock Price Index; Nikkei Dow Jones

Country	City					Index
Korea	Seoul	2.7	334	0	4.4	Korea Composite stock Price index – 334 issues
Luxembourg	Luxembourg	N/A	88	138	4.7	Domestic Share Price Index – 7 issues
Malaysia	Kuala Lumpur	1.4	194	67	13.9	Kuala Lumpur Stk Exch Indust. Index – 30 issues
Netherlands	Amsterdam	5.1	216	260	25.7	ANP–CBS General Index – 51 issues
Norway	Oslo	0.1	112	6	2.4	Oslo Bors Stock Index – 52 issues
Singapore	Singapore	2.4	112	176	31.2	SES Industrial and Commercial Index – 32 issues
South Africa	Johannesburg	2.6	470	24	77.8	JSE Actuaries Index – 141 issues
Spain	Barcelona	0.2	426	1	11.5	General Index of Barcelona Stk Exch – 73 issues
	Madrid	1.1	448	0	11.2	Madrid Stock Exchange Index – 69 issues
Switzerland	Basel	18.6	101	157	33.2	Societe de Banque Suisse – 90 issues
	Geneva	N/A	106	172	36.8	Societe de Banque Suisse – 90 issues
	Zurich	N/A	119	155	38.7	Societe de Banque Suisse – 90 issues
United Kingdom	London	32.7	2279[1]	485[2]	196.2[4]	Financial Times All Ordinaries Index
United States	American	19.7	784	50	45.0	AMEX Market Value Index – over 800 issues
	New York	488.4	1482	44	1258.7	NYSE Composite; S&P 500; Dow Jones
	OTC (NASDAQ)	100.2	3008	268	153.1	NASDAQ OTC Composite Index – over 3000 issues
	Regionals	67.8	N/A	N/A	N/A	None

Notes:
1. Includes some companies with fixed income issues only.
2. Includes Ireland.
3. 12/31/1981.
4. Excludes Ireland.

Source: FIBV Statistics 1983 (Federation Internationale des Bourses de Valeurs, Paris, France); additional information by the authors.

(e.g., Ireland, whose equity trading is done in England). Also, some countries classified as emerging markets have sizable stock exchanges.

The equity capitalization of a country cannot be computed by adding the capitalizations of the securities on its stock exchanges. This is because stocks are frequently listed on more than one exchange, and sometimes on exchanges in different countries. For example, the NYSE lists dozens of foreign stocks. Likewise, the Tokyo and Osaka exchanges have approximately the same capitalization since they list roughly the same stocks; yet almost all trading occurs on the Tokyo exchange. Switzerland has three exchanges with almost identical listings, including a large proportion of non-Swiss stocks. Let's now briefly describe the world's principal equity markets.

The Foreign Equity Arena

Canada.   The Canadian stock market is more familiar to U.S. investors than any other foreign market. The dominant marketplace is the Toronto Stock Exchange. While the Toronto exchange has traditionally served as a haven for penny mining and energy stocks, the list has become much more industrial in recent years.

Mexico.   Following decades of decentralized capital markets, the Mexican government in the 1970s established a central stock exchange at Mexico City, the Bolsa de Valores de Mexico. In addition, U.S. investors may easily buy and sell most Mexican securities through U.S. brokers, or may purchase shares of mutual funds specializing in Mexican investments.

United Kingdom and Ireland.   The Stock Exchange, named as if it were the only one in the world, is the central securities marketplace for the United Kingdom and the Republic of Ireland. It was formed in 1973 by consolidation of all regional stock exchanges with the old London Stock Exchange. The London Stock Exchange was one of the oldest exchanges in the world, dating to the 1600s. The Stock Exchange lists thousands of issues, and by that measure is the world's largest. The list is large because almost any reputable security in any developed country can be listed. In fact, the list includes more than 100 NYSE and AMEX stocks. Moreover, fixed-income issues outnumber equities on The Stock Exchange. Thus, the number of issues on The Stock Exchange vastly overstates the size of the British stock market. Although the largest in Europe, the British market is only about one-eighth as large as the U.S. market in equity value.

Germany. Germany's publicly traded stock market is small compared with its huge debt market, the private equity market, and the integrated commercial and investment banking houses. Yet Germany's public stock market is the second largest in Europe and provides important investment opportunities. The market is decentralized, with the Frankfurt exchange dominant in fixed-income and international securities and the Dusseldorf exchange dominant in domestic industrial stocks. An over-the-counter market flourishes and is competitive with the exchanges.

France. The French equity market is the third largest in Europe and one of the world's oldest. The Paris Bourse, or exchange, originated in the 1500s, but equity trading was not its major activity until 200 years later. In the twentieth century, French stocks have assumed a substantial role in world markets. Despite nationalizations in the early 1980s, the French economy provides substantial opportunities to U.S. investors.

Switzerland. The Swiss stock market, while playing a secondary role to its credit markets, ranks fourth in size in Europe and has an aggregate market value far out of proportion to the Swiss population. The three principal stock exchanges, Zurich, Geneva, and Basel, function essentially as one, since trades are executed wherever terms are most favorable. The Swiss exchanges list a large number of fixed-income issues and foreign securities. Of the few hundred Swiss equities, only several dozen have large enough markets for institutional trading.

Belgium and Luxembourg. Belgium's principal stock exchange, the Brussels Bourse, is a dynamic market where foreign investment is welcomed. Most domestic Belgian stocks are industrials. An approximately value-weighted portfolio of Belgian equities can be held by purchasing the shares of one company, Société Générale de Belgique, which is said to own 30 percent of the value of all publicly traded Belgian stocks. Nearby Luxembourg, a small grand duchy, is closely tied to but independent of Belgium. Unlike Belgium, Luxembourg does not tax security trades, so that some investors employ its brokers to buy and sell Belgian and other securities.

Italy. It surprises many Americans not to see Italy listed as a major stock market. Yet the Italian stock market, situated in Milan, was in an almost unbroken decline from 1962 to 1979. The 1980s have seen a dramatic resurgence in Italian stocks, but they remain at the bottom of the pack in long-run performance.

Netherlands. The Netherlands, historically a world trading and financial center, houses a major equity market. The principal exchange is at

Amsterdam, where shares of the Dutch East India Company were first listed in 1602. The Dutch were pioneers in international investing because their domestic market is so specialized. Robeco, a global investment trust formed in the 1930s, is the country's largest shareowner and a model international equity portfolio. Robeco is listed on 19 stock exchanges, more than any other firm in the world.

Norway. Resource-rich Norway became financially prominent in the 1970s, when rising energy prices pushed Norwegian stock prices to dizzying heights. Much of the market value of Norwegian stocks is represented by Norsk Hydro, the national electric company.

Spain. Despite the autocratic rule of Francisco Franco, Spain emerged in the 1960s and early 1970s as a growing economy with a rapidly rising stock market. After 1959, considerable economic and political liberalization occurred, causing an influx of foreign capital. Since the mid-1970s, however, returns have been poor. Foreign investment on the Madrid, Barcelona, and Bilbao stock exchanges is welcomed, and traditional corporate secrecy is giving way to fuller disclosure.

Sweden. Sweden is the industrial powerhouse of the Scandinavian group, with the best historical equity returns in Europe. Interestingly, Sweden's adoption of certain aspects of socialism does not preclude very large, profitable private enterprises. The stock market is open to foreigners who are willing to abide by various complex rules.

Japan. Japan's equity market, like its population and overall economy, is roughly half the size of that of the United States and is by far the most important non-U.S. equity market in the world. The Tokyo Stock Exchange (TSE), Japan's principal trading venue, has about 1400 stocks, making it only slightly smaller than the NYSE in the number of stocks listed. The exchange has two tiers or categories of listings. The "first section" of the TSE corresponds very roughly with the NYSE in listing requirements and the "second section" with the AMEX. In trading volume, the TSE ranks first in the world. The price of an average share is under $5, and consequently daily trading is measured in the hundreds of millions of shares. The market is also extremely liquid, with a high trading volume as a percentage of its aggregate value. Many Japanese stocks are traded in the United States, usually in the form of American Depositary Receipts (ADRs).

Japanese business tradition encourages companies doing business with one another to hold each other's shares. Thus corporate holdings of corporate stocks form an appreciable portion of Japan's aggregate equity value. This portion is not nearly enough to cut into the liquidity of the market, but it creates a double-counting problem in estimating the size of the market.

Hong Kong. Hong Kong has a highly volatile stock market, subject to extreme price swings. Stock prices rose twentyfold in the early 1970s and then came crashing down in 1973–1974. After another surge in the late 1970s, the market plunged in 1983, when diplomatic talks between the United Kingdom and the People's Republic of China over the colony's future stalled. When an agreement was reached, in the mid-1980s, specifying that Hong Kong will become part of China in 1997 with the right to retain a capitalist economy for at least 50 years, the stock market soared once again.

Singapore. Following its separation from the Malay Federation in 1965, Singapore emerged as the richest Asian country outside Japan. Banking is the largest industry and the principal vehicle for stock investment. While Singapore's stock market has fluctuated wildly in the past, like that of Hong Kong, Singapore's market has become more stable in recent years as the country has become more developed.

Australia. Australia is a resource-rich country with a standard of living comparable to that of the United States and Canada. Although the country has wealthy mining regions, the principal Australian stocks are industrial and financial companies. Many are traded in the United States. The largest Australian company, Broken Hill Proprietary, is a diversified conglomerate offering a cross section of the Australian economy.

Advice to Investors

Institutional investors in foreign equities can use a number of strategies to cope with the high information and transaction costs associated with international equities. Foreign money managers, particularly those in Japan, the United Kingdom, and Switzerland, have become popular. Institutions may also build relationships with foreign brokers, since U.S. brokers are often at a disadvantage in executing trades abroad. One drawback to trading in some foreign markets is that commission rates are high. Also, bid-asked spreads are large, and the thin markets are subject to price-pressure effects.

While active stock selection may yield superior results for some managers, a passive strategy reduces trading costs and avoids the costs of gathering and evaluating information on foreign stocks. As a quasi-passive strategy, institutions may achieve diversification by holding shares of global investment companies, such as Robeco, or regional investment companies, such as Société Générale de Belgique.

Individual investors seeking a diversified international portfolio can choose from a number of U.S.-based open-end mutual funds. Since no-load international stock funds exist, investors should avoid "load" funds. For those who favor a particular country, regional portfolios are available either as open-end or closed-end mutual funds. Since almost all international equity funds available to individual investors are actively managed, fees will probably be high.

Individuals seeking to buy specific foreign stocks may wish to concentrate on those which are traded in the United States in the form of ADRs. ADRs are generally very liquid and have transaction costs comparable to U.S. stocks. U.S. brokers are well represented in the largest foreign markets and can execute trades for American investors seeking shares of many companies not traded as ADRs. Foreign brokers are required to purchase some foreign securities. Both U.S. and foreign brokers face high transaction costs in foreign countries, but U.S. brokers may be more attuned to the needs of an individual investor in the United States.

Suggested Reading

Bernstein, Peter L. (ed.): *International Investing*, Institutional Investor, Inc., New York, 1983. Diverse readings on the subject, compiled by a master editor and writer on finance.

Esslen, Rainer: *The Complete Book of International Investing: How to Buy Foreign Securities and Who's Who on the International Investment Scene*, McGraw-Hill Book Company, New York, 1977. Although dated due to the rapid changes in the field, Esslen provides a flavor of the "hands-on" side of foreign equity investing.

Lessard, Donald R. (ed.): *International Financial Management: Theory and Application*, 2d ed., John Wiley & Sons, Inc., New York, 1985. This book of readings includes some of the best articles on the subject.

PART 3

Bond Markets

8

Cash Returns and Hierarchies of Financial Need

Although proponents of modern portfolio theory assume that rational investors construct portfolios to maximize their returns and diversify away risk, actual investors may be less rational and more idiosyncratic than academics suspect. Some people find it more comfortable to compartmentalize various facets of their lives, including their investments. Richard Thaler, Hersh Shefrin, and Meir Statman, among others, suggest that many people have unconsciously devised shortcuts to help them set financial priorities and to cope with spending impulses. Such people avoid spending money saved for future expenditures by separating assets into mental compartments.

Money in each compartment has a purpose, and is used only for that purpose. The first compartment could include cash to spend and cash for emergencies. Other compartments might be for investments with various characteristics: different degrees of risk, different maturities, and different taxability. A last compartment could incorporate speculative activities.

Individuals find compartmentalization useful because it helps them meet financial objectives with a minimum of effort and attention. In economic terms, it helps individuals maximize financial and psychological utility. Sometimes people's compartments crumble, as with compulsive gamblers who risk even the cash meant for groceries and rent. When the distinctions break down, these individuals and their families can be ruined.

While compartmentalization can help adults control spending impulses and achieve diverse objectives, it may also be expensive. For example, an investor may retain cash in a money market fund that earns 7 percent and at the same time accrue credit card charges at 18 percent.

By deciding not to raid the money market account to finance current spending, this investor may be able to restrict his or her spending to the credit limit on the card. Yet the price of this distinction is 11 percent annually. Still, this compartmentalization, even if costly, may help investors maintain several financial objectives simultaneously.

Hierarchies of Human and Financial Needs

The psychologist Abraham Maslow proposed a hierarchy of human needs, which are listed in Figure 8.1. Basic needs must be satisfied before those higher up come into play. Maslow's pyramid has five levels:

- Basic physiological needs, such as satisfaction of hunger and thirst
- Safety and security, e.g., security from attack, avoidance of pain, and preservation of privacy

---

Maslow's Personal Hierarchy of Needs

Basic Physiological Needs
Safety and Security
Love and Belongingness
Self-Esteem
Self-Actualization

Individual Investment Hierarchy

Immediate Cash Needs
Saving for a Purchase
Security and Safety
Investment
Speculation

Institutional Investment Hierarchy

Working Capital Management
Dedication and Immunization
Passive Management and/or Portfolio Mix Policies
Active Management and/or Dynamic Asset Allocation
Speculation

Figure 8.1. Personal and financial hierarchies of need. (*Source: Abraham Maslow's hierarchy of needs can be found in "Self-Actualizing People: A Study in Psychological Health,"* Personality Symposia, *New York, Grune and Stratton, 1950.* The individual and institutional investment hierarchies are provided by the authors.)

- Love and belongingness
- Self-esteem, including pride and confidence
- Self-actualization, or fulfillment through creativity, insight, and achievement

When investors compartmentalize their financial lives, a hierarchy of financial needs occurs that parallels those identified by Maslow. The financial hierarchy of individual investors, also illustrated in Figure 8.1, is built with five levels: immediate cash needs, like money to pay the rent; savings for a purchase, such as a car for next year; security and safety, like saving for retirement; investments, including various forms of capital accumulation; and speculation, such as money to bet on penny stocks or football pools.

Institutions might have a similar hierarchy of financial needs, and this third hierarchy is also depicted in Figure 8.1. Its most basic levels are cash for working capital management, such as money to pay management fees and to facilitate redemptions of mutual fund shares, and provisions for dedication and immunization of fixed obligations, such as defined-benefit pension obligations known in advance. Only after these two categories are satisfied do some institutional managers set portfolio mix objectives and engage in passive management through techniques such as indexing. When the static portfolio mix is set, some institutions then introduce active management. As well as selection of securities to beat the market, this may include strategies for dynamic asset allocation, where the mix changes as market conditions and wealth positions change. Finally, institutions might be said to speculate in venture capital or other high-risk instruments.

Most of this book concerns investments that fit into the bottom three categories of both individuals' and institutions' financial hierarchies. In this chapter, investing to meet short-term cash needs (the top two categories) is discussed. Securities with minimal risk, such as U.S. Treasury bills, are appropriate investments for these foundation categories, and their returns, or interest rates, are discussed first.

Real and Nominal Interest Rates

Defining Terms

Before describing how real and nominal interest rates have changed over time, a few definitions are in order. In this chapter only, the expression *interest rate* refers to short-term interest rates. These rates are the returns on cash or securities equivalent to cash. *Cash equivalents*, in turn, can be defined as any short-term, interest-bearing security or bill. For example, Treasury bills with 30 days to maturity are cash equivalents, as are short-term corporate securities with small default risk, such as commercial paper and bankers' acceptances.

In the following tables, interest rates, or yields, on short-term securities are assumed to be equal to the *returns* on these instruments. Strictly speaking, this relation holds only for a hypothetical security with an instantaneous maturity, because of the risk of interest rate changes inherent in longer-than-instantaneous instruments. Yields and returns diverge as the maturity of the security extends into the future. Since maturities of cash equivalents range from a day to a year, the actual returns on these securities will only approximate their yields.

Real Interest Rates in the United States

Economists define the short-term, real riskless interest rate as the Treasury bill yield minus anticipated inflation. Since anticipated inflation cannot be measured, the most recent realized inflation rate is substituted. In Table 8.1, then, real interest rates for any year are calculated as the U.S. Treasury bill return less the inflation rate. Over the last 60 years, the short-term real riskless rate of interest averaged 0.29 percent, practically indistinguishable from zero. This lends weight to the hypothesis that the pure time value of money is near zero on average.

Real Interest Rates since the 1920s. Yet during the deflationary 1920s and early 1930s, real interest rates climbed to great heights as Treasury yields approached zero but rarely dipped below it. Investors do not buy securities with negative yields when they can leave cash in their checking accounts and avoid a negative return. Thus, when the purchasing power of a dollar is increasing, real interest rates roughly equal the deflation rate. That is, if cash investments earn a near zero (but not negative) interest rate, deflation causes the cash to be worth more over time, producing high real rates of interest.

Later, in the 1940s, real interest rates were persistently negative because the government fixed Treasury bill yields below the high inflation rates of the war and postwar years. Then, beginning with the Treasury–Federal Reserve accords of 1951, Treasury bill yields were deregulated and tracked inflation very closely. Since real interest rates were low and stable, around 1 percent, some academics came to believe that the "natural" real riskless rate was 1 percent.

Again, in the 1970s, the financial winds shifted. While nominal interest rates soared, real interest rates plunged to sharply negative levels—

Table 8.1. U.S. Nominal and Real Interest Rates, 1926–1985

Year	T-Bill Returns	Inflation Rates	Real Interest Rates*
1926	3.27%	-1.49%	4.76%
1927	3.12	-2.08	5.20
1928	3.24	-0.97	4.21
1929	4.75	0.19	4.55
1930	2.41	-6.03	8.44
1931	1.07	-9.52	10.60
1932	0.96	-10.30	11.26
1933	0.30	0.51	-0.21
1934	0.16	2.03	-1.87
1935	0.17	2.99	-2.82
1936	0.18	1.21	-1.03
1937	0.31	3.10	-2.79
1938	-0.02	-2.78	2.76
1939	0.02	-0.48	0.50
1940	0.00	0.96	-0.95
1941	0.06	9.72	-9.66
1942	0.27	9.29	-9.02
1943	0.35	3.16	-2.81
1944	0.33	2.11	-1.78
1945	0.33	2.25	-1.92
1946	0.35	18.17	-17.81
1947	0.50	9.01	-8.50
1948	0.81	2.71	-1.90
1949	1.10	-1.80	2.91
1950	1.20	5.79	-4.60
1951	1.49	5.87	-4.38
1952	1.66	0.88	0.77
1953	1.82	0.62	1.20
1954	0.86	-0.50	1.36
1955	1.57	0.37	1.20
1956	2.46	2.86	-0.40
1957	3.14	3.02	0.12
1958	1.54	1.76	-0.22
1959	2.95	1.50	1.45
1960	2.66	1.48	1.19
1961	2.13	0.67	1.45
1962	2.73	1.22	1.51
1963	3.12	1.65	1.47
1964	3.54	1.19	2.35
1965	3.93	1.92	2.00
1966	4.76	3.35	1.40
1967	4.21	3.04	1.17
1968	5.21	4.72	0.48
1969	6.58	6.11	0.47
1970	6.53	5.49	1.03
1971	4.39	3.36	1.03
1972	3.84	3.41	0.43
1973	6.93	8.80	-1.87
1974	8.00	12.20	-4.20
1975	5.80	7.01	-1.21
1976	5.08	4.81	0.27
1977	5.12	6.77	-1.65
1978	7.18	9.03	-1.85
1979	10.38	13.31	-2.93
1980	11.24	12.40	-1.16
1981	14.71	8.94	5.77
1982	10.54	3.87	6.67
1983	8.80	3.80	4.83
1984	9.85	3.95	5.69
1985	7.72	3.77	3.82

SUMMARY STATISTICS 1926-1985

Compound Annual Return	3.41%	3.06%	0.18%
Arithmetic Mean Return	3.46%	3.17%	0.29%
Standard Deviation	3.35%	4.87%	4.61%
First Order Autocorrelation	0.92	0.65	0.62

SUMMARY STATISTICS 1952-1985

Compound Annual Return	5.27%	4.26%	0.98%
Arithmetic Mean Return	5.32%	4.32%	1.00%
Standard Deviation	3.26%	3.56%	2.36%
First Order Autocorrelation	0.88	0.78	0.70

INDEX VALUES FOR 1985 (12/31/1925=1.000)

	7.473	6.097	1.199

* T-bill returns minus inflation rates.

Source: *Stocks, Bonds, Bills, and Inflation: 1986 Yearbook,* Chicago: Ibbotson Associates, 1986.

the difference being made up by high inflation rates. Nevertheless, these negative real rates were often smaller (and thus better) than the negative real returns on stocks and bonds. In the 1980s, however, returns on stocks and bonds both picked up again; cash, too, performed well relative to the moderate inflation rates of the period. Setting aside deflationary periods, the real riskless rate has risen to record levels in this decade.

Over the short term, then, Treasury bill yields have deviated substantially from the inflation rate, producing real interest rates which can be markedly positive or negative. Some economists claim that the variation of real interest rates occurs because investors misforecast near-term inflation. If this were so, lenders, as investors, must have accepted negative real rates in 65 out of 90 months from January 1973 to June 1980. Similarly, borrowers, or Treasury bill and commercial paper issuers, must have paid positive real rates to investors in 62 of the 66 months from July 1980 to December 1985. Rational borrowers and lenders would not behave in this way. Most academics believe that, in addition to both expected and unexpected inflation, real interest rates move in tandem with economic variables such as the supply and demand for credit and the varying time value of money.

Commercial Paper and Bankers' Acceptances. While Treasury bills are the primary cash equivalent issued by the federal government, commercial paper and bankers' acceptances are the principal cash equivalents issued by corporations. Historically, these private-sector securities have had higher returns than Treasury bills. Measured over almost 60 years, U.S. commercial paper had a compound annual return of 4.1 percent, compared with 3.3 percent for Treasury bills. The standard deviation of annual returns was 3.4 percent for commercial paper and 3.3 percent for Treasury bills. Thus, over the long run, investors in commercial paper have received a substantial incremental return (0.8 percent) while absorbing very little additional default risk. This presumes a diversified portfolio of commercial paper, in which a default by one issuer would make only a small dent in the portfolio's value. In practice, most money market funds (except "government only" funds) invest in private-sector cash equivalents to reap these higher yields.

Cash Investments

Why Hold Cash?

Until the 1970s, individual investors and portfolio managers downplayed cash equivalents, considering them to be a "parking place" for funds not yet "invested," presumably in securities with higher expected returns. Their treatment of cash is consistent with the mental compartments that Thaler and others might predict.

Now, however, cash can be regarded as a permanent part of investors' portfolios. Historically the real rate of interest was zero, but lately, it has been significantly positive. Thus investors have altered their conception of cash equivalents, thinking of them now as investments.

Aside from their positive returns, cash equivalents are also desirable because they are a good inflation hedge. Statistically, cash returns, or more precisely short-term interest rates, are very highly correlated with inflation. Thus, the inflation risk of cash equivalents is minimal.

Furthermore, cash is now the safest of any investment alternative. Recent returns on cash have been far less volatile than those of either stocks or bonds. Over the short and medium term, the stock market has soared and plummeted in unpredictable gyrations; only the truly long-term investor holds for a period long enough to erase the stock market's occasional very poor returns. Likewise, even bonds, the traditional haven for conservative investors, have become much riskier. A a result, cash has assumed the new role of a statistically safe and conservative investment with a modest real return.

Investing in Cash Equivalents

Institutional investors can buy a diversified portfolio of cash equivalents with any of several risk levels. Those with the lowest risks are used for the compartments of working capital and cash for spending, as well as for savings with a defined time horizon, while those with higher risks are appropriate for other investment categories.

Most institutionally managed money is exempt from tax, so that institutions generally seek those cash equivalents which would be highly taxable to taxpaying investors. These include securities like Treasury bills, bonds with a short term to maturity, commercial paper, bankers' acceptances, and "jumbo" certificates of deposit (CDs) issued by banks in denominations of $100,000 or greater.

Individual investors, however, rarely have the financial resources to invest in these securities. Jumbo CDs are out of the reach of all but the richest individuals. Treasury bills are issued in $10,000 denominations. To allow individuals to participate in the cash equivalent markets, financial intermediaries have created money market funds which purchase the large-denomination cash equivalents. They then sell shares in such funds for a small premium. Typical minimum investments in money market funds are $1000, and in a few cases as little as $100.

Money Market Funds

Money market funds each have their own "personality." Depending on the securities that make up the portfolios, these funds have different levels of default and maturity risk. Since default means loss of principal, default risk is the first factor to consider. Most money market funds invest in private-sector cash equivalents, so that individual issues have some default risk if the underlying borrowers fail in business. By diversifying among hundreds of issues, money market funds avoid most of this risk; "government only" funds avoid it entirely.

Second, the average maturity of money market funds ranges from a few days to several months. Funds with longer maturities may incur capital losses in a period of rising interest rates, yet have higher average returns. Investors must decide how much default risk and maturity risk to absorb, and choose their fund accordingly.

There is substantial evidence that very long-term cash equivalents offer the best risk-return combination. Empirical work done by Eugene Fama shows that securities with around 6 months to 1 year to maturity and short-term bonds with 1 to 5 years to maturity have higher returns than securities with very short maturities for little additional risk. Investors who do not object to occasional, small capital losses in their cash accounts should consider funds which invest in this maturity range. Although few such funds exist at present, more may be formed as investors learn of this profit opportunity and demand them.

Investors in high tax brackets, or institutions managing money for such investors, should hold cash in tax-exempt money market instruments. These are either short-term borrowings by "municipal" (state and local) entities, or long-term borrowings which have nearly matured and which therefore have a short remaining term. Such investments have approximately the same default and interest rate risk as taxable cash equivalents, but the income from municipals is exempt from the federal government's personal income tax. Because of this tax advantage, tax-exempt cash equivalents have lower yields than taxable cash equivalents. After subtracting taxes paid, however, tax-exempts provide higher yields to investors in the higher tax brackets. Using the yields on two alternative securities and their tax brackets, investors must calculate whether they will receive a higher after-tax yield from the taxable or the tax-exempt cash equivalent, and invest accordingly.

Other Money Market Instruments

Other money market instruments compete with those already described. One is the money market deposit account offered by banks. These are operated like checking accounts and pay interest at approximately money market rates. Such accounts are far less diversified than true money market funds because they are secured by the assets of only one bank, not hundreds of borrowers. On the other hand, they have one significant advantage over money market funds. The principal (although not the interest) of money market deposit accounts is insured by the Federal Deposit Insurance Corporation. Other money market investments include cash management accounts, savings accounts with check-writing privileges, and smaller-denomination CDs issued by banks.

Conclusion

The first levels of financial need, whether of individual or institutional investors, are often satisfied by holding cash equivalents. Such an asset is useful for immediate cash needs like cash to spend or working capital, as well as for needs that will arise at specific dates in the future. For these reasons, investors often compartmentalize and segregate such holdings.

With short-term investments like cash, the type of instrument purchased is important. Even unsophisticated investors can distinguish between the yields on a NOW account and those on a CD, cash management account, or tax-exempt fund. Differences due to the grade of the instrument are less obvious; with high-yielding, low-quality instruments subject to possible default, investors only discover at maturity whether or not default has occurred.

Compartmentalization, which helps investors organize their financial affairs, has a monetary cost. On the other hand, failure to compartmentalize has costs too. By understanding the costs of each kind of behavior, investors may be able to alter their portfolios and improve their financial returns and/or their psychological well-being, of which financial security is an important part.

Suggested Reading

Fama, Eugene: "Term Premiums in Bond Returns," *Journal of Financial Economics*, vol. 13, no. 4, December 1984, pp. 529–546. Shows that expected returns on 6- to 12-month fixed-income securities may exceed those for both longer- and shorter-term securities.
Shefrin, Hersh, and Meir Statman: "How Not to Invest in the Stock Market," *Psychology*

Today, February 1986. Drawing on psychology, this article applies behavioral finance to investment markets in a creative way.

Stigum, Marcia: *The Money Market,* 2d ed. Dow Jones-Irwin, Homewood, Ill., 1983. A comprehensive manual for investment professionals, with a how-to slant.

Thaler, Richard, and Hersh Shefrin: "An Economic Theory of Self-Control," *Journal of Political Economy,* vol. 89, no. 2, April 1981, pp. 392–406. One of the seminal papers setting forth a behavioral, or bounded rational, theory of finance.

9

Introduction to Bond Yields and Returns

Bonds are financial securities, or contracts, that usually entitle holders to a series of cash flows or interest payments as well as a return of principal. Because these contracts have a fixed date of maturity and a predetermined schedule of coupon payments, they are known as *fixed-income securities*. The bond document sets forth the bondholder's rights and the issuer's obligations.

Investors must first understand the basics of bond yields and returns as well as the economic factors that influence them if they are to interpret the historical returns on bonds presented in Chapter 10. To begin the explanation, the factors that affect bond pricing are identified, different types of bonds are described, and the concept of duration is introduced. Those familiar with the basics should turn straightaway to Chapter 10.

The Basics of Bonds

Factors in Bond Pricing

The *par value* of a bond is the value printed on the face of a bond certificate. This principal, or face, amount is the amount that must eventually be repaid, and is also approximately the amount borrowed by the issuer. The most common par value of U.S. government and corporate bonds is $1000. In this country, bond prices are usually quoted in a price per $100 of face value; United Utilities' 10 percent bonds, maturing in 20 years, might sell for $90, or about 90 percent of face value, which means they have an actual price of $900 per $1000 bond.

As the United Utilities example illustrates, a bond's *market price* is usually not equal to its face value. This price is determined in the market by the bond's coupon rate, maturity date, call provisions, tax status, and default risk, as well as prevailing interest rates. Each of these factors is considered in turn.

In addition to a return of principal, most bonds promise a series of cash payments. The amount of those payments is determined by the *coupon rate*, usually expressed as a percentage of the principal (par) amount. For example, the United Utilities bond with a 10 percent coupon produces 10 percent interest on the $1000 face value, or annual interest of $100. If the bond sells above or below $1000, the coupon remains at $100. The bond would have an annual yield greater than 10 percent if the bond were to sell for less than $1000. If the bond sold above $1000, the annual yield would be less than 10 percent. Coupons are usually paid semiannually, and yields are slightly higher than the stated coupon rate because the interest compounds.

When bonds are sold between interest dates, they are usually priced to include part of the interest payment that the new owner will receive. Consequently, the seller must allocate part of the purchase price to *accrued interest*. The *flat price* of a bond is the quoted price plus accrued interest.

A bond's *maturity date* is the date on which the issuer must repay the bond's principal value. *Long-term debt* is usually considered to be any obligation repayable 10 years or more from the date of issue, while *medium-term debt* is greater than 1 year and less than 10 years. *Short-term debt* is debt due in 1 year or less.

Some bonds are issued with the proviso that the issuer may pay back the principal on, or "call," them prior to maturity. Bonds are likely to be called if the issuer observes that interest rates have dropped dramatically and the issuer believes that a new issue at a lower rate will substantially reduce its interest expense. If a bond is *callable,* its price must be lower than that of comparable, noncallable bonds to compensate bondholders for the cost of reinvesting bond proceeds at what will presumably be lower rates.

Some bonds have a different *tax status* from others, which significantly affects their prices and yields. While the income from corporate bonds is taxable to bondholders as ordinary income, the income from the bonds of state and local governments is exempt from federal tax. The tax-exempt status of municipal bonds makes them very attractive to investors in high tax brackets. It also results in lower before-tax yields on these bonds.

Finally, a bond's riskiness affects its price. In the following description of markets for government and corporate securities, various *default risks* are identified. Bond rating houses have evolved systems to estimate the riskiness of bonds and assist investors in pricing these securities fairly.

Types of Bonds

Bonds can be divided into three classes. Depending on the form its principal and interest payments take, a bond can be classed as:

- A coupon bond
- A zero coupon bond
- An annuity

The focus of this chapter will be on the first two, which are what are generally thought of as bonds.

Coupon bonds, the most common type, have already been described. Typically, these are issued near face value. Coupon bonds also pay a fixed dollar amount of interest, determined by the coupon rate. Such payments are made to bondholders semiannually until maturity.

A *zero coupon, or discount, bond* is a bond issued below its par value, or at a discount. For example, a $1000 zero coupon bond that matures in 3 years might sell for $780, the underlying present value of the bond. The *present value* is the value today of the cash flows (in this example, $1000 3 years hence) discounted at the yield (in this example, an annual yield of 8.6 percent). The return on a "zero" comes from an increase in principal value alone, for this type of bond pays no interest on face value. The price of such a bond without default risk is the present value of the face amount, assumed to be received with complete certainty. Some corporate bonds and all U.S. Treasury bills (but not Treasury notes or bonds) are issued at a discount. Some investors find "zeros" advantageous because these bonds are not callable before maturity and because, over the investment horizon, they have no reinvestment risk. (*Reinvestment risk* is the uncertainty as to the rate in which income can be reinvested.) Zeros were developed for investors with well-defined time horizons. Strictly speaking, zeros are called *original issue discount bonds* to distinguish them from coupon bonds selling below face value, which bond traders sometimes refer to as "discount bonds."

An *annuity* is the third type of bond payment scheme. A house mortgage and an insurance annuity contract are examples of annuities. Each payment contains principal and interest. Payments are level over a finite term, and there is no "balloon" payment of principal at maturity. The amount of principal and interest changes because the interest is computed on a decreasing outstanding balance; the interest portion is less and the principal portion greater with each payment.

Bond Yields and Returns

Yield to Maturity. A bond's *yield to maturity* (or simply the "yield") is its internal rate of return, or the discount rate that equates the present value of future income to the bond's current market value. This calculated return of a bond is dependent upon three factors:

- The money received as annual interest
- The difference between purchase price and redemption value
- The number of years to maturity

In bond trading, yields to maturity are typically quoted on a semiannual compounding basis. For comparability with the other annual returns in this book, however, all bond yields and returns are quoted here on an annual compounding basis.

Consider again the United Utilities bond with a 10 percent coupon, a face value of $1000, a term of 20 years, and a market value of $900. (For ease of explanation, assume annual coupons instead of the more prevalent semiannual coupons observed in the marketplace.) The present value of its income is the value of an income stream of $100 annually plus the value of the $1000 principal payment 20 years later. (The interest has a present value of $781.85, while the principal has a present value of $118.15, summing to $900.) If the security's market value is $900, its yield to maturity is determined by iteration, or trial and error, i.e., by trying various discount rates to see which produces that market value. Using present-value tables or a calculator in such a process, the discount rate is found to be about 11.3 percent. Thus the bond's yield to maturity is about 11.3 percent. A bond's yield to maturity changes if interest rates change, if its default risk increases or decreases, or if expectations about inflation change.

Expected Return. A bond's yield to maturity would be the bond's *expected return* if there were no possibility of default and if interest rates were constant through time. If default is possible, the bond's expected return will be less than its yield to maturity because of the expected loss from default.

Yet there is a problem with thinking about yields as constant returns. The calculation assumes that the same rate is used to discount all payments, but bondholders may demand different rates over different future periods. The yield is really an average, and hides the variability of rates at which interest payments might be reinvested. The return expected by investors may vary from period to period in the future.

Actual Return. A bondholder's *actual return* is the amount of money earned from holding the bond over one period, divided by the investment at the beginning of the period. Only if the bond is held to maturity is the bond's actual return equal to its expected return or yield. If the bond is sold before maturity, its actual return includes the capital gain or loss on its sale. If interest rates change at any time during the period, interest payments may be reinvested at rates higher or lower than expected.

Consider yet again the United Utilities bond, this time 1 year later. The coupon is still 10 percent and the face value is still $1000. But now the remaining term is 19 years and the market price is $950. Assuming the bond is then sold, its actual return can be calculated as the difference between the purchase price, $900, and the sale price, $950, or $50, plus the income from the period, $100, both divided by the purchase price. Therefore, the actual return is 16.7 percent in that year, while its yield to maturity at the end of the year has fallen to 10.6 percent.

After-Tax Return. So far, the before-tax returns on bonds have been described. To obtain the *after-tax returns,* the taxes on interest income and on capital gains or losses from principal must be taken into account. The interest income from coupon bonds, determined by the coupon rate, is all subject to tax. Likewise, the increase in a discount bond's principal value over its purchase price must be treated as interest income. In addition, the difference between a bond's purchase price (less accrued interest, if any) and its sales price is taxed at capital gains rates, which are traditionally different from ordinary rates, although they are the same under the 1986 tax revision.

Discount Yield. The yields on short-term bills are often quoted as discount yields. This is the market price divided by par, subtracted from 1, then divided by the time to maturity. For example, a bill selling at 98 with one-half year to maturity is quoted as having a discount yield of $(1 - \$98/\$100) \div (1/2) = .04$, or 4 percent. Because long-term bond yields include compound interest, short- and long-term bond yields are not directly comparable. Of course, short-term bond yields can be converted to the yield to maturity, which is referred to as the *bond equivalent yield* and which is comparable. The bond equivalent yield in the above example is 4.12 percent.

Current Yield. Sometimes people measure a bond's *current yield,* which is the ratio of its promised or current income to its current market price. Again, this is not to be confused with a bond's yield to maturity (usually shortened to "yield"). If the 10 percent United Utilities bond sells for $950, its current yield would be the coupon, $100, divided by the market value of $950 or a current yield of 10.5 percent, in contrast to its yield to maturity of 10.6 percent. In this example, the yield to maturity is higher than the current yield because the investor expects a $50 capital gain at maturity, which is included in the yield to maturity.

Note that a bond's coupon rate is different from its current yield. The coupon rate is the bond's return as a percent of its par, or principal amount, while its current yield is the income return on the investment at the market price. Yield to maturity, however, measures the total expected return—including both income and capital gain or loss—on the overall investment. To reiterate, in this book, when the term *yield* is used, *yield to maturity* is implied.

A Bond's Duration

The duration of the bond is a weighted average of the times when payments are due. Each payment's weight is determined by its present value as a percentage of the present value of the bond as a whole. Consider two bonds, both with 4-year terms and 12 percent yields to maturity. The first is a 4-year zero coupon bond with a price of $635.50. This bond has a duration of 4 years because there is a single payment at maturity which makes up 100 percent of its present value. By contrast, the second is a 4-year bond with a 9 percent coupon and a price of $908.87. This bond has a shorter duration—3.5 years—because each coupon payment figures into the weighting (the payments are compounded annually to simplify the illustration). The calculations of these bond durations are shown in Table 9.1.

Duration thus measures the present-value-weighted average time that investors have money owed to them. In Table 9.2, the effects of increasing maturity and decreasing coupon rates on a bond's duration are illustrated. When a bond's yield and coupon are held constant but its maturity is increased, its duration increases, but much more slowly than the bond's maturity in years. While a 5-year, 12 percent bond has a duration of 3.9 years, a similar 10-year bond has a duration of 6.1 years, and a comparable 20-year bond has a duration of only 8.0 years.

The higher the bond's coupon rate, the shorter its duration. This is because the coupons have larger weights, relative to the principal, the higher the coupon rate. A 30-year bond with a coupon of 12 percent has a duration of 8.6 years, while a 30-year bond with a coupon of 6 percent has a duration of 9.2 years, and a 30-year discount bond with a zero coupon has a duration of 30 years.

Duration also measures the interest rate sensitivity of a bond. The

Table 9.1. A Four-Year Discount and Four-Year Coupon Bond Have Different Durations (with Annual Compounding)

Type of Bond (1)	Time (years) (2)	PV of Payment (3)	PV of Pmt as Fraction of PV of Bond (4)	Col 2 x 4 (years) (5)
DISCOUNT BOND:				
Coupon = 0% Annual YTM = 12%	4	$635.50	1.00	4
COUPON BOND:				
Annual coupon = 9% Annual YTM = 12%				
Interest	1	$ 80.36	.088	.088
	2	$ 71.75	.079	.158
	3	$ 64.06	.071	.213
	4	$ 57.20	.063	.252
Principal	4	$635.50	.699	2.796
Total		$908.87	1.000	3.5 yrs

closer the bond price is to par, the more exact this measure becomes. Take a bond with a duration of 5 years, a coupon of 12 percent, and a yield to maturity of 12 percent, selling at par, or 100. If the yield to maturity rises 10 basis points, or 0.10 percent, to 12.10 percent, the price will fall 5 *times* 0.10, or 0.50, to 99.50.

Table 9.2. Maturities and Durations of Selected Bonds (with Semiannual Compounding)

Coupon (%)	YTM (%)	Maturity (Years)	Price ($)	Duration (Years)
12	12	5	1,000.00	3.901
12	12	10	1,000.00	6.097
12	12	20	1,000.00	7.975
12	12	30	1,000.00	8.566
6	12	30	515.14	9.196
0	12	30	33.40	30.000

Bond Markets

Federal Government Bonds

Securities of the federal government and its agencies are the largest sector of the U.S. bond market; the government's old debt is maturing, current debt is being refinanced, and new debt is sold to obtain additional funds. These securities are very safe investments with respect to default because both principal and interest are guaranteed by the federal government. In addition to safety, federal debt issues also have tax advantages. While income from federal securities is subject to federal tax, it is exempt from state and local tax.

The federal government issues various types of debt instruments. A principal type is *Treasury bills,* which are sold at a discount, pay no coupon, and have maturities up to 1 year. These can be purchased through various banks and brokers, or directly at issue from the Federal Reserve Board, in $10,000 denominations. *Treasury notes* are another security issued by the U.S. government, with maturities that vary from 2 to 10 years. These pay interest semiannually, and are issued at or close to par in denominations of $1000 or more. Prior to 1983, Treasury notes were sold in bearer form, with detachable interest coupons; now all Treasury note holders are registered to help the IRS identify taxable income. Finally, *Treasury bonds* are the federal bonds with the longest maturities, 10 years or greater. Like Treasury notes, Treasury bonds are issued in denominations starting at $1000. Government security dealers maintain an active secondary market for all three Treasury issues, which means that such investments are highly liquid.

Aside from the U.S. government itself, many federal agencies also issue securities, with various degrees of government backing. Agency securities are second only to those of the U.S. government in safety. The Federal National Mortgage Association, a government agency that issues bonds to increase the availability of mortgage money, is, after the Treasury, the largest borrower in U.S. capital markets. Other agencies include the Tennessee Valley Authority, the Postal Service, and the U.S. Merchant Marine.

Corporate Bonds

Corporate bonds are bonds issued by firms from the utility, industrial, transportation, and finance sectors of the economy. Most corporates are coupon bonds, although some firms issue zero coupon bonds. Because the risk of bankruptcy is greater for firms than for the U.S. government, corporate bonds have a higher yield to maturity, to compensate for default risk. Such bonds sell at a *yield spread* over government bonds.

Various restrictive covenants, like sinking fund requirements, exist to protect bondholders from loss of principal.

Corporate bonds can be unsecured or secured. Most short-term corporate bonds are backed by issuers' guarantees alone, and consequently by the firm's credit rating. Such unsecured bonds, called *debentures,* have a kind of collateral, the revenues of the corporation. With an *income bond,* a type of unsecured bond, the issuing corporation is not required to pay bond interest if corporate income is insufficient.

Secured bonds, such as mortgage or equipment bonds, have two forms of collateral. They are secured both by a pledge of specific property and by the revenues of the firm. Mortgage bonds are secured by real estate, while equipment bonds are collateralized with equipment and other movable corporate property. Because utilities are capital intensive and have extensive real property holdings, many issue mortgage bonds. Railroads typically issue *equipment trust certificates,* bonds collateralized by railroad rolling stock (cars). In general, secured bonds are much more common than unsecured bonds.

State and Local Bonds: The Tax-Exempt Market

Many state and local governments, such as states, counties, municipalities, townships, and special districts, also issue debt. Issues with maturities of from 1 month to 3 years that are used to enhance cash flow are typically called *municipal notes.* Those with terms from 1 year to 30 years that are used to finance long-term capital projects are called *municipal bonds.* All municipal note and bond income is exempt from federal income tax.

The *general obligation (GO) bonds* of governmental units are unsecured, and are backed by their full faith and credit. These securities are thus a general lien on the unencumbered revenues of the government body. Other municipal securities are simply a "moral obligation" of the government. Still others, called *revenue bonds,* are repayable only from designated funds, such as public utility revenues.

State and local bonds are subject to default risk. Some municipal entities, like Washington Public Power Supply System, have defaulted on their coupon payments, and bondholders cannot sue bankrupt issuers, even municipal or state governments. In general, then, municipal securities have higher default risk than federal securities. Municipal bond issuers often buy insurance to protect buyers against default. This insurance facilitates selling the bonds and lowers the interest rate issuers have to pay to investors.

State and local bonds are usually issued in serial form, meaning that some are redeemed each year until all are retired. These bonds may also be callable at specific dates and prices. The issuing agency is sometimes required to contribute to a sinking fund to guarantee that resources will exist to repay bondholders at maturity.

Investment banking houses acting as underwriters handle the public and private placement of municipal bond issues. While many investors buy municipal bonds to hold until maturity, an active secondary market exists to resell these securities in the interim.

International Bonds

A *domestic bond* of any country is a bond that meets two tests. First, the currency of the bond is the currency of the borrower's home country, and second, the bond is principally bought by nationals of the borrower's home country. Such bonds are usually underwritten by domestic syndicates of banks and sold primarily to local investors.

Crossborder bonds, then, are bonds issued in a currency different from the borrower's home currency, or bonds primarily bought by foreigners. They include what have traditionally been called both *foreign bonds* and *Eurobonds*. (When domestic bonds are bought primarily by foreigners, these bonds are usually classified as foreign bonds.) Crossborder bonds are primarily issued in three currencies: dollars, yen, and marks. Examples are Samurai bonds, which are issued in dollars in Japan; Eurodollar bonds, which are issued in Europe in dollars; Euroyen bonds, which are issued in Europe in yen; and Euro-Deutschmark bonds, which are issued in Europe (outside Germany) in marks.

The major bond markets outside the United States are in Canada, Germany, Japan, the Netherlands, Switzerland, and the United Kingdom. The debt instruments in each of these markets are different, because of local traditions and regulations. For example, the main Japanese instruments of interest to foreign investors are bonds of the Japanese government and its agencies, Japanese bank debentures, *Gensaki*, yen certificates of deposit, Samurai bonds, and Euroyen bonds.

From the point of view of U.S. investors, U.S. dollar crossborder bonds are exposed to political risks such as sovereign risk and repatriation of funds risk, while U.S. dollar domestic bonds are not. (Sovereign risk is the risk of a government's refusing to honor its debts. Repatriation of funds risk is the risk of a government's blocking payment of interest and principal to foreign debtors.) Likewise, the German investor finds Deutschmark crossborder (but not domestic) bonds exposed to political risk.

When foreigners purchase domestic bonds of another country, these bonds are also subject to currency or exchange risk. That is, exchange risk exists if the bond's currency does not match the currency with which the bondholder intends to buy goods. Thus, in addition to yield, investors must consider potential appreciation or depreciation of the bond's currency against the dollar.

The Economics of Bond Markets

Horizon Premiums

A bond's maturity, or more precisely its duration, significantly affects its sensitivity to prevailing interest rates. Long-term bond prices are more sensitive to interest rate changes than those of short-term bonds. As previously indicated, the difference between the yields in long- and short-term bonds, or between any two bond yields, is called a yield spread. Investors seem to demand such a spread, or premium, for assuming the interest rate risk of long-term bonds. This spread is called the bond maturity premium, *horizon premium,* or liquidity premium.

In economic terms, the yield on a default-free bond is equal to the expected inflation, plus the expected real interest rate, plus the bond's horizon premium. If inflation is 6 percent, the real interest rate is 3 percent, and the bond's horizon premium is 1 percent, such a default-free bond should yield 10 percent. The horizon premium constitutes the compensation for interest rate risk.

Default Premiums

If a bond is subject to default, the promised yield must be not only high enough to cover this probability, but also high enough to provide compensation for taking default risk. The total of these compensations is the *default premium.* If the expected loss from default is 1 percent and if the compensation for taking default risk is 1 percent, then the total default premium would be 2 percent. When a riskless bond yields 10 percent, the corresponding yield on a bond subject to the default probability described above would be 12 percent. The expected return would be approximately 12 percent conditional on no default, but only 11 percent after allowing for the probability of default.

Inflation and Real Returns on Bonds

Changes in expected inflation cause changes in nominal interest rates, and consequently changes in bond yields. The economist Irving Fisher was the first to observe that the nominal rate of interest must equal the real rate of interest, plus the prospective rate of inflation. Thus, if investors generally revise their estimates of expected inflation downward by 1 percent, the nominal interest rate may also fall by 1 percent.

In practice, changes in expectations about inflation do often cause a shift in bond yields. In fact, the change may affect bonds of different durations in different ways. If investors expect that near-term inflation will increase, the yields on bonds of short duration rise. If investors do not increase their expectations about long-term inflation as much, yields on bonds of longer duration will increase, but less sharply.

Yield Curves—The Term Structure of Interest Rates

The yields to maturity on default-free bonds of various maturities are shown together in Figure 9.1 to portray what is called the *yield curve* on Treasury securities. As before, the difference between the yields of two otherwise similar securities with different maturities is called the yield spread. In June 1986, 30-day Treasury bills are shown to yield about 6

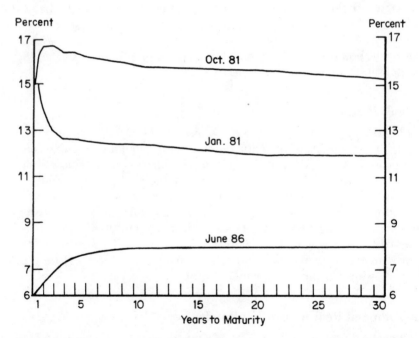

Figure 9.1. Term structure of U.S. Treasury yields. (*Source: Ibbotson Associates, Chicago.*)

percent, while 5-year notes yield about 8 percent, the 2.0 percent difference being the yield spread between these two securities. The yield curve on such riskless securities is also called the *term structure of interest rates*.

The yield curve or term structure takes three basic forms, as also shown in Figure 9.1. In an upward-sloping curve, such as the June 1986 curve, short-term rates are lower than long-term rates. When the curve is downward-sloped, as in January 1981, short-term rates are higher than long-term rates. The curve can also be hump-backed, as it was in October 1981; here, short-term rates are low, medium-term rates are high, and long-term rates are in between. Long-term bonds usually have a higher expected return, or a horizon premium, because there is greater interest rate risk over longer periods than for an investor with a short-term horizon. Hence, the June 1986 curve is the most common form. Yield curves provide forecasts of future short-term interest rates; a downward sloping yield curve, for example, implies lower short-term rates in the future.

Finally, the market price of bonds, like that of any debt instrument, varies inversely with changes in interest rates. As interest rates decline, bond prices rise because the fixed coupon and principal payments associated with bonds become more valuable. Likewise, when interest rates rise, they become less valuable, and bond prices fall.

Bond Dedication and Immunization Strategies

Liabilities are in essence the obligation to make payments in the future. An individual might be planning to put a child through college, or a pension fund manager might anticipate paying pension benefits to retirees. Both invest their assets in the interim to meet these future demands. Shrewd investors have observed that by matching the duration of such assets to that of anticipated liabilities, the risk of insufficient wealth to meet these obligations is reduced.

Dedication.   When the liability is known and its amount fixed, certain assets can be set aside, or *dedicated,* to meet that liability. To continue the example, the parent may buy a zero coupon bond to assure that funds will be available when a child reaches college age, and the pension fund manager may buy bonds with interest payments that exactly match the monthly amount of expected retirement obligations to retired employees. For example, a portfolio of zero coupon bonds with durations of 6, 7, and 8 years can be used to meet a series of liabilities with maturities of 6, 7, and 8 years.

Immunization. If liabilities of differing amounts mature at different times, the matching of cash flows can be complicated or impossible. In this situation, it is possible to *immunize* the liabilities with a portfolio. Immunization is a mathematical procedure that minimizes the risk of changes in nominal value of a portfolio of assets over a specified time horizon. The objective is to replicate as closely as possible with bonds that have coupons the results of a dedication strategy using zero coupons. If interest rates go up, the coupons can be reinvested at higher rates to offset the loss of principal. As bond prices fall, interest rates increase, and thus coupons can be reinvested at higher rates. There is a trade-off between the reinvestment rate and the bond's price.

Use of Duration in Immunization. Immunization can most easily be accomplished with bond durations. The durations of liabilities are matched as closely as possible with the durations of various assets. Duration measures the sensitivity of the bond price to changes in its yield to maturity. When the duration of the assets (the bond portfolio) and the liabilities are matched, changes in prevailing interest rates change the value of the assets and liabilities by the same amount, assuming the entire yield curve shifts by the same amount.

Immunization and Interest Rate Elasticity. When long- and short-term interest rates change by the same amount, the yield curve shifts in parallel. In this case, only a bond's duration need be known to determine the effect on a bond's price. However, typically, long-term rates are more stable than short-term rates. Thus, the short end of the yield curve is more volatile, or more sensitive to interest rate changes. In economic terms, short-term rates are more interest-rate elastic than long-term rates.

Empirically, short rates usually adjust by a greater amount than long rates. For every 1 percent change in the yield to maturity on a 1-year bond, 2-year bond yields change about 0.8 percent on average. For longer-term bonds, the changes are smaller: 5-year bond yields change only about 0.4 percent relative to 1-year bond yields, and 15-year bond yields change only 0.2 percent.

When elasticity factors are computed, long-term bonds are less elastic than short-term bonds. If the factor was 1 for short-term bonds, the factor will be less than 1 for long-term bonds. When such factors are multiplied by a bond's duration, the expected change in price can be determined. Specifically, the expected change in price is equal to the elasticity factor (expressed as a negative number) times the bond's duration times the expected short-term change in yield.

Conclusion

The yield to maturity of a bond best measures its approximate expected return. This is true especially for default-free bonds over the life of the bond, ignoring reinvestment risk. For bonds with default risk, the bond's expected return will be below its promised yield to maturity, because there is some probability that the bond will default.

The actual return on a bond equals its yield to maturity, plus the return in excess of this yield, whether positive or negative. Gains and losses on bonds occur primarily because of changes in prevailing interest rates.

The duration of a bond measures its price sensitivity to changes in its yield to maturity. Long-term bond prices are more sensitive to changes in yield to maturity than short-term bonds. On the other hand, this is partially offset by the empirical fact that short-term interest rates fluctuate more than long-term interest rates.

Dedication and immunization are techniques for protecting a bond portfolio's nominal value from changes in interest rates over a given horizon. When the liabilities are fixed, zero coupon bonds can be dedicated so that their maturities match the horizon. In this way, nominal risk is eliminated at the end of the horizon.

Immunization is desirable when there are many liabilities with complicated payment schedules, and when coupon bonds are used to match these liabilities. As interest rates change, there is a trade-off between the bond's price and the rate at which coupon payments are reinvested. Immunization is a mathematical procedure for implementing such trade-offs.

Suggested Reading

Fabozzi, Frank J., Sylvan G. Feldstein, Irving M. Pollack, and Frank G. Zarb (eds.): *The Municipal Bond Handbook*. vols. 1 and 2, Dow Jones-Irwin, Homewood, Ill., 1983. A textbook designed for brokers, money managers, and other professionals.

Fisher, Irving: *The Theory of Interest*, 1930. Reprinted by Augustus M. Kelly, Publishers, New York, 1965. Sets forth the principles of fixed-income capital theory still widely accepted more than 50 years later.

Fong, H. Gifford, and Frank J. Fabozzi: *Fixed Income Portfolio Management*, Dow Jones-Irwin, Homewood, Ill., 1985. Provides good technical information along with general descriptions of bond management.

Granito, Michael R.: *Bond Portfolio Immunization*, Lexington Books, Lexington, Mass., 1984. A technical treatment of bond immunization.

Homer, Sidney, and Martin L. Liebowitz: *Inside the Yield Book: New Tools for Bond Market Strategy*, Prentice-Hall, Inc., Englewood Cliffs, N.J., 1972. A seminal work on bonds, oriented to the professional bond manager.

10
The U.S. and International Bond Markets

"I decided to go East and learn the bond business," said the narrator of F. Scott Fitzgerald's *The Great Gatsby*. Why the bond business? A young man must work even if he is rich. But the work should be dignified and easy, and above all, safe. And so it was in the spring of 1922. No business was safer than bonds, whose yields moved only within the astonishingly narrow range of three-tenths of 1 percent from 1922 to 1929. The bond business did not require much technical expertise, but it was very important to have a good tennis arm.

Today bonds are nearly as risky as stocks. It is a dull year when long-term bond yields move only three-tenths of 1 percent—as much as the cumulative move in yields over most of the 1920s. Quantitative analysts and aggressive traders swarm about the bond markets; the Treasury bond futures contract is by far the most actively traded future in existence.

Recall that a bond's total return is a measure of achieved results, and includes both income and capital appreciation. (The basics of bonds are presented in Chapter 9.) By contrast, its yield, or yield to maturity, is a forward-looking measure related to its expected return. It can also be thought of as the discount rate at which the present value of the bond's future cash flows equals its current market price.

Bond returns and yields move in an inverse relationship. Bond prices fall (that is, returns are negative) as yields rise, because a fixed-income contract is worth less, the higher the discount rate. Conversely, as a bond's yield falls, the price rises, producing positive returns. Thus, bond yields and returns move in opposite directions, even though part of a bond's total return is its yield.

Let's now examine returns and yields, first on U.S. and then on international bonds.

The U.S. Bond Market

Cumulative Returns on U.S. Government Bonds

With respect to default, U.S. government bonds are among the safest of any bonds that investors might choose. Consequently, these bonds provide a good indication of the basic risk and return levels of bond investments in general. Returns on other categories of bonds, such as corporates, are described later.

The value of a dollar invested in 1789 in government bonds grew to over $4400 by the mid-1980s. This result assumes reinvestment of cash flows at prevailing yields, and excludes taxes (which were negligible for most of the period) and transaction costs. All of this growth, and then some, comes from income returns (coupon payments), since an investor would have suffered a capital loss over the period studied. Inflation, by contrast, pushed consumer prices up only seventeenfold over the nearly 200 years. Thus bond investors would have beat inflation by roughly 3 percent per year over the period, which over centuries amounts to considerable growth in real wealth.

Historical U.S. Government Bond Yields

Yields tell a different and perhaps more relevant story. In Figure 10.1, we see yields and inflation rates moving in tandem over most of U.S. history. Long-term yields moved less than yearly inflation rates because the yield represents the market's inflation expectation over the life of the bond, not just over the current year. For example, during the Civil War, yearly inflation rates exceeded 30 percent, but long-term yields rose only to 7 percent because investors expected inflation to decrease later.

For the first 150 years of American history, bond yields rose in wartime, corresponding to the inflationary character of such periods. Yields peaked during the War of 1812, the Civil War, and World War I. Each peak was below the previous one, indicating the increasingly good credit of the government, and/or lowered inflation expectations over the period. Although there were wide swings in yields over time, the general trend was downward, producing capital gains (a bull market) for bondholders.

Interestingly, World War II, the largest military effort ever undertaken by the United States, was not associated with an increase in long-term bond yields, even though there was substantial inflation during the war. Investors appeared to anticipate very low inflation rates beyond the immediate time frame.

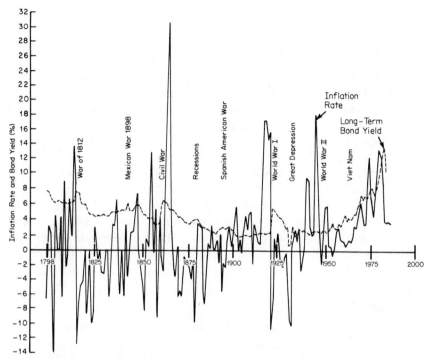

Figure 10.1. Long-term U.S. government bond yields and inflation, 1798 to 1985.   (*Source: Bond yields from Sidney Homer, "Long-Term Bond Yields from Medieval Time to 1975," in A History of Interest Rates. Copyright © 1963, 1977 by Rutgers, the State University. Data used with permission of Rutgers University Press, with updates by the authors. Inflation rates from Table 11.3.*)

After World War II, yields started to rise. The rise was considerable in the 1950s, larger in the 1960s, and astounding in the 1970s. By September 1981, the yield on a long-term government bond had passed 15 percent. The practically unbroken rise in yields from 1945 to 1981 represented the most disastrous bond bear market in history; investors who maintained a constant 20-year-maturity portfolio would have lost two-thirds of their principal due to falling bond prices over that period.

The bear market, or rise in yields, was due to the unprecedented peacetime inflation that accelerated almost continuously over the same years. In previous inflations, investors had anticipated a return to stable prices, or to deflation, within the life of long-term bonds, keeping long-term bond yields under 8 percent even in the most inflationary years of the nineteenth century. But in the postwar inflation, investors eventually learned from bitter experience that inflation was not only durable but likely to accelerate over the life of a long-term bond. Yields soared and bond prices crashed.

The great bond bear market ended suddenly in 1981. By the middle of 1982, yields were falling even more rapidly than they had risen. Bond prices skyrocketed, but since they were rising from extremely depressed levels, most investors were simply recovering a portion of what they had lost. The lucky few who bought bonds when yields were at their highest enjoyed a real bonanza. By the middle of the 1980s, yields had fallen to about 8 percent—in perspective, roughly the maximum level reached over the country's history until late in the previous decade.

In Table 10.1, yields and returns on government issues are presented for bonds of short, medium, and long maturities since 1926. The effect of a change in yield on a bond's capital appreciation return is measured by the bond's duration, described in Chapter 9. All other things being equal, the duration of a bond is directly related to its maturity. Thus, returns on long-term bonds are more sensitive to changes in yield than those of short-term bonds. Hence capital gains and losses are larger with long-term than short-term bonds, as shown in the return data.

The National Debt

The size of the U.S. government bond market is of particular interest because, in essence, it is the national debt. In Figure 10.2, the U.S. national debt is portrayed as a percentage of U.S. gross national product. The debt percentage gyrates widely. In particular, wars cause the debt percentage to skyrocket. Issuing debt is one of the three ways that any government finances wars, in addition to raising taxes and printing money. During peacetime, GNP growth has generally outpaced growth of the national debt, so that the debt percentage has fallen.

It is interesting to compare the more recent national debt levels with historical debt levels. There have been various attempts by Congress to control government deficits, the latest being the Gramm-Rudman legislation, which mandates that the federal budget be balanced. Despite the problem that Congress has in controlling the federal deficit, the long-run level of debt as a percentage of GNP has decreased dramatically since the end of World War II. Nevertheless, it is reasonable that Congress should limit spending, since its failure to do so in the 1980s may cause debt levels to rise again, even in peacetime.

The U.S. Corporate Bond Market

Corporate bonds have default risk, which government bonds do not, and consequently they command a risk premium (i.e., a higher yield) in the market. The primary types of corporate bonds are those issued by

Table 10.1. U.S. Government Yields and Returns, 1926–1984

Year	Short-Term (1 - 2 Year Maturities) Yield	Total Return	Intermediate (5 - 10 Year Maturities) Yield	Total Return	Long-Term (10 - 15 Year Maturities) Yield	Total Return
1926	3.30 %	4.80%	-0.23%	2.83%	3.33%	4.49%
1927	3.35	3.34	0.52	1.75	3.27	5.71
1928	4.48	2.78	1.99	1.87	3.74	-0.08
1929	3.32	5.45	3.11	4.85	3.59	2.42
1930	1.01	4.51	2.97	3.29	2.73	8.17
1931	1.96	0.92	1.68	-0.25	4.00	-3.25
1932	0.69	5.57	0.81	4.64	3.29	14.12
1933	2.19	0.41	3.43	1.25	3.55	0.30
1934	-0.16	4.66	2.53	8.62	2.98	10.76
1935	0.11	1.33	1.83	6.76	2.72	5.55
1936	0.39	0.45	1.45	4.83	2.22	7.70
1937	0.49	1.67	1.75	1.16	2.45	0.36
1938	-0.10	1.80	1.50	5.55	1.96	5.88
1939	-0.35	1.09	1.06	3.94	1.85	5.00
1940	-0.35	0.42	0.70	3.37	1.56	5.80
1941	0.49	-0.30	1.24	-0.53	1.98	0.72
1942	0.58	0.62	1.55	1.64	1.90	0.72
1943	0.67	0.97	1.47	2.50	1.61	4.78
1944	0.85	0.80	1.39	2.38	1.36	3.65
1945	0.81	1.13	1.08	3.27	1.57	3.77
1946	0.93	0.93	1.21	0.57	1.79	1.58
1947	1.08	0.91	1.53	0.14	2.14	-2.49
1948	1.29	1.20	1.46	2.23	2.19	3.96
1949	1.10	1.60	1.12	2.72	1.94	6.34
1950	1.45	0.99	1.43	0.19	2.36	-0.47
1951	2.04	1.45	1.63	0.61	2.71	-1.89
1952	2.19	1.93	2.10	1.38	2.77	2.07
1953	1.49	3.07	1.83	2.87	2.70	3.93
1954	1.15	1.69	1.85	2.35	2.58	4.36
1955	2.67	0.74	2.48	-0.46	2.88	-1.30
1956	3.57	1.90	3.24	-0.80	3.53	-5.12
1957	2.69	4.94	2.50	6.30	3.26	14.00
1958	3.08	2.61	3.60	-2.15	3.86	-3.71
1959	4.47	2.11	4.56	-1.83	4.54	-4.30
1960	2.61	7.13	3.56	13.32	3.80	13.80
1961	3.24	2.59	3.96	1.75	4.04	0.65
1962	3.08	3.82	3.70	6.53	3.90	6.02
1963	3.70	2.63	4.04	2.01	4.16	1.03
1964	3.82	3.93	4.10	4.17	4.18	3.99
1965	4.73	2.73	4.65	0.91	4.50	0.23
1966	4.69	5.29	4.61	5.15	4.58	3.67
1967	5.49	3.60	5.69	-0.13	5.66	-7.53
1968	5.97	4.74	6.16	3.99	5.99	2.01
1969	8.11	3.69	7.80	-1.27	7.21	-6.17
1970	5.37	11.86	6.20	16.56	6.45	16.72
1971	4.72	6.95	5.75	10.22	6.51	15.67
1972	5.79	4.36	6.24	4.34	6.47	5.99
1973	7.10	4.74	6.74	4.30	7.32	-0.78
1974	7.39	7.18	7.18	5.32	7.72	4.00
1975	6.06	9.08	7.50	6.90	7.78	7.27
1976	4.85	9.10	6.31	14.42	6.82	17.17
1977	6.96	4.15	7.61	-0.35	7.71	1.07
1978	10.11	5.07	9.27	0.19	8.85	-1.53
1979	11.66	7.18	10.35	2.61	9.79	-0.16
1980	13.44	8.69	12.38	2.07	11.58	-4.49
1981	13.08	14.61	13.52	1.14	13.41	1.57
1982	8.48	19.48	10.87	32.19	10.46	43.28
1983	10.25	9.35	11.62	5.29	11.87	1.95
1984	9.73	13.34	11.42	13.97	11.65	14.65

Source: "Returns and Yields on U.S. Government Bonds," in progress by Thomas S. Coleman and Roger G. Ibbotson.

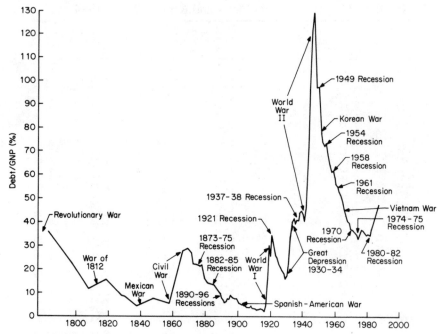

Figure 10.2. U.S. national debt as a percentage of GNP, 1790–1985. (*Source: Ibbotson Associates, Chicago.*)

utility, industrial, financial, and transportation firms. Composite returns on various corporate bonds are presented in Table 10.2.

The creditworthiness of a bond is inversely related to its return. In Table 10.2, corporates since 1926 were ranked by their Moody's credit rating, and on average the relatively risky Baa-rated bonds have achieved about 1.5 percent higher annual returns than the much safer Aaa-rated bonds. Thus, bonds rated as risky have had historically higher returns than more creditworthy bonds. In economic terms, bondholders are rewarded with higher returns for assuming more risk, even after taking defaults into account.

When bonds are ranked by maturity, the returns on long-term bonds are lower than those on short-term bonds. At first this may seem counterintuitive, because bondholders are generally thought to demand a horizon premium for assuming interest rate risk. Recall, however, that total returns include capital gains and losses. As just described, bond yields have risen since the 1940s, which means that bond prices fell steadily since then. Thus long-term bonds had capital losses, and consequently, lower returns than short-term bonds. During this period at least, bondholders have not been rewarded for assuming maturity risk.

Table 10.2. The U.S. Corporate Bond Market, 1926–1983

	Total Returns				Return in Excess of Yield
Portfolio	Geometric Mean	Arithmetic Mean	Standard Deviation(a)	Year-end 1983 Value of $1.00 Invested 12/31/25	Geometric Mean
Composite	4.25%	4.50%	7.28%	$12.13	-1.62%
Industry:					
Utility	4.02%	4.24%	6.98%	$10.58	-1.71%
Industrial	4.46	4.71	7.41	13.48	-1.36
Financial(b)	2.52	2.67	5.82	4.45(c)	-2.01
Transportation	4.44	4.83	8.96	13.41	-1.66
Moody Rating:					
Aaa	3.54%	3.71	6.12%	$7.89	-1.45%
Aa	3.58	3.77	6.36	8.21	-1.64
A	3.73	4.03	7.90	9.04	-1.90
Baa	5.06	5.23	6.07	19.20	-0.80
Below Baa	5.19	5.93	12.00	21.41	-2.54
Maturity:(d)					
5 - <15 years	5.06%	5.23%	6.07%	$19.20	-0.80%
15+ years	3.84	4.16	8.18	$9.55	-2.03

Notes

(a) Standard deviations reflect a small sample size and thus do not exactly reflect the underlying dispersion of returns.

(b) Data for financial category is for 1950–1983.

(c) Year-end 1949 = $1.00

(d) Results omitted for 0–5 years to maturity due to small sample size.

Source: Roger G. Ibbotson and Michael J. Gibbs, "The Corporate Bond Market: Structure and Returns," in progress, 1986.

There is no economic reason to believe that this debacle will be repeated, and long-term bondholders can expect to receive positive horizon premiums in the future. In fact, updating Table 10.2 to include the tremendous bond rally of the mid-1980s would substantially change these results.

International Bond Returns

Major Bond Markets

Thus far, the U.S. bond market has been the focus of attention. This market is the largest in the world, almost two-thirds of all publicly issued debt. But the Euromarkets and the domestic Japanese, British, and, to a lesser extent, German markets are also significant. Overall, the world bond market is huge, $3.4 trillion in value. This is significantly larger than the aggregate market value of the world's stock markets. Thus, by value, world bonds are a larger investment market than world stocks.

In Table 10.3, the dollar values of the government, agency, and cor-

Table 10.3. How Big Is the World Bond Market?

Country/ Currency	Central Gov't	Central Gov't Agency & Gov't Guar.	State & Local Gov't	Corp. (incl Cvts)	Other Domestic Publicly Issued	Crossborder Bonds Foreign Bonds	Euro- Bonds	Total Publicly Issued	As Pct. of Public Issues in All Markets	Private Placement Unclassif.
U.S. Dollar	$873.0	$543.4[b]	$538.3	$420.7	$ 15.3	$ 66.4	$195.9	$2,653.0	56.7%	$178.3
Japanese Yen	477.6	56.3	22.0	49.9	154.1	16.6	3.0	779.2	16.7	154.0
West German DM	64.9	—	6.8	0.7	196.2	30.5		299.1	6.4	156.7[c]
Italian Lira	126.8	10.0	—	2.3	46.3	—	0.1	185.4	4.0	—
U.K. Sterling	132.1	—	1.1	9.1	—	3.6	6.3	152.0	3.2	—
Canadian Dollar	49.9	0.2	40.7[c]	24.8	0.9	0.5	4.8	121.7	2.6	—
French Franc	27.6	58.4	2.4	20.2	—	0.8	1.1	110.5	2.4	—
Belgian Franc	34.0	25.0[d]	2.7[d]	4.9[d]	11.2[d]	0.2	—	78.1[d]	1.7	—
Swedish Krona	38.6	—	1.1	6.2	29.6	—	—	75.7	1.6	—
Danish Krone	26.1	—	—	—	45.0	—	0.1	71.0	1.5	—
Swiss Franc	4.6	—	4.8	11.2	13.2	22.1	—	55.9	1.2	28.8
Australian Dollar	27.7	9.9	—	12.1	—	—	0.5	50.2	1.1	31.2
Dutch Guilder	28.0	—	2.8	12.0	—	3.2	2.0	48.0	1.0	39.7[c]
Total	$1,910.9	$703.2	$622.7	$574.1	$511.8	$357.7		$4,679.8	100.0%	$588.7[c]

Nominal Value Outstanding. Billion U.S. Dollars Equivalent[a]

[a] Exchange rates prevailing as of December 31, 1984, used for conversion to U.S. dollars in this figure are as follows: Y251.8/US$, 3.159DM/US$, 1,934.0 Lire/US$, 0.864 £/US$, 1.322 Can$/US$, 9.645 Ffr/US$, 63.225 Bfr/US$, 8.989 Skr/US$, 11.260 Dkr/US$, 2.600 Sfr/US$, 3.651 Dfl/US$ and 1.227 A$/US$.

[b] Includes mortgage pool issues.

[c] Only the marketable portion of provincial bonds was used in calculating this figure.

[d] As of October 31, 1984.

Source: Jeffrey D. Hanna and Richard Segal, "How Big is the World Bond Market?" Salomon Brothers Inc. New York, 1985.

porate debt markets of the United States and 12 other countries are presented. Details on the size of each country's central government debt, combined government and agency debt, state and local debt, corporate debt, other domestic public debt, and private placements are shown, as well as figures for crossborder bonds issued in the currency of the particular country.

The U.S. central government swamps the debt of other central governments, with 45 percent of the total. Japan ranks second, but its central government debt is only half that of the United States. In the corporate debt market, the United States is the undisputed leader, with 72 percent of this market. U.S. corporate debt amounts to over twice as much as all publicly traded non-U.S. corporate debt, which totaled about $150 billion in the mid-1980s. Much foreign corporate debt is privately held, or held by banks (and consequently not included in the bond markets).

Germany stands out as a country with a disproportionately large bond market. Recall, however, that most German firms are privately owned, and that the German stock market is rather small. In this context, Germany's large market for "other domestic publicly issued bonds," with a value of over $195 billion, is less surprising.

Indebtedness as a percent of GNP suggests the degree of leverage of each country's economy. By this measure, the United States, Japan, and Switzerland are highly leveraged, with ratios in the 50 to 60 percent range. France and the Netherlands, on the other hand, have little leverage in their economies: 16.9 and 25.6 percent of their GNPs, respectively.

The pie chart of Figure 10.3 shows 12 countries' shares of total publicly issued bonds by aggregate value in 1980. In contrast to the previous table, this figure excludes all U.S. bonds except U.S.-dollar-denominated

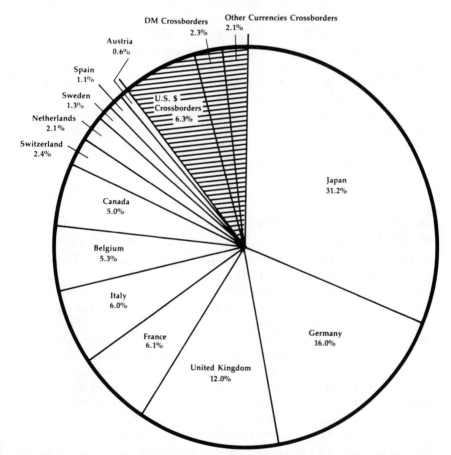

Figure 10.3. Foreign bond markets: Aggregate values as a percentage of the total. (Percentages are as of year-end 1980.) (*Source: Roger G. Ibbotson, Richard C. Carr, and Anthony W. Robinson, "International Equity and Bond Returns,"* Financial Analysts Journal, *July–August 1982.)*

crossborder bonds, which are foreign. Note that while the bond markets of Japan and Germany were destroyed by World War II, these two countries alone make up about half the non-U.S. bond market 30 years later. Also, crossborder bonds, which were almost nonexistent in 1946, now make up almost 11 percent of the international bond market as investors continuously traverse national boundaries in search of diversification and performance opportunities.

Returns on International Bonds

Not only have Japan's and Germany's bond markets mushroomed in size, but these two countries have been the hot performers since 1960. When cumulative indices of dollar-adjusted total returns are computed for various countries, Japan and Germany come out on top. As Figure 10.4 suggests, a dollar invested in bonds in Japan in 1960 has grown to $13.70 by year-end 1985, and in Germany to $10.89, far exceeding the United States with $4.16 and the United Kingdom with $3.91. Some of this differential comes from an increase in the currency value of these two countries. If the theory of interest rate parity were to hold, U.S.-dollar-converted returns on the bonds of each of these countries would be expected to be the same. This theory is explained next.

The Theory of Interest, Inflation, and Exchange Rates

Economists, notably Irving Fisher, have proposed theories of both domestic and international prices and returns, based on the principles of economic equilibrium and rational investor expectations. For clarity, let's first look at the domestic and then the international relationships.

Inflation rates have an important effect on bond yields. The interest rates on such securities are based on investors' expectations about inflation over the term of the security, plus a positive or negative real interest rate. This relationship is known as the Fisherian relation for a single economy. In the last half century, the average real interest rate has been near zero; returns on short-term U.S. Treasury bills, the prototype cash equivalent, exceeded the U.S. inflation rate by only 0.3 percent per year.

Between countries, interest rates should, like other prices, obey the *law of one price*. This economic law states that the price of two identical goods in separate places cannot differ by more than the transaction or transportation costs needed to bring the two goods to the same place. Thus, shares of IBM stock should sell for approximately the same price

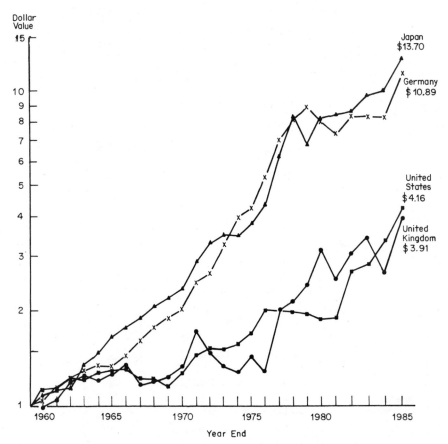

Figure 10.4. U.S. dollar-adjusted cumulative wealth indexes of selected domestic bond markets, 1960–1985. (Year-end 1959 = $1.) (*Source: Roger G. Ibbotson, Richard C. Carr, and Anthony W. Robinson, "International Equity and Bond Returns," Financial Analysts Journal, July–August 1982, with updates by the authors.*)

in Paris as in New York. Extending this principle to bonds, the price of obtaining money—i.e., the interest rate—should not differ greatly between countries *when this price is converted to a single currency*, such as the U.S. dollar. The interest rates of two countries may be dissimilar because each country has different monetary and fiscal policies. When their exchange rates are anticipated to diverge, interest rates between the countries move to equalize any differences.

This principle, called the *principle of interest rate parity*, is sketched out in Figure 10.5. First, consider the implications of different inflation rates in two countries. If the U.S. inflation rate is 6 percent and British inflation 11 percent, then investors generally expect the British pound to

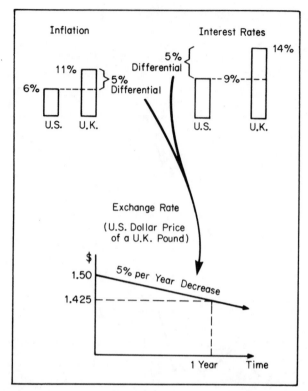

Figure 10.5. The relationship between foreign and domestic inflation, interest, and exchange: Hypothetical illustration.

decline by 5 percent per year. This expected decline would show up
in the relative prices of spot and forward currency. (The *spot currency
price* is the price of purchasing a currency to be delivered now,
while the *forward price* is the price for delivery at a specified time in
the future.)

Next, consider the effects of differing inflation rates on interest rates.
If the U.S. interest rate were 9 percent under this scenario, the British
rate would be 14 percent. A U.S. holder of British bonds would receive
only 9 percent in U.S. dollar terms, however, because the British pound
would decline by 5 percent over the year's holding period. Thus, interest
rates, converted to U.S. dollars, would be identical in Britain and the
United States. The theory of interest rate parity, then, suggests that
dollar-adjusted interest rates should be the same in every country.

Tests of the Theories

To see if the Fisherian relation and interest rate parity hold, the short-term interest rates of 14 countries were correlated with both their inflation rates and changes in their exchange rates against the U.S. dollar. If the Fisherian relation in a single economy is precisely true, short-term interest rates should be positively correlated with inflation at a level of 1.0, assuming constant real interest rates. If interest rates and inflation do not move in lockstep, the correlations would be less than 1.0. As Table 10.4 shows, all countries had relatively high, but not perfect, correlations between interest and inflation, ranging between 0.88 for Italy and 0.33 for the Netherlands. Thus, to some extent, interest rates incorporate investor expectations about inflation.

Statistics on the correlation of short-term interest and exchange rates weakly confirm interest rate parity. The theory predicts that the two series should move perfectly in opposite directions and that the correlation coefficients would all be −1. Yet in Table 10.4, few countries show a high negative correlation. Thus an increase in interest rates may not always cause a decline in the exchange value of a country's currency.

Interest rate parity may not be proved in the data for several reasons. Market segmentation and market imperfections could be one cause. Segmentation occurs if some securities are not bought for their yields.

Table 10.4. Correlation of Short-Term Yield in Local Currency with Local Inflation and Exchange Rates

Countries	Correlation of Yield with:[*]	
	Local Inflation	Exchange Return[**]
Austria	0.50	−0.07
Belgium	0.55	−0.29
Canada	0.82	−0.09
Denmark	0.61	−0.44
France	0.83	−0.53
Germany	0.58	−0.17
Italy	0.88	−0.75
Japan	0.44	−0.60
Netherlands	0.33	−0.03
Spain	0.51	−0.39
Sweden	0.67	−0.30
Switzerland	0.57	0.15
United Kingdom	0.77	−0.23
United States	0.85	N/A

[*] Correlations are based on annual data over 1960–1982.
[**] Exchange return is defined as the change in U.S. dollars per foreign currency unit.
Source: Roger G. Ibbotson, Richard C. Carr, and Anthony W. Robinson, "International Equity and Bond Returns," *Financial Analysts Journal*, July–August 1982, with updates by the authors.

For example, a non-interest-bearing or low-interest security might be purchased to secure protection from robbers, or to obtain bank services such as free checking and preferential loans. Another cause may be governments' interference with Treasury bill and exchange rates. U.S. yields were controlled in the 1940s and early 1950s. More recently, Swiss interest rates have been set by the major banks. Some of the discrepancies are likely to be real divergences from interest rate parity, while others reflect economists' inability to accurately measure the various interest rates on a comparable basis.

The Very Long View of Bond Yields

Historical Perspective on Bond Yields

Business enterprises have existed for thousands of years. Bond, or loan, yields from the distant past provide evidence of early economic activity, and give information on the interest rates that lenders charged. To get a feel for historical rates, a continuous series of returns and information on daily trading are unnecessary. Thus, it is easier to describe this market historically than other investment markets like real estate or equities.

The data on bond yields in this section are designed only to provide such a long-term perspective. Where data were missing, interpolations were made to complete the return series. Thus the precision of data in this section is lower than that on more recent returns, which originate from extremely reliable sources. The purpose of this section is to obtain an impression of long-term trends, while the purpose of measuring more recent returns is often to set standards for investment performance.

Bond Yields from Medieval Times to the Present

Bond yields are available anecdotally back to the preclassical period of history. The economist Sidney Homer finds that bond yields in ancient times formed a bow-shaped pattern. These yields reached a low of about 10 percent in Babylon, 6 percent in Greece, and 4 percent in Rome, each at the time of the empire's economic heyday. From these patterns, he theorizes that as trust between business participants increases and as economies mature, interest rates decrease. One reason is that creditworthiness becomes easier to evaluate, so that borrowers with the best credit pay closer to the true riskless rate. When trust decreases with

political and economic disruptions, and when information becomes unreliable, interest rates increase correspondingly.

More continuous information on bond markets exists from the thir-
teenth century on. Such quotes, shown in Table 10.5 (covering A.D.
1200–1799) and Table 10.6 (1800 to the present), indicate which countries were most active economically. Before 1500, these were Italy and
the Netherlands, while after that date, economic activity is evident

Table 10.5. Long-Term Bond Yields from Medieval Times to 1799

Date	England	France	Nether-lands	Germany	Sweden	Switzer-land	Italy
		Minimum Rates on Best Credits by Half Century					
13th Century							
1st Half			8.00				
2nd Half		14.00	8.00				6.62
14th Century							
1st Half			8.00				4.88
2nd Half			8.00				5.25
15th Century							
1st Half		10.00	8.00				6.00
2nd Half		10.00	8.00	5.00			5.00
16th Century							
1st Half	10.00	8.33	4.00	4.00			4.00
2nd Half	10.00	8.33	4.00	4.00			4.00
17th Century							
1st Half	8.00	8.33	5.00				
2nd Half	4.00	5.00	3.00				
18th Century							
1st Half	3.05	5.00	3.00	4.00		5.00	4.00
2nd Half	3.13	5.00	2.50	4.00		4.00	4.00

Decennial Averages

	England	France	Holland	United States
18th Century				
1700–1709	7.00			
1710–1719	6.00			
1720–1729	3.40			
1730–1739	3.05			
1740–1749	3.22			
1750–1759	3.13			
1760–1769	3.59			
1770–1779	3.75			
1780–1789	4.64			
1790–1799	4.54	14.00	6.42	7.49

Source: "Long-Term Bond Yields from Medieval Time to 1975," from *A History of Interest Rates*, by Sidney Homer.
Copyright © 1963, 1977 by Rutgers, the State University. Reprinted by permission of Rutgers University Press.

Table 10.6. Long-Term Bond Yields in Europe and the United States, 1800–1985

	England	France	Nether-lands	Germany	Sweden	Switzer-land	Italy	United States*
				Decennial Averages				
19th Century								
1800–1809	4.80	8.66						6.23
1810–1819	4.57	7.29	5.95	5.45				6.39
1820–1829	3.72	4.21	4.79	4.91				4.55
1830–1839	3.40	4.06	5.11	4.05				4.95
1840–1849	3.26	4.14	4.53	3.84				5.41
1850–1859	3.16	4.45	4.02	4.08	4.64			4.33
1860–1869	3.27	4.37	4.21	4.03	5.41			5.34
1870–1879	3.19	4.71	4.17	4.29	4.91			4.98
1880–1889	2.97	3.68	3.55	3.82	3.73			3.60
1890–1899	2.47	3.03	2.93	3.53	3.68			3.23
20th Century								
1900–1909	2.79	3.06	3.20	3.64	3.74	3.68		3.17
1910–1919	3.81	4.06	4.00	4.72	5.10	4.52		3.93
1920–1929	4.63	5.22	4.50	7.25	4.72	5.20	5.68	4.26
1930–1939	3.54	3.98	3.50	6.26	3.48	3.94	4.74	3.34
1940–1949	3.06	3.60	3.24	4.70	3.04	3.31	4.16	2.31
1950–1959	4.31	5.68	3.52	6.01	3.65	2.96	6.12	2.99
1960–1969	6.53	5.39	5.30	6.59	5.16	3.84	5.70	4.51
1970–1979	12.18	9.69	8.18	8.03	8.72	5.19	11.18	7.60
1980–1985	12.42	13.16	9.10	8.18	12.71	4.81	17.85	11.95

* Municipal yields are used for various years in the 19th century when there was no U.S. Treasury debt.
Source: "Long-Term Bond Yields from Medieval Time to 1975," from *A History of Interest Rates,* by Sidney Homer. Copyright © 1963, 1977 by Rutgers, the State Univesity. Reprinted by permission of Rutgers University Press, with updates by the authors.

throughout Europe. In the nineteenth and twentieth centuries, bonds are issued as business activity picks up in the United States and Canada.

Investment Advice

Historically, bonds have had substantially lower returns than equities. But, even with their recent volatility, the risks of bond investments are also lower than those for common stocks. In the last 4 decades, bonds have been particularly dismal, with high risk and poorer returns than common stocks. On the bright side, bonds have consistently outpaced inflation over the very long run. Also, bonds have performed very well in the mid-1980s, and bond yields continue to be well in excess of anticipated inflation.

Bond investors have been rewarded with higher returns for holding bonds with higher risks. When bond returns are grouped by credit rating, returns increase as creditworthiness decreases. Investors should diversify, however, to pick up the high returns available from lower-rated bonds, or else a single default may severely damage the returns on their portfolios.

Bondholders who assumed interest rate risk by purchasing bonds of longer maturities, however, have not been rewarded. In the period analyzed, long-term bonds had lower returns than short-term bonds. But in the mid-1980s, bond issuers anticipate more interest rate fluctuations than before, so bond returns should be higher in the future to compensate for this anticipated risk.

Some international bond markets, such as Japan and Germany, have had excellent returns since World War II. This suggests that U.S. investors can increase their returns and diversify the risks of bond investments by spreading their holdings among several countries.

Interest rate risk has not been substantially rewarded since the last world war. Thus, bondholders might wish to take advantage of relatively new vehicles to reduce such risks. By understanding and using bond dedication and immunization techniques (discussed in the previous chapter), bond investors can lock in returns and reduce the risks of their portfolios.

Suggested Reading

Aliber, Robert Z.: *Exchange Risk and Corporate International Finance,* Halsted Press, New York, 1978. Summarizes the basic international parity relationships.
First Boston Corporation: *Handbook of Securities of the United States Government and Federal Agencies,* New York, 1986. Describes the characteristics of principal U.S. government securities.
Hickman, W. Braddock: *Corporate Bond Quality and Investor Experience,* Princeton University Press, Princeton, N.J. 1958. A major historical study of bond prices and returns in the United States.
Homer, Sidney: *A History of Interest Rates,* 2d rev. ed., Rutgers University Press, New Brunswick, N.J., 1977. An encyclopedic compilation of interest rates, with commentary including implications for society.

PART 4

Inflation, Tangible Assets, Options, and Futures

11
Inflation around the World

If a latter-day Rip Van Winkle had gone to sleep a half century ago, cash in pocket, he would face some surprises on waking up now. His $10,000 fortune, which would have bought a very fine house in the 1930s, would barely suffice to purchase a car. Of the change in his pocket, Rip's dollar, which would have bought dinner before he went to sleep, would now be insufficient to obtain a "dime novel," and a dime would probably purchase only one "penny candy." The value of Rip Van Winkle's cash would have lost a decimal place; put another way, prices inflated by a factor of 10 between the 1930s and the 1980s.

The Great Inflation

A moment of historical reflection gives the background for the "Great Inflation." Historically, wars have usually been accompanied by dramatic increases in the price level. After a war, deflation typically brings prices back to their previous level. Prices during prolonged times of peace, while fluctuating year to year, frequently remain stable over time. In fact, prices in the United States in 1914 were approximately the same as they had been a century earlier.

After World War II, however, the usual deflation did not occur. Instead of falling back to their prewar levels, prices continued to rise. In some countries, prices escalated at an even faster pace than during wartime. Throughout the world, price levels climbed to dizzying heights, and inflation appeared to be a new fixture in the peacetime economy. This environment of steadily increasing prices can be called the Great Inflation, and its occurrence internationally is unprecedented.

Foreign Inflation after 1940

The Great Inflation came to Europe and other countries before it came to the United States. While the U.S. inflation rate settled at about 1 percent in the 1950s, the United Kingdom suffered 4 percent annual inflation in that decade, France 6 percent, and Japan 2.5 percent. In Table 11.1, decade-by-decade inflation rates are documented for nine developed countries, including the United States, over the last 60 years. While foreign inflation rates after World War II are modest by today's standards, they represent rising, not falling, prices after a wartime inflation and are a sign of more trouble to come.

Inflation rates in the 1960s repeated the 1950s, with prices rising steadily at moderate rates. The 1970s, however, brought much more severe inflation. Of the eight foreign countries in Table 11.1, all had compound annual inflation rates over 4 percent in the 1970s; six had inflation rates over 7 percent; and two had inflation rates over 12 percent. These rates continued, with some dampening, into the 1980s. Many other countries had even higher inflation. Such a worldwide price explosion has never before occurred.

The arithmetic of compounding illustrates the magnitude of the Great Inflation. Prices increasing by 4 percent per year will double every 18

Table 11.1. International Consumer Price Indexes, 1926–1985

Decade	Canada Rate of Change[1]	Index[2]	France Rate of Change[1]	Index[2]	Germany Rate of Change[1]	Index[2]	Italy Rate of Change[1]	Index[2]	Japan Rate of Change[1]	Index[2]
1926–29	0.18%	1.01	8.52%	1.39	0.33%	1.01	-2.82%	0.89	-4.46%	0.83
1930–39	-1.80	0.84	3.08	1.88	-1.96	0.83	0.24	0.91	2.11	1.03
1940–49	4.52	1.31	31.48	29.02	5.23	1.38	47.72	45.19	66.80	171.17
1950–59	2.36	1.65	6.40	53.97	1.05	1.53	2.65	58.69	2.42	217.50
1960–69	2.59	2.13	3.78	78.17	2.47	1.96	3.66	84.09	5.51	371.97
1970–79	7.54	4.41	9.09	186.66	5.02	3.20	12.88	282.43	8.94	876.08
1980–85	7.61	6.85	9.75	326.20	4.14	4.01	14.68	642.45	3.32	1065.74

	Sweden Rate of Change[1]	Index[2]	Switzerland Rate of Change[1]	Index[2]	United Kingdom Rate of Change[1]	Index[2]	United States Rate of Change[1]	Index[2]
1926–29	-0.98%	0.96	-1.05%	0.96	-1.68%	0.93	-1.09%	0.96
1930–39	0.10	0.97	-1.53	0.82	-0.41	0.90	-2.05	0.78
1940–49	4.10	1.45	4.76	1.31	5.69	1.56	5.41	1.32
1950–59	4.39	2.23	1.08	1.46	4.36	2.39	1.02	1.64
1960–69	3.52	3.15	3.20	1.99	3.68	3.44	2.52	2.10
1970–79	8.72	7.27	4.99	3.25	13.04	11.71	7.37	4.28
1980–85	9.52	12.55	4.17	4.15	8.81	19.43	6.07	6.10

Notes: 1. Annual compound rate of change in percent, for the decade or subperiod indicated.

         2. Cumulative price index initialized at 1.00 on 12/31/1925.

Source: Starting 1960, *International Financial Statistics* (various issues), published by the International Monetary Fund, Washington, D.C.; and DRI-FACS, a service of Data Resources, Inc., Lexington, Mass. Prior to 1960, the authors collected government statistics from diverse sources.

years and rise fiftyfold in a century. At a 10 percent inflation rate, prices double every 7 years and rise a staggering 14,000-fold in a century.

U.S. Inflation in the Postwar Period

Immediately after the World War II price controls were removed, U.S. prices shot up spasmodically, with 18 percent inflation in 1946—still the all-time U.S. record, excepting the Revolutionary and Civil Wars. But the inflation rate quickly headed downward, settling in a range of 0.5 percent deflation to 3 percent inflation over 1952–1965. The compound annual inflation rate over these 14 years was an exemplary 1.3 percent. Thus, while inflation was accelerating in the rest of the world, the United States went its own way, experiencing a degree of price stability comparable to peacetime periods earlier in its history.

Starting in 1966, U.S. inflation rates rose steadily and alarmingly. Inflation reached 6 percent by 1969 and peaked for the first time at 12 percent in 1974. After a period of "low" (5 to 7 percent) inflation in the mid-1970s, inflation surged to a new high in 1979—13 percent. At the end of 1981, the Consumer Price Index stood at triple its end of 1965 level. Starting with 1982, inflation rates were much lower, around 4 percent. In the mid 1980s, they approached the lows of the 1952–1965 period, due to a decrease in energy prices worldwide.

The Great Inflation's Effect on Investable Assets

Inflation affects the returns on various investable assets differently. To determine these effects, returns from major capital assets are regressed on the U.S. inflation rate, and the results are displayed in Table 11.2. Assets with an inflation beta of 1 keep up with inflation; such an asset is called an inflation hedge. Returns on assets with a zero beta are unaffected by inflation. Assets with betas in excess of 1.0 have rates of return very sensitive to the inflation rate. During inflationary periods, particularly when inflation is unexpected, investors make money holding assets with inflation betas over 1. Holding assets with inflation betas of less than 1 or assets with negative inflation betas, investors lose real value during periods of inflation.

According to Table 11.2, almost all categories of equities and bonds have negative betas when regressed on inflation. The longer the term of the bond, the more money investors lose in real terms when inflation is unexpected. In general, higher inflation rates hurt returns on bonds and stocks, while lower inflation rates help. Cash and real estate had betas

Table 11.2. Capital Market Returns, 1960–1984, Regressed on U.S. Inflation

Dependent Variable	Independent Variable	Alpha (%)	Alpha T Statistic	Beta	Standard Error of Beta	Adjusted R^2	Standard Deviation of Residuals	1st Order Autocorr of Residuals
U.S. Equities:	U.S. Inflation							
NYSE	"	14.22	2.39	-0.80	0.93	-0.01	16.73	-0.11
AMEX	"	10.43	1.26	-0.24	1.26	-0.00	24.49	-0.07
OTC	"	14.50	2.51	-0.81	0.96	-0.01	17.34	-0.09
U.S. Total Equities	"	10.76	1.87	-0.34	0.89	-0.01	16.19	-0.21
Europe Equities	"	24.75	2.17	-1.19	1.75	-0.02	31.73	-0.07
Asia Equities	"	9.06	1.17	-0.22	1.22	-0.04	21.75	-0.08
Other Equities	"	12.95	2.18	-0.36		-0.04	16.70	-0.08
Foreign Total Equities	"							
World Total Equities	"	13.75	2.46	-0.67	0.88	-0.02	15.73	-0.10
.U.S. Corporate Bonds:								
Intermediate Term	"	7.45	2.82	-0.16	0.41	-0.04	17.43	0.37
Long Term	"	10.42	2.61	-0.91	0.62	0.05	11.23	0.18
U.S. Total Corporate Bonds	"	9.49	2.75	-0.70	0.53	0.03	9.69	0.26
U.S. Government Bonds								
Treasury Notes	"	6.72	3.46	-0.66	0.28	0.04	5.49	0.15
Treasury Bonds	"	8.59	3.22	-0.05	0.55	-0.04	9.81	-0.01
Agencies	"	7.58	2.76	-0.05	0.33	-0.04	6.40	-0.05
U.S. Total Government Bonds	"	6.58			0.38	-0.02	6.70	-0.14
U.S. Total Bonds	"	7.56	2.88	-0.31	0.41	-0.02	7.38	0.22
Foreign Corporate Bonds	"	9.37	3.49	-0.15	0.43	-0.04	7.55	0.35
Foreign Government Bonds	"	8.86	2.13	-0.03	0.38	-0.04	7.72	0.28
Crossborder Bonds	"	8.84		-0.22	0.38	-0.02	5.95	0.28
Foreign Total Bonds	"	7.30	2.86	-0.05	0.36	-0.04	7.17	0.31
World Total Bonds	"	7.28	3.55	-0.15	0.33	-0.03	5.77	0.28
U.S. Cash:								
Treasury Bills	"	3.11	3.77	0.60	0.13	0.46	2.32	0.74
Commercial Paper	"	3.63	3.48	0.65	0.13	0.51	2.28	0.74
U.S. Total Cash	"	3.18	3.97	0.53	0.38	0.48	2.36	0.75
Foreign Cash	"	2.37		0.73	0.10	0.10	6.88	-0.01
World Total Cash	"	3.05	4.52			0.60	1.90	-0.39
U.S. Business Real Estate	"	5.08	4.01	0.66	0.20	0.30	3.56	0.44
U.S. Residential Real Estate	"	4.61	5.26	0.81	0.14	0.59	2.47	-0.08
U.S. Farm Real Estate	"	7.18	2.72	0.80	0.41	0.15	2.43	-0.46
U.S. Total Real Estate	"	5.23	7.53		0.11	0.69	1.95	0.13
Gold	"	-15.97	-1.90	5.39	1.31	0.40	23.65	0.03
Silver	"	-25.73	-1.01	8.72	3.96	0.19	71.39	0.19
Total Metals	"	-15.96	-1.92	5.39	1.30	0.40	23.40	0.06
U.S. Market Wealth Portfolio	"	7.88	4.23	0.16	0.29	-0.03	5.24	-0.09
Foreign Market Wealth Portfolio	"	9.59	3.07	-0.28	0.48	-0.03	8.77	-0.04
World Wealth excl. metals	"	8.32	4.28	0.03	0.33	-0.04	5.47	-0.00
World Wealth incl. metals	"	6.71	3.19	0.35	0.33	-0.01	5.90	-0.17

Source: Roger G. Ibbotson, Laurence B. Siegel, and Kathryn S. Love, "World Wealth: Market Values and Returns," *Journal of Portfolio Management*, Fall 1985.

below but near 1 when regressed on inflation, indicating that these assets are inflation hedges, although imperfectly so.

Metals are extremely responsive to inflation, with a small rise in inflation producing a large rise in metals prices and vice versa. When inflation increases, *real* returns on gold and silver are very high. In other words, investors in these metals actually make money during periods of accelerating inflation.

The adjusted R-squared statistic indicates the percent of an asset's return explained by the U.S. inflation rate. For example, inflation explains 40 percent of gold's movement and 69 percent of U.S. real estate's movement, making real estate a more reliable inflation hedge than gold. Low or negative R squareds should be ignored; inflation has unpredictable effects on these assets.

Causes of Inflation

Many economists believe that the *quantity theory of money* explains inflation. According to this theory, inflation results from an increase in the money supply in excess of increases in the amount of goods which the money can buy. An example often given is an island economy consisting only of mangoes and dollars. Given a fixed supply of both dollars and mangoes, the exchange rate between dollars and mangoes (i.e., the dollar price of a mango) remains stable. Assume that an airplane drops a sack of dollars on the island. Because dollars are now more plentiful and mangoes are not, the dollar price of mangoes rises. (The magnitude of the price rise is related to the size of the sack.) In other words, the exchange rate between real goods and money changes in proportion to the quantity of money.

In more complex economies, however, the supply of goods is neither fixed nor homogeneous. There are many goods, and the supply of each grows or shrinks at varying rates. Moreover, the money supply is not clearly defined, with many different instruments used as money or quasimoney. Therefore, the relationship between money and prices is not nearly as simple as in the mango-dollar economy. Nonetheless, empirical evidence from different countries and time periods suggests a direct causal relationship between various measures of the money supply and the price level.

A few economists cite other causes of inflation. Some claim that disequilibrium in goods markets causes "demand-pull" or "cost-push" inflation. Others have formulated expectations hypotheses, which suggest that today's inflation is caused by anticipation of future inflation and can be lowered by altering people's expectations about the future.

Measuring Inflation with the Consumer Price Index

In the United States, inflation is tracked with the Consumer Price Index (CPI). The CPI is an index of reported prices of a "market basket" of consumer goods. Unique among economic statistics, the CPI both measures inflation and helps to dictate the course of the economy. Wage contracts, pension agreements, business contracts, and social security legislation often contain clauses requiring price or wage adjustments based on changes in the CPI. Thus, investors should understand the characteristics and limitations of this frequently used index.

As an inflation measure, the CPI has three main problems:

- Short-run substitutability

- Long-run substitutability

- Changes in the quality of goods for which costs are measured

In the short run, say week to week, the prices of goods which are close substitutes may fluctuate relative to one another. The relative prices of chicken and fish, for example, commonly change by 20 percent or more on a weekly basis. The CPI does not capture this week to week fluctuation. Any shopper can beat the index simply by buying more chicken than fish when chicken is relatively cheaper, and vice versa.

Substitutability of goods in the long run is even more difficult to incorporate in the index. For example, scientific calculators fell in price from about $800 in 1970 to about $100 in 1980 for a similar but better (programmable) model. Less powerful calculators, selling for about $10 in 1980, did not even exist in 1970. The CPI began to include calculators in about 1975, after most of the price decline had already occurred. This is appropriate because the CPI should reflect the market basket of typical consumers, not mechanical engineers. Nevertheless, the CPI missed the dramatic 5-year drop in the price of a calculation. Judgment is necessary to determine when goods or services become cheap enough to be part of a typical market basket.

Quality changes also complicate the construction of price indexes. Almost everything undergoes quality changes over long periods. Automobile tires and electronic devices have become more durable and reliable. Today's supermarkets contain a variety and quality of foods unimaginable in the era before cheap refrigeration and rapid transport. On the other hand, labor-intensive services—such as mass transit and artisan's crafts—have declined in quality. Ideally, the CPI should include the cost of these qualitative changes by denominating goods in terms of the services they provide. An automobile tire provides miles of "safe" travel;

thus a 40,000-mile radial tire should be counted as providing four times the consumer utility or satisfaction as a 10,000-mile tire of 40 years ago.

These three difficulties with the CPI all bias the measured inflation rate upward. In other words, the actual inflation rate is likely to be less than the rate as measured by the CPI. Another bias exists because the CPI is not an instantaneous "snapshot" of prices but rather a mixture of old and new prices. Thus, during inflation the CPI understates the price level (setting aside all the other biases) and during deflation the CPI overstates the price level.

Despite these problems, the CPI remains a useful and important barometer of inflation. Researchers may wish to revise or even backdate the consumer price index using more sophisticated construction methods. For practical purposes, however, CPI measurements can be safely used by those aware of their limitations.

The Long-Term Record of Inflation and Deflation

In recent decades, rampant inflation has occurred around the world. Historically, however, inflation and deflation have alternated, making long-term changes in the price level quite moderate.

The United Kingdom

In England, a record of inflation exists from the 1200s to the present. That is the longest period for which records have been kept in a single country, probably because England had one government (more or less) and one monetary system for the whole time. The level of consumer prices in England from 1260 to the 1970s is illustrated in Figure 11.1.

Prices were quite stable across amazingly long periods of time. Setting the year 1600 equal to 1, the price index almost always remained within the range of 0.1 to 0.4 for 2½ centuries, between the years 1260 and 1510. In the sixteenth century, considerable inflation occurred, and the price level quintupled. England's inflation index rose from a level of 0.2 in 1510 to 1.4 in 1597, settling around 1.0 during the stable Elizabethan years in the first part of the seventeenth century. Between 1510 and 1610, inflation averaged a compound 1.6 percent per year. This inflation is usually attributed to an increase in the European money supply brought about by Spanish gold and silver importation from the New World.

From about 1610 to 1750, the English (later U.K.) price level remained within the relatively narrow range of 0.8 to 2.0. After 1750,

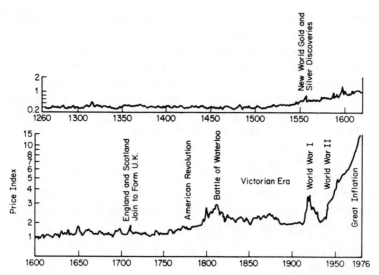

Figure 11.1. Seven hundred years of consumer prices: Inflation in the United Kingdom, 1260–1976. (1600 = 1.) (*Source: M. Jefferson, T. Mann, A. D. White, and W. W. Rostow, Inflation, Riverrun Press, Dallas, 1978, p. 75.*)

however, prices began to rise steadily, with the peak at the Battle of Waterloo. Wartime financing and the demand for money associated with the booming economy of the Industrial Revolution were to double the price level from 1.2 in 1750 to about 2.4 in the 1820–1870 period. Although this doubling of prices represents only a 1 percent compound rate of inflation, inflation rates in individual years were occasionally extreme in the modern sense, reaching 42 percent in 1799.

The Victorian Era was one of price stability. World War I brought on a rapid inflation of the kind associated with the financing of war expenditures. Afterward, prices fell sharply through the 1920s and the Great Depression of the 1930s. World War II caused another inflation of the classic type. After the end of the war in 1945, however, England entered the Great Inflation along with the rest of the world.

The United States

Year-by-year inflation rates for the United States beginning with the year 1720 are illustrated in Figure 11.2 and shown in Table 11.3. Prices were quite stable until the Revolutionary War began in 1775, causing rapid inflation. Introduction of a stable currency in 1782 brought prices back to their prewar level, producing a spurious 97 percent deflation rate for the year. Since the new currency was not convertible on a one-

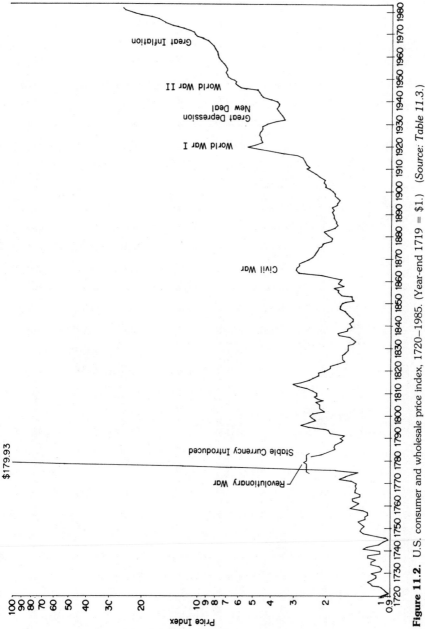

Figure 11.2. U.S. consumer and wholesale price index, 1720–1985. (Year-end 1719 = $1.) (*Source: Table 11.3.*)

Table 11.3. Inflation and Deflation in the United States, 1719–1985 (Yearly Percent Change and Index of Consumer and Producer Prices)

18th Century			19th Century			20th Century		
Year	Percent Change	Price Index	Year	Percent Change	Price Index	Year	Percent Change	Price Index
			1800	2.38	2.4061	1900	2.42	1.7712
			1801	-1.96	2.3589	1901	4.28	1.8471
			1802	-14.00	2.0287	1902	5.95	1.9569
			1803	4.65	2.1230	1903	0.00	1.9569
			1804	0.00	2.1230	1904	1.74	1.9910
			1805	0.00	2.1230	1905	-0.13	1.9883
			1806	4.44	2.2174	1906	2.89	2.0459
			1807	-6.38	2.0758	1907	4.86	2.1453
			1808	9.09	2.2646	1908	2.93	2.2081
			1809	-2.08	2.2174	1909	4.98	2.3180
			1810	0.00	2.2174	1910	5.08	2.4357
			1811	6.38	2.3589	1911	-1.72	2.3939
			1812	2.00	2.4061	1912	3.57	2.4793
			1813	13.73	2.7363	1913	2.41	2.5392
			1814	8.62	2.9722	1914	1.35	2.5734
			1815	-12.70	2.5948	1915	1.00	2.5990
			1816	-7.27	2.4061	1916	7.57	2.7957
			1817	-5.88	2.2646	1917	17.43	3.2830
			1818	-4.17	2.1702	1918	17.45	3.8558
1719		1.0000	1819	0.00	2.1702	1919	14.86	4.4286
1720	0.00	1.0000	1820	-8.70	1.9815	1920	15.83	5.1297
1721	-8.87	0.9113	1821	-4.76	1.8871	1921	-10.67	4.5825
1722	3.93	0.9471	1822	0.00	1.8871	1922	-6.34	4.2918
1723	3.24	0.9778	1823	-10.00	1.6984	1923	1.79	4.3688
1724	5.41	1.0307	1824	-8.33	1.5569	1924	0.20	4.3773
1725	8.77	1.1212	1825	3.03	1.6041	1925	2.54	4.4885
1726	4.57	1.1724	1826	0.00	1.6041	1926	-1.49	4.4216
1727	-3.49	1.1314	1827	0.00	1.6041	1927	-2.08	4.3297
1728	-4.83	1.0768	1828	-2.94	1.5569	1928	-0.97	4.2879
1729	-0.32	1.0734	1829	-3.03	1.5097	1929	0.19	4.2962
1730	5.88	1.1365	1830	0.00	1.5097	1930	-6.03	4.0371
1731	-11.11	1.0102	1831	0.00	1.5097	1931	-9.52	3.6526
1732	-2.03	0.9898	1832	-6.25	1.4153	1932	-10.30	3.2765
1733	2.93	1.0188	1833	-3.33	1.3682	1933	0.51	3.2932
1734	12.23	1.1433	1834	3.45	1.4153	1934	2.03	3.3601
1735	-1.04	1.1314	1835	3.33	1.4625	1935	2.99	3.4604
1736	-5.58	1.0683	1836	6.45	1.5569	1936	1.21	3.5022
1737	10.70	1.1826	1837	3.03	1.6041	1937	3.10	3.6103
1738	0.14	1.1843	1838	-5.88	1.5097	1938	-2.78	3.5105
1739	-14.12	1.0171	1839	0.00	1.5097	1939	-0.48	3.4938
1740	0.00	1.0171	1840	-6.25	1.4153	1940	0.96	3.5272
1741	23.49	1.2560	1841	3.33	1.4625	1941	9.72	3.8699
1742	-5.30	1.1894	1842	-4.29	1.3997	1942	9.29	4.2294
1743	-14.35	1.0188	1843	0.19	1.4023	1943	3.16	4.3631
1744	-4.36	0.9744	1844	2.43	1.4363	1944	2.11	4.4550
1745	-5.95	0.9164	1845	2.55	1.4729	1945	2.25	4.5553
1746	2.42	0.9386	1846	4.80	1.5436	1946	18.17	5.3828
1747	19.27	1.1195	1847	7.46	1.6587	1947	9.01	5.8676
1748	13.26	1.2679	1848	-0.47	1.6508	1948	2.71	6.0264
1749	2.42	1.2986	1849	-3.17	1.5985	1949	-1.80	5.9177
1750	-2.89	1.2611	1850	-4.42	1.5279	1950	5.79	6.2604
1751	-2.57	1.2286	1851	-9.25	1.3866	1951	5.87	6.6282
1752	5.00	1.2901	1852	1.32	1.4049	1952	0.88	6.6867
1753	3.44	1.3344	1853	0.37	1.4101	1953	0.63	6.7285
1754	-8.70	1.2184	1854	12.99	1.5933	1954	-0.50	6.6951
1755	-0.28	1.2150	1855	5.25	1.6770	1955	0.37	6.7202
1756	-2.39	1.1860	1856	-0.31	1.6718	1956	2.86	6.9124
1757	0.14	1.1877	1857	5.32	1.7607	1957	3.02	7.1214
1758	6.18	1.2611	1858	-9.06	1.6011	1958	1.76	7.2467
1759	16.10	1.4641	1859	4.08	1.6665	1959	1.50	7.3554
1760	-5.01	1.3908	1860	-1.10	1.6482	1960	1.48	7.4641
1761	-4.91	1.3225	1861	-2.86	1.6011	1961	0.67	7.5142
1762	7.61	1.4232	1862	7.84	1.7267	1962	1.22	7.6062
1763	0.12	1.4249	1863	21.21	2.0930	1963	1.65	7.7315
1764	-7.54	1.3174	1864	30.75	2.7366	1964	1.19	7.8235
1765	-0.65	1.3088	1865	3.35	2.8281	1965	1.92	7.9739
1766	6.52	1.3942	1866	-0.65	2.8098	1966	3.35	8.2414
1767	0.00	1.3942	1867	-3.63	2.7078	1967	3.04	8.4921
1768	-1.22	1.3771	1868	0.68	2.7261	1968	4.72	8.8933
1769	0.62	1.3856	1869	-6.14	2.5587	1969	6.11	9.4366
1770	-1.48	1.3652	1870	-5.42	2.4200	1970	5.49	9.9549
1771	6.13	1.4488	1871	-6.05	2.2735	1971	3.36	10.2892
1772	15.69	1.6757	1872	-0.69	2.2578	1972	3.41	10.6403
1773	-7.43	1.5512	1873	-1.85	2.2159	1973	8.80	11.5764
1774	-7.26	1.4385	1874	-1.89	2.1741	1974	12.20	12.9890
1775	-1.89	1.3310	1875	-2.29	2.1244	1975	7.01	13.9000
1776	38.46	1.8430	1876	-3.94	2.0407	1976	4.81	14.5687
1777	205.19	5.6244	1877	-1.03	2.0197	1977	6.77	15.5550
1778	81.47	10.2064	1878	-9.84	1.8209	1978	9.03	16.9592
1779	396.41	50.6660	1879	-1.15	1.8000	1979	13.31	19.2160
1780	255.13	179.9291	1880	3.63	1.8654	1980	12.40	21.5981
1781	-51.77	86.7863	1881	3.51	1.9308	1981	8.94	23.5289
1782	-97.26	2.3822	1882	3.12	1.9910	1982	3.67	24.4399
1783	-14.68	2.0324	1883	-5.78	1.8758	1983	3.80	25.3686
1784	-5.37	1.9232	1884	-7.39	1.7372	1984	3.95	26.3707
1785	-6.83	1.7918	1885	-2.71	1.6901	1985	3.77	27.3649
1786	0.10	1.7935	1886	1.08	1.7084			
1787	-1.14	1.7730	1887	0.15	1.7110			
1788	-6.26	1.6621	1888	3.21	1.7660			
1789	-3.49	1.6041	1889	0.44	1.7738			
1790	4.65	1.6787	1890	0.00	1.7738			
1791	-5.56	1.5854	1891	1.47	1.8000			
1792	10.59	1.7533	1892	-1.89	1.7660			
1793	8.51	1.9026	1893	2.37	1.8078			
1794	5.88	2.0144	1894	-5.50	1.7084			
1795	21.30	2.4434	1895	-1.68	1.6796			
1796	11.45	2.7232	1896	-2.02	1.6456			
1797	-10.27	2.4434	1897	1.59	1.6718			
1798	-6.87	2.2755	1898	3.13	1.7241			
1799	3.28	2.3501	1899	0.30	1.7293			

Source: *Historical Statistics of the United States,* U.S. Bureau of the Census, Dept. of Commerce, Washington, D.C.; various tables. The Consumer Price Index is used starting 1913.

for-one basis with the old, those who held cash would not have realized a tremendous real gain. Therefore, the index line in Figure 11.2 is broken rather than shown as true deflation.

The nineteenth century, along with the early Federal period immediately preceding it, was a period of great price stability. Prices fluctuated in a two-to-one range from 1782 to 1915, exceeding even the British record of price stability. The severest inflation of this period occurred during the Civil War, when the inflation rate reached 31 percent, but prices fell quickly and steadily after the Civil War to a level equal to that of 1860.

The inflation index broke out of its two-to-one range in World War I, with sharp price increases in each year from 1916 to 1920. The economic boom of the roaring twenties then followed, with prices slowly *declining* over the period. (As the quantity of goods grew but the money supply did not, prices fell.) The Great Depression of the 1930s was associated with an extremely sharp contraction in the money supply and hence a deflation. Prices then began to rise, in response first to New Deal measures of the early 1930s and later to World War II in the 1940s. The 1950s and the first half of the 1960s exhibited price stability almost as impressive as that of Victorian Britain and America. But starting around 1966, as previously indicated, the United States too experienced the Great Inflation.

The histogram in Figure 11.3 reveals the distribution of annual U.S. inflation rates. Moderate inflation, from zero to 4 percent, is much more common than any other category.

Hyperinflation

The record of inflation is incomplete without a consideration of hyperinflation. *Hyperinflation* is an unchecked and radical increase in the price level. While the United States and most industrial countries have not approached hyperinflation in the recent past, it is a constant reality for many third world countries and is a conceivable outcome in any unbacked-money economy. Thus it merits attention here.

Two types of hyperinflation can be distinguished. The traditional kind is characterized by a gradual building from mere inflation to fabulously high rates of price increase. German inflation in 1923 typifies *traditional hyperinflation;* in that country, a cup of coffee reportedly doubled in price while being sipped. Such a hyperinflation ends when no one is willing to accept the currency as payment. The government is then forced into a true currency reform, which gives money a sound footing. In recent decades, a second type of hyperinflation has occurred in Israel

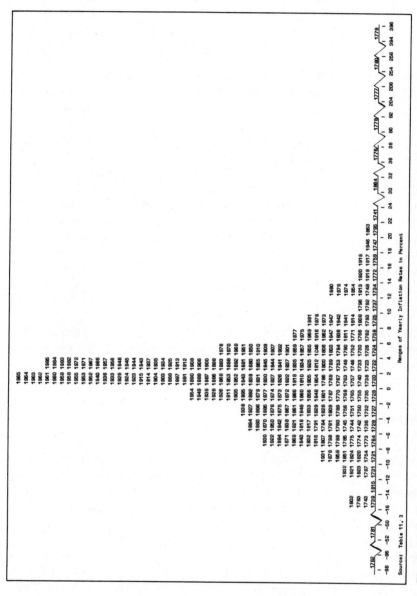

Figure 11.3. Two hundred and sixty-six years of U.S. inflation and deflation. (*Source: Table 11.3.*)

and many Latin American states. It is termed *managed hyperinflation* because double- or triple-digit inflation, or even higher rates, persists year after year.

Traditional Hyperinflation

The first traditional hyperinflation to be carefully documented was the one after the French Revolution of 1789. Because the new popular regime was expected to provide prosperity through easy credit, the Revolutionary government issued *assignats,* or paper money supposedly backed by land, in ever-increasing quantities. But the land backing proved to be worthless, and free-market prices rose to astronomical levels. Meanwhile, the government, which became known for its "Reign of Terror," prescribed death as the penalty for trading at prices other than low official prices. Ultimately the French government repudiated the national debt, and a stable monetary policy was imposed under the dictatorship of Napoleon. This French hyperinflation set the pattern for future hyperinflations.

A hundred and thirty years after the paper money inflation in France, neighboring Germany experienced a similar inflation. The two causes here were probably exorbitant war reparations and massive government debts incurred to finance World War I. German hyperinflation has been cited as a principal reason for the rise of Hitler and the totalitarian state, a connection popularized by the novelist Thomas Mann in *The Witches' Sabbath.*

In Table 11.4, month-by-month German price levels in 1921–1923 are documented, along with month-by-month (and later week-by-week) price levels in post-World War II Hungary. The 50-billion-fold rise in the German price index in the 28 months from July 1921 to November 1923 speaks for itself. This price spiral ended only when the German government repudiated its debts, stopped its reparation payments, and issued a new mark tied to gold.

In Hungary after World War II, inflation reached even more preposterous proportions, with a 4 octillion to one rise in prices in a single year of furious money printing. (An octillion is 1 followed by 27 zeros.) Such numbers defy analysis.

Managed Hyperinflation

Managed hyperinflation has been a way of life in Israel since its founding and has become prevalent in many third world countries, especially in Latin America. In countries with managed hyperinflation, such as

Table 11.4. Hyperinflation in Germany and Hungary

	Germany		Hungary	
	July 1921–Nov. 1923		July 1945–July 1946	
Elapsed Month	Calendar Month	Price Index	Calendar Month	Price Index
0	7–1921	1.00	7–1945	1.00
1	8	1.34	8	1.63
2	9	1.45	9	3.61
3	10	1.72	10	23.15
4	11	2.39	11	123.61
5	12–1921	2.44	12	395.03
6	1–1922	2.57	1–1946	688.86
7	2	2.87	2	4,151.30
8	3	3.80	3	17,837.27
9	4	4.44	4	340,860.58
10	5	4.52	5	107.3 millions
11	6	4.92	6–1946[1]	8,212.0 millions
			6–1946[2]	9,085.7 millions
12	7	7.03	7–1946[3]	29,202,419,050 millions
			7–1946[4]	108.82 quintillions
			7–1946[5]	343,037.70 quintillions
			7–1946[6]	3,805,933,333 quintillions
13	8	13.43		
14	9	20.07		
15	10	39.58		
16	11	80.70		
17	12–1922	103.51		
18	1–1923	194.76		
19	2	390.56		
20	3	341.47		
21	4	364.48		
22	5	571.33		
23	6	1,335.59		
24	7	5,229.86		
25	8	66,016.85		
26	9	1.7 millions		
27	10	496.2 millions		
28	11–1923	50,769.2 millions		

[1] First two week period. [3] First week of the month. [5] Third week of the month.
[2] Second two week period. [4] Second week of the month. [6] Fourth week of the month.

Sources: For Germany, David F. De Rosa, "Rates of Return on Common Stock and Inflation: Theories and Tests," University of Chicago Ph. D. Dissertation, 1978. For Hungary, Michael Jefferson et al., *Inflation,* Dallas: Riverrun Press, 1978.

those in Table 11.5, very high rates of inflation have persisted without any meaningful currency reform. Token reforms, such as moving the decimal place and/or changing the name of the currency, do not affect the inflation rate. Nevertheless, this is done all the time, presumably so that people do not have to figure their transactions in billions. In a couple of generations, Brazil has gone from the reis to the milreis (1000 reis) to the cruziero (1000 milreis), and now the cruzado.

Table 11.5. Accelerating Inflation in Three High-Inflation Economies

Period	Brazil Rate of Change[1]	Index[2]	Israel Rate of Change[1]	Index[2]	Mexico Rate of Change[1]	Index[2]
1960–1969	44.20%	38.88	5.22%	1.66	2.53%	1.29
1970–1979	29.95	533.79	31.01	24.78	14.45	4.97
1980–1982	95.23	3972.25	122.62	273.36	36.96	12.76

Notes   1. Annual compound rate of change in percent, for the decade or subperiod indicated.
2. Cumulative return index initialized at 1.00 on 12/31/1959.
Source: *International Financial Statistics* (various issues), published by the International Monetary Fund, Washington, D.C.

In economies with managed hyperinflation, consumers, investors, and institutions adjust to changing price levels. Ownership of short-term money market instruments is the investor's first line of defense against managed hyperinflations. Index-linked bonds, which have a payoff tied to the consumer price index, have been popular in Argentina, Israel, Brazil, and other countries. Stocks and real estate are often held as inflation hedges, with varying success. Finally, tangible or consumable assets are bought in lieu of money-denominated assets. In Brazil, for example, a vintage Volkswagen is often stored for years in a garage to preserve the owner's capital. Whatever the course of the cruzado or the Brazilian economy, the car owner will receive a return in the form of transportation when this capital asset is used.

The spread of managed hyperinflation in the 1970s and 1980s is astonishing. There are probably as many hyperinflations taking place today as in the remainder of recorded history. Nevertheless, the drop in energy prices in the mid-1980s has moderated inflation in most countries.

Conclusion

In summary, then, sustained inflation is a relatively recent phenomenon. In the past, inflation typically occurred only in countries fighting wars or undertaking rapid economic expansion. Inflation may have been minimal in the past because many currencies were tied to monetary metal. The present era is unusual because inflation persists throughout the world. Inflation will probably remain a factor in contemporary society, primarily because governments spend more than they receive in taxes, creating inflationary deficits.

When inflation rates are stable, inflation risk—the risk of a person's wealth changing due to a change in the inflation rate—is minimized. Except where wages are unconditionally indexed for inflation, persons whose main wealth is their earning power bear most of society's inflation risk and should be most interested in stabilizing inflation. They should also prefer lower inflation, since low inflation rates are almost always more stable than high rates.

Investors with financial as well as human capital should consider price level changes when making decisions about assets in their portfolios. Metals such as gold and silver are good hedges against inflation, but unpredictable ones. Investors holding gold and silver actually make money when inflation accelerates. Real estate, and to a lesser extent cash equivalents, largely track inflation, and both are less volatile than monetary metals. Equities and bonds of all types usually lose ground in inflationary periods. Thus, investors who believe inflation will continue or increase should hold large parts of their portfolios in metals, real estate, and cash. All investors should own *some* assets that are inflation hedges to protect their wealth against inflation risk.

Inflation has moderated in the mid-1980s. Future inflation rates depend on many unpredictable factors, such as wars, monetary policies, and economic catastrophes like the oil crisis. The Great Inflation may be coming to an end, or a new economic shock could send international inflation rates soaring again.

Suggested Reading

De Rosa, David: *Rates of Return on Common Stocks and Inflation: Theories and Tests,* doctoral dissertation, University of Chicago, 1978. Analyzes stock returns relative to U.S. inflation and studies German hyperinflation.

International Monetary Fund: "Consumer Prices 1959 to Present," *International Financial Statistics,* Washington, D.C., various issues. Reference work updated frequently; series include international inflation, interest rates, trade statistics, etc.

Jefferson, M., T. Mann, A. D. White, and W. W. Rostow: *Inflation,* Riverrun Press, Dallas, Tex., 1978. Excellent set of essays on inflation, with data, from a disparate group of authors.

U.S. Bureau of the Census: *Historical Statistics of the U.S.,* Government Printing Office, Washington, D.C., annual. Extensive compilation of historical data from Colonial times to the present on U.S. population, economy, etc, including inflation rates.

12
Gold and Silver

With an ounce of gold, a man could buy a fine suit in the time of Shakespeare, in that of Beethoven and Jefferson, in the Depression of the 1930s, and today. Gold is a remarkably constant store of value across time.

Because its purchasing power is steady, gold investments historically have had a real return near zero. Silver prices have paralleled gold prices and also have had an inflation-adjusted return near zero. Although these metals do not have positive real returns in the long run, you may find gold useful as an "insurance asset," to diversify against catastrophic events and to hedge against inflation. You may also want to own gold because it is a significant part of the world's wealth.

The Supply of and Demand for Gold

For centuries, Britain and other countries used copper metal for small change, silver for intermediate coins, and gold for valuable currency. With an ounce of copper, beggars could buy a morsel of food; with an ounce of silver, commoners could purchase household necessities; and with an ounce of gold, families could rent cottages with thatched roofs. Because these metals are portable, durable, and divisible, they have been a store of value throughout the world.

Gold, in particular, is sought after and precious. The quantity of gold relative to other metals is low, while the demand for it—for adornment, industrial uses, dentistry, speculation, investment, and as a store of value—is high. Consequently, its total value is about one-twentieth of the world's wealth.

Major groups of gold owners are portrayed in Figure 12.1. Much gold is tied up in the reserves of central banks, but more than half is outside governmental control. When private holdings and mostly private deco-

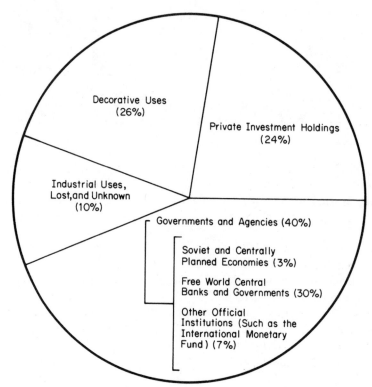

Figure 12.1. Who owns the gold? (*Source: Jeffrey A. Nichols, American Precious Metals Advisors, Inc., New York.*)

rative uses are taken together, they comprise over half of the world's gold, a fact which suggests that the gold market is relatively liquid.

Governments and agencies account for 40 percent of gold ownership. Of this, governments and central banks in the noncommunist world hold three-quarters (30 percent of the total). While collectively they are a major producer, Soviet and other centrally planned economies hold relatively little gold, about 3 percent of the world total.

About 10 percent of the world's gold is either in industrial use or lost. But little is lost to robbers or conquerors, who eventually trade their gold for goods. Most lost gold is buried and unrecovered, or lost at sea. Treasure hunters are slowly placing this wealth back in private hands.

Monetary Metals and Inflation

For centuries, gold and silver *were* money. A gold or silver *standard* exists when a country's currency and its banking and international trading structures are based to some degree on gold or silver. Governments either use the metals to make coins or define their currencies in terms of gold's and silver's values. When these metals are equivalent to money, the money prices of gold and silver by definition do not change.

If gold and silver are money, what does it mean to measure returns from investing in monetary metals? When a metal like gold is monetized, it *becomes* the unit of account by which investment returns are measured. For instance, when the United States was on a gold standard, a $20 gold piece was legally worth $20. Thus, a monetized metal, considered as an investment asset, always has a return of zero relative to the currency.

By way of contrast to gold-standard money, *fiat money* is money, such as the unbacked paper currency now used in the United States and most other countries, that is not convertible into metal of equal value. When a fiat currency prevails and when gold and silver trade freely, returns are computed like those on any other investment. If gold rises in price from $400 to $480 an ounce, it is meaningful to say that the investment provides a 20 percent return. Thus, when a monetary system has employed fiat currencies, gold returns can be computed using market prices.

Yet even under gold or silver standards, investors often could trade gold and silver freely, at prices different from the official price. In these periods, returns are measured using market rather than official prices. When market prices are lacking, official prices are employed to complete the data series.

Inflation-adjusted returns on gold and silver indicate the relationship of gold and silver values to consumer goods values. Monetary metals are often viewed as prototype commodities—that is, commodities which track or reflect the price changes of consumer market baskets. Inflation-adjusted returns on these metals, then, indicate the divergence between the price of gold and that of consumer goods. When gold tracks consumer goods exactly, the inflation-adjusted return on gold is by definition zero. When gold and consumer goods diverge, as they did in the 1970s when gold raced ahead of inflation, the inflation-adjusted return on gold may be highly positive. As will be demonstrated, inflation-adjusted returns on gold are extremely close to zero when measured over long periods. This result indicates that gold is in fact a store of value or a prototype commodity.

Next, the monetary history of the United States and United Kingdom is summarized to suggest how these governments' policies affected metal prices over time. Returns on monetary metals in the United Kingdom are documented to encompass returns before the founding of the United States. Not only are price data available for both countries, but also their monetary denominations are unchanged for long periods. Most importantly, both countries have been internationally significant financial and commercial centers in modern times, sharing common political and economic traditions. Prices here are expressed in nominal (dollar and pound) terms, while returns are also presented as inflation-adjusted.

Prices and Returns from Gold and Silver

Gold and Silver Prices in the United Kingdom

In the Anglo-American world, silver substantially predates gold as a monetary metal. In Britain, the silver standard lasted from Saxon times (circa A.D. 800) to the beginning of the eighteenth century. The British pound was originally a measure of weight, with a pound of "sterling" silver taking on the monetary value of a pound sterling. This relationship has not held up well, with a pound (12 troy ounces) of fine silver costing over 70 British monetary pounds in the mid-1980s.

Gold prices from 1343 to 1799 are presented in Table 12.1, while prices for the nineteenth and most of the twentieth century are shown in Table 12.2. Gold coins first circulated widely in England in the eighteenth century. By defining a gold guinea of a specific weight to be worth 21 shillings in 1717, Britain—acting under the powerful influence of the philosopher John Locke—adopted a gold standard as official policy. From 1717 to 1759, gold's price per ounce hovered around 3.88 pounds. Then, due to political uncertainty caused by the Napoleonic Wars, commoners began to withdraw gold guineas from banks and bury them. Consequently, the government ordered the Bank of England to stop redeeming bank deposits in gold, temporarily lifting the gold standard. By 1814, at the climax of the Napoleonic Wars, gold's price had escalated to 5.50 pounds.

After the wars' end, the United Kingdom returned to a gold standard. In 1820, Sir Robert Peel invoked the ghost of Locke and persuaded Parliament to fix the price of gold at "the ancient standard of 3.8938 pounds per ounce, a magic price for gold from which England ought never to stray and to which, if she did, she must always return as soon as possible."

And stray she did not. Exactly one century later, gold stood at the same price, 3.89 pounds. For the entire eighteenth century and from 1820 until 1919, gold's price was 3.89. The First World War's inflation brought the price of gold to a high of 5.18 pounds. The British did not tolerate this deviation from the Lockean tradition for long, and restored

Table 12.1. The Price of Gold in the United Kingdom, 1343–1799

Year	Price (£/troy ounce)	Year	Price (£/troy ounce)
Fourteenth Century			
1343	1.24	1611	3.21
1344	1.14	1612–1618	3.28
1345	1.15	1619–1662	3.31
1346	1.20	1663–1695	3.69
1351	1.30	1696–1698	4.06
1355	1.31	1699	3.96
1363	1.32		
		Eighteenth Century	
Fifteenth Century		1700–1716	3.96
1412	1.47	1717–1759	3.88
1464	1.64	1760	3.95
1465	1.92	1761	4.00
1467	1.95	1762	3.99
1471	1.98	1763	4.02
1492	2.00	1764	3.95
		1765	3.90
Sixteenth Century		1766	3.96
1526	2.25	1767	3.98
1544	2.40	1768	3.97
1545	2.50	1769	4.01
1546	2.60	1770	4.02
1547	2.90	1771	3.99
1549	3.00	1772	4.00
1560–1589	2.72	1773	3.89
1590–1599	2.71	1774–1781	3.88
		1782	3.89
Seventeenth Century		1783	3.85
1600	2.71	1784–1785	3.89
1601–1603	2.74	1786–1796	3.88
1604–1610	2.96	1798–1799	3.89

Source:

1343–1549. Sir Albert E. Feavearyear, *The Pound Sterling* (first edition), Humphrey Milford, Oxford University Press, London, 1931. Quoted in shillings and coverted by the authors to pounds using 20 shillings per pound.

1560–1799. Prices reconstructed by the authors from indexes in *The Golden Constant* by Roy W. Jastram. Copyright © John Wiley & Sons, Inc., 1977. Jastram constructed his indexes using free market prices, Bank of England buying prices, and Mint prices, in that order of preference.

the price of 3.8938 pounds with the Gold Standard Act of 1925. (The 1926 gold price is the first in Table 12.2 to reflect the Act.) The ancient price of gold was to last until 1931. England's actions in 1925 lend credence to John Maynard Keynes's famous statement that "practical men, who believe themselves to be quite exempt from any intellectual influences, are usually the slaves to some defunct economist." When Britain went off the gold standard in 1931, gold's price rose slowly at first and then at an unprecedented speed, from 12.43 pounds in 1950 to over 240 pounds in the 1980s.

Table 12.2. The Price of Gold in the United Kingdom (Pounds Sterling per Ounce) and United States (Dollars per Ounce), 1800–1985

Year	Price £/oz	Price $/oz	Year	Price £/oz	Price $/oz
1800	4.25	19.39			
1801	4.30	19.39	1878	3.89	20.84
1802	4.15	19.39	1879–1919	3.89	20.67
1803–1808	4.00	19.39	1920	4.13	20.67
1809	4.53	19.39	1921	5.18	20.67
1810	4.60	19.39	1922	4.90	20.67
1811	5.00	19.39	1923	4.28	20.67
1812	5.40	19.39	1924	4.14	20.67
1813	5.40	19.39	1925	4.29	20.67
1814	5.50	19.39	1926–1930	3.89	20.67
1815	5.25	19.39	1931	4.24	20.67
1816	4.00	19.39	1932	5.41	20.67
1817	3.92	19.39	1933	5.72	20.67
1818	4.07	19.39	1934	6.31	35.00
1819	4.05	19.39	1935	6.51	35.00
1820	3.89	19.39	1936	6.43	35.00
1821	3.89	19.39	1937	6.45	35.00
1822–1824	3.87	19.39	1938	6.53	35.00
1825	3.89	19.39	1939	7.10	35.00
1826–1828	3.87	19.39	1940–1949	8.60	35.00
1829–1833	3.89	19.39	1950–1959	12.43	35.00
1834	3.89	20.05	1960	12.45	35.00
1835–1861	3.89	20.67	1961–1967	12.43	35.00
1862	3.89	23.42	1968	16.31	39.27
1863	3.89	30.01	1969	16.37	35.45
1864	3.89	42.02	1970	14.75	37.65
1865	3.89	32.51	1971	15.78	43.85
1866	3.89	29.12	1972	24.26	65.20
1867	3.89	28.57	1973	40.46	114.55
1868	3.89	28.88	1974	64.65	186.75
1869	3.89	27.49	1975	72.58	140.35
1870	3.89	23.75	1976	66.11	134.75
1871	3.89	23.09	1977	86.60	164.96
1872	3.89	23.23	1978	111.19	226.00
1873	3.89	23.52	1979	230.40	512.00
1874	3.89	22.99	1980	245.54	586.00
1875	3.89	23.75	1981	209.16	401.00
1876	3.89	23.05	1982	282.04	456.90
1877	3.89	21.66	1983	262.66	381.50
			1984	266.56	309.00
			1985	226.27	327.00

Source: *The Golden Constant* by Roy W. Jastram. Copyright © John Wiley & Sons, Inc., 1977. Updated by the authors using year-end prices from *The Wall Street Journal.*

Gold and Silver Prices in the United States

American gold prices for the nineteenth and twentieth centuries are also shown on Table 12.2. In the Colonies, first the Spanish silver dollar and later paper was the dominant currency. Then, in the Coinage Act of 1791, the United States adopted a bimetallic standard, with the prices of gold and silver officially linked in a 15 : 1 ratio.

When the Civil War began in 1861, the United States returned to paper money, the Union's greenback. With the war's inflation, gold prices doubled to $42.02, but by 1878, gold had fallen back to its prewar level of $20. When in 1897 the United States again required banks to exchange paper currency for monetary metal, gold was the only coin that could be freely minted. Thus, the United States operated on a *de facto* gold standard until the Gold Standard Act of 1900 gave gold official recognition.

During the Depression, the United States made owning gold illegal, prohibited gold exports, and stopped exchanging dollars for gold. Between 1934 and 1971, the dollar was loosely defined in gold, at a value determined by the U.S. Treasury.

Since the gold standard was abolished in 1971, the price of gold has fluctuated wildly, rising to unprecedented levels in this period of high inflation. From a price of $35 at the beginning of 1968, gold escalated to more than $800 per ounce for a few days in 1980, and bookmakers took bets on when the first gold quote of $1000 an ounce would occur. Like gold, silver rocketed upward with other tangible assets. Silver's highest year-end price, shown in Table 12.3, was $28 per ounce in 1979. For a few days in January 1980, however, silver sold above $50 per ounce. Both gold's and silver's prices had dropped substantially by the mid-1980s.

Inflation-Adjusted Returns from Monetary Metals

The historical purchasing power of gold must be examined to determine the real returns from gold and silver investments. An index is constructed with the real (inflation-adjusted) price of gold in 1930 set equal to 100. Real returns for the United Kingdom and United States are graphed in Figure 12.2. The most remarkable feature of these graphs is the constancy of gold's value. Over long periods, the real price indexes for both countries are extremely stable. Historically, silver and gold prices move together, with peaks and troughs at approximately the same time. This is evident from the graph of gold and silver's returns, shown in Figure 12.3.

Table 12.3. The Price of Silver in the United States, 1700–1985

PRICES IN BRITISH POUNDS 1700-1749

Year	£/oz	Year	£/oz	Year	£/oz
1700–1704	0.35	1722	0.71	1735	1.38
1705–1710	0.40	1723	0.75	1736	1.34
1711	0.42	1724	0.81	1737	1.34
1712	0.42	1725	0.78	1738	1.35
1713	0.42	1726	0.80	1739	1.42
1714	0.45	1727	0.80	1741	1.40
1715	0.45	1728	0.86	1744	1.50
1716	0.50	1729	1.02	1745	1.80
1717	0.50	1730	1.00	1746	1.92
1718	0.55	1731	0.94	1747	2.75
1719	0.60	1732	1.00	1749	3.00
1720	0.62	1733	1.10		
1721	0.65	1734	1.28		

PRICES IN U.S. DOLLARS 1792-1985

Year	$/oz	Year	$/oz	Year	$/oz	Year	$/oz
1792–1833	1.29	1890	1.05	1925	0.69	1960	0.91
1834–1836	1.21	1891	0.99	1926	0.62	1961	1.03
1837–1859	1.29	1892	0.88	1927	0.56	1962	1.20
1860	1.35	1893	0.78	1928	0.58	1963	1.29
1861	1.33	1894	0.63	1929	0.53	1964	1.29
1862	1.35	1895	0.65	1930	0.38	1965	1.29
1863	1.34	1896	0.67	1931	0.29	1966	1.29
1864	1.34	1897	0.60	1932	0.28	1967	2.06
1865	1.34	1898	0.58	1933	0.35	1968	1.96
1866	1.34	1899	0.60	1934	0.50	1969	1.80
1867	1.33	1900	0.61	1935	0.64	1970	1.63
1868	1.33	1901	0.59	1936	0.45	1971	1.38
1869	1.32	1902	0.52	1937	0.45	1972	2.04
1870	1.33	1903	0.54	1938	0.43	1973	3.28
1871	1.32	1904	0.57	1939	0.39	1974	4.37
1872	1.32	1905	0.60	1940	0.35	1975	4.16
1873	1.30	1906	0.67	1941	0.35	1976	4.37
1874	1.28	1907	0.65	1942	0.38	1977	4.48
1875	1.24	1908	0.53	1943	0.45	1978	6.07
1876	1.16	1909	0.52	1944	0.45	1979	28.00
1877	1.20	1910	0.53	1945	0.52	1980	15.65
1878	1.15	1911	0.53	1946	0.80	1981	8.25
1879	1.12	1912	0.61	1947	0.72	1982	10.90
1880	1.15	1913	0.60	1948	0.74	1983	8.95
1881	1.13	1914	0.55	1949	0.72	1984	6.36
1882	1.14	1915	0.50	1950	0.74	1985	5.83
1883	1.11	1916	0.66	1951	0.89		
1884	1.11	1917	0.81	1952	0.85		
1885	1.06	1918	0.97	1953	0.85		
1886	1.00	1919	1.11	1954	0.85		
1887	0.98	1920	1.01	1955	0.89		
1888	0.94	1921	0.63	1956	0.91		
1889	0.94	1922	0.68	1957	0.91		
		1923	0.65	1958	0.89		
		1924	0.67	1959	0.91		

Note: Prices are year-end except where unavailable.

Sources:

1700-1791: Price of silver trades in Boston, from Series Z586, *Historical Statistics of the United States,* U.S. Department of Commerce, Bureau of the Census, Washington, D.C., 1975.

1792-1859: The authors converted gold to silver prices using ratios established by Congress on April 2, 1792 of 15:1, on June 28, 1834 of 16.002:1, and on January 18, 1837 of 15.988:1.

1860-1975: Beryl W. Sprinkel and Robert J. Genetski, *Winning with Money,* Homewood, Ill.: Dow Jones-Irwin, 1977, pp. 244-246.

1976-1985: Handy and Harman closing prices for the year, as reported in *The Wall Street Journal.*

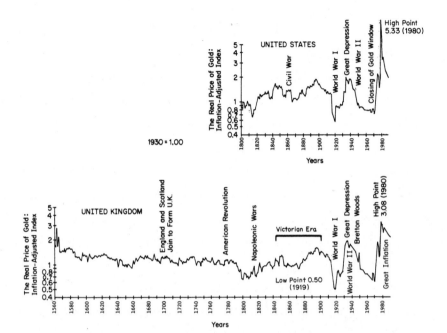

Figure 12.2. The inflation-adjusted index of gold prices in the United States and United Kingdom. (Prices are plotted in inflation-adjusted terms as an index. This index reflects the inflation-adjusted [real] price of gold, with the 1930 base year equal to 1.00. It shows the changing consumption value in an ounce of gold over time in the United States and United Kingdom.) (*Source: Roy W. Jastram, The Golden Constant. Copyright © John Wiley & Sons, Inc., 1977;* updates by the authors.)

Gold, like other cash instruments, has an expected real return near zero. In Britain, the compound real return from gold over 4 centuries was 0.1 percent per year, and in the United States it was 0.7 percent per year over 2 centuries. In other words, gold prices and commodity indexes track one another over the long run. Gold can thus be viewed as a prototype commodity, one whose price represents commodity prices in general.

In America as in Britain, gold and silver have behaved as prototype commodities up to 1970. More recently, though, prices have been extremely unstable. An investor who bought an ounce of gold at the end of the 1960s realized a thirteenfold increase in nominal dollars by the early 1980s, for a compound return of 21.7 percent per year over the period. Adjusted for inflation, the compound return was 14 percent per year. Silver had a similar price history. Thus, both American and British experience suggests that gold and silver prices track inflation over the long term, but not the short term.

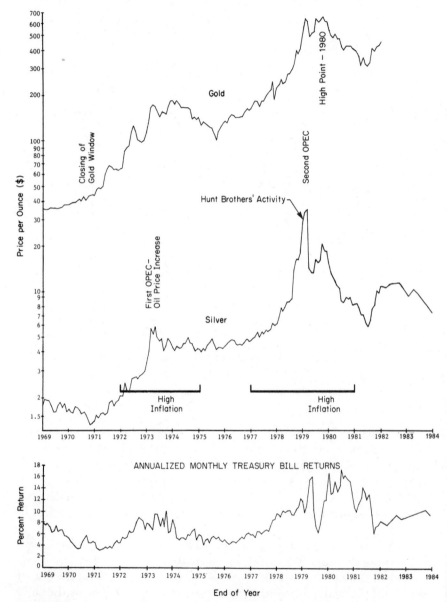

Figure 12.3. U.S. gold, silver, and interest rates move in tandem. (*Sources: Gold and Silver monthly prices: DRI-FACS. T-bills: Stocks, Bonds, Bills, and Inflation 1985 Yearbook.*)

Why Include Gold and Silver in Your Portfolio?

Institutional and individual investors have many investment alternatives, one of which is monetary metals. Either type of investor may want to hold gold or silver in their portfolio.

Because gold and silver have real returns near zero, do not hold these metals over the long term to reap high returns. While both had tremendous returns in the 1970s, expect that, over the longer term, their real return will be near zero. As a practical matter, even the relatively small costs of trading and holding monetary metals may bring their returns below zero.

Some institutional investors regard gold as simply another form of cash. However, gold is far riskier than short-term bills over the short term. When choosing between gold and interest-bearing paper as a *short-term* defensive instrument, paper is the proper choice.

Why, then, might you want to invest in gold and silver? There are three primary reasons:

- To insure against catastrophes
- To diversify your holdings
- To hold assets that are part of the world's wealth

Gold and Silver as Insurance Assets

More than other assets, gold and silver provide insurance against catastrophic changes such as economic collapse or hyperinflation, since these metals are a sort of international money, constituting a portable store of value in hard times.

Because both gold and silver usually gain in value during inflationary periods, they are held as a hedge against inflation. Over the long run, the purchasing power of gold has been remarkably constant, but recently its price has been unstable. Thus, gold and silver are hedges against inflation, but not perfectly dependable ones.

To insure against hyperinflation and economic collapse, gold is a suitable medium. Pension funds, for example, might hold a small amount of gold to insure that, if other economic institutions fail, beneficiaries would have some residual wealth. Individuals also might want to hold a *small* portion of their wealth in gold or silver in case of war, hyperinflation, or radical changes in the economic system.

Gold and Silver
as Diversification Tools

Another argument for the inclusion of gold in your portfolio comes from the diversification of risk it can provide. Low correlations with other assets make a given asset a powerful diversification tool. From 1960 through the mid-1980s, gold had a correlation of −0.09 with U.S. equities and −0.32 with U.S. corporate bonds, the most commonly held individual and pension assets. No other asset had such low correlations with the major investment assets. This suggests that when traditional assets perform poorly, gold fares well. Silver has a similar track record, but has higher, and thus less favorable, correlations with all assets except real estate.

Additional correlation coefficients round out the diversification argument. Between 1960 and the mid-1980s, gold had a correlation of:

+0.04 with foreign equities

−0.21 with U.S. government bonds

+0.00 with foreign corporate bonds

+0.68 with U.S. real estate

+0.08 with the world market portfolio, excluding metals

Statistically, then, gold reduces portfolio risk.

If you want to reduce the risk of your portfolio, holding gold or silver will increase diversification and thus reduce risk. Gold appears to be a better diversifier than silver. Even in small amounts, monetary metals provide substantial diversification and should be included in most portfolios.

Gold and Silver as a Share
of World Assets

Gold and silver are a significant part of the world's wealth. In 1960, gold alone accounted for 3.7 percent of investable assets. By 1980, when metal prices reached historical highs, gold and silver made up an astonishing 14 percent of the world's investable assets, exceeding even U.S. equities. Later in this decade, gold and silver's proportion has dropped to about 7 percent of investable assets or 3 percent of all assets. This lower percentage may better reflect the relative value of monetary metals over long periods.

The aggregate value of silver is only about one-seventieth the aggregate value of gold. Consequently, the market for silver is very thin compared to the market for gold. During the January 1980 silver "bubble," the price of silver was almost four times higher than its price a year earlier. In contrast, when large and small investors caught gold fever in 1979–1980 and bid up gold's price, the peak price was only twice as high as the price that prevailed a year later. Rich individual investors or institutional investors manage billions of dollars and could easily have a powerful impact on prices in relatively thin markets like that for silver. Thus, if you want to hold an asset that is a significant part of the world's wealth, you might wish to buy gold.

Suggested Reading

Jastram, Roy W.: *The Golden Constant: The English and American Experience 1560–1976,* John Wiley & Sons, Inc., New York, 1977. A readable history of the gold market, revealing monetary policies of two major financial powers.
Sherman, Eugene: *Gold Investment Papers,* International Gold Corporation, Ltd., New York, 1984. Updated occasionally. A series of pamphlets that describe the investment market for gold.

13

Real Estate

The nineteenth-century Chicago retailer Marshall Field once said, "Buying real estate is not only the best way, the quickest way, and the safest way, but the only way to become wealthy." A great rise in real estate values since World War II confirms that real estate investment is one major way to strike it rich. From 1947 to the 1980s, an index of total returns on unleveraged real estate increased over twentyfold, representing a compound annual rate of 8.3 percent.

Most twentieth-century investors held mortgaged, or *leveraged*, real estate, and earned even higher returns. Some became multimillionaires. According to *Forbes*, 83 of the 400 richest individuals in the United States during 1985—including shopping center developer A. Alfred Taubman, highrise developer Donald Trump, and real estate syndicator and Empire State Building owner Harry Helmsley—acquired their fortunes primarily through real estate.

Real Estate Markets

The real estate market is larger than the stock and bond markets combined. According to Figure 13.1, real estate makes up about 55 percent of the major U.S. investment assets in the mid-1980s, while stocks and bonds comprise less than 45 percent.

Both individuals and institutions participate in this market, many holding real property for their own use. Individuals primarily buy houses, condominiums, and cooperatives to inhabit. Owner-occupied single family homes make up over 60 percent of the market value of U.S. real estate. Businesses own property to carry on their operations. Although they can rent space, firms often construct or buy office buildings, retail stores, hotels, and factories for their own use.

Individual and institutional investors also hold real property for its potential income and capital gains. Investment real estate includes:

Figure 13.1. Real estate market dominates other assets. (Value of capital market security groups as a percentage of the total, 1947–1984.)   (*Source: Roger G. Ibbotson and Laurence B. Siegel, "Real Estate Returns: A Comparison with Other Investments,"* AREUEA Journal, *vol. 12, no. 3, Fall 1984, p. 226.*)

- Office and apartment buildings
- Hotels
- Shopping centers
- Industrial property
- Raw land

Real estate partnerships and institutional investors such as insurance companies and pension funds dominate the market for investment properties other than small apartment buildings.

Many of the largest pension funds aim to hold about 10 to 15 percent of their assets in real estate. A 1985 survey by *Pensions and Investment Age* found that investments by tax-exempt institutions in real estate

equity, hybrid debt (debt with equity participation), and mortgages totaled $52.1 billion. If all U.S. pension fund assets are estimated to be
$1.3 trillion, then the real estate component is about 4 percent. Sum-
ming taxable and tax-exempt funds under institutional management,
real estate assets amount to $192 billion, consisting of $84.6 billion in
equity, $12.3 billion in hybrid debt, and $95 billion in mortgages. The
same study broke down institutional holdings by type of property. The
percentage breakdowns were:

- Office: 45 percent
- Industrial: 16 percent
- Retail: 16 percent
- Undeveloped land: 7 percent
- Residential: 5 percent
- Research and development projects: 4 percent
- Hotel: 3 percent
- Other: 4 percent

The nature of property ownership is changing in the mid-1980s. In
particular, ownership is becoming more "securitized" through investors'
use of partnerships, syndications, real estate investment trusts (REITs),
and various mortgage-backed securities. Real estate securities have the
advantage of being more liquid and homogeneous than the properties
themselves, although most are not traded in central markets, limiting the
availability of current price information.

Real Estate Returns

Real Estate Returns Compared to Other Assets

Compared with other assets in roughly the last 40 years, real estate has
had spectacular returns. Unleveraged returns on real estate were second
only to those of common stocks. When leveraged, real estate returns far
exceeded common stocks'. Cumulative wealth indexes of returns on six
capital assets including real estate are shown graphically in Figure 13.2.
Over the entire period, and especially in the 1970s, real estate surpassed
a composite index of investment assets and far exceeded U.S. government bonds, bills, and inflation rates.

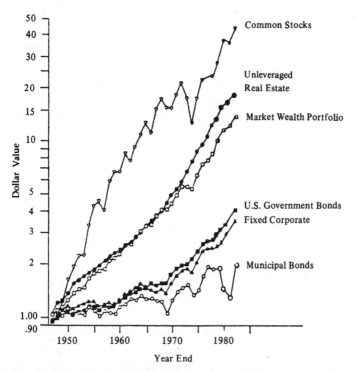

Figure 13.2. Cumulative wealth indexes of capital market security groups, 1947–1984. (Year-end 1946 = $1.) (*Source: Roger G. Ibbotson and Laurence B. Siegel, "Real Estate Returns: A Comparison with Other Investments,"* AREUEA Journal, *vol. 12, no. 3, Fall 1984, p. 225.*)

Returns on Residential, Farm, and Business Real Estate

The three sectors of the real estate market have had rather different returns in the postwar period. Total returns on residential and farm property since the 1940s and on business real estate since the 1960s are shown as three sets of annual indexes in Table 13.1. Also, returns on these subcategories are weighted by the market value of the residential, farm, and business components to form a composite index of real estate returns. Total returns for each sector include both capital appreciation and income returns, the latter net of operating expenses—that is, what a landlord would earn. Returns are unleveraged by mortgage or other debt financing.

Over almost 40 years, farm real estate had higher average returns, 9.6 percent per year, than residential housing with 7.7 percent. Since 1960, farmland also had returns superior to business real estate; compound

Table 13.1. U.S. Real Estate by Sector, 1947–1984: Year by Year Returns (in Percent) and Indexes (December 31, 1959 = 1.000)

	Business		Residential		Farmland		Composite	
Year	Return	Index	Return	Index	Return	Index	Return	Index
1947			8.22%	0.547	16.33%	0.396	10.79%	0.481
1948			9.28	0.598	13.13	0.448	10.42	0.532
1949			1.49	0.607	5.56	0.473	2.65	0.546
1950			5.75	0.642	21.90	0.577	10.19	0.601
1951			11.32	0.715	17.97	0.680	13.19	0.681
1952			5.30	0.753	7.06	0.635	5.80	0.720
1953			3.76	0.781	0.98	0.642	3.00	0.742
1954			4.30	0.815	7.12	0.687	5.04	0.779
1955			3.29	0.841	5.97	0.728	3.98	0.810
1956			4.13	0.876	7.75	0.785	5.04	0.851
1957			6.03	0.929	7.77	0.846	6.47	0.906
1958			4.05	0.966	12.80	0.954	6.28	0.963
1959		1.000	3.50	1.000	4.83	1.000	3.84	1.000
1960	2.49%	1.025	4.99	1.050	4.07	1.041	4.57	1.046
1961	2.69	1.052	5.28	1.105	9.10	1.136	5.82	1.107
1962	3.29	1.087	4.79	1.158	8.98	1.238	5.51	1.168
1963	4.29	1.134	6.78	1.237	9.79	1.359	7.15	1.252
1964	2.99	1.168	5.83	1.309	7.58	1.462	5.91	1.326
1965	4.09	1.216	6.24	1.391	12.64	1.647	7.34	1.423
1966	4.89	1.275	5.76	1.471	12.23	1.848	7.02	1.523
1967	6.39	1.356	6.83	1.571	10.30	2.038	7.49	1.637
1968	10.69	1.501	8.25	1.701	8.71	2.216	8.62	1.778
1969	6.09	1.592	11.02	1.888	7.24	2.376	9.73	1.951
1970	9.99	1.751	12.16	2.118	7.77	2.561	11.09	2.167
1971	15.49	2.022	8.16	2.291	11.70	2.861	9.71	2.377
1972	9.49	2.214	6.73	2.445	18.94	3.403	9.21	2.596
1973	7.39	2.378	6.97	2.615	35.27	4.603	11.94	2.906
1974	8.09	2.570	13.50	2.968	19.80	5.514	13.99	3.313
1975	6.60	2.740	13.23	3.361	18.52	6.535	13.29	3.753
1976	8.55	2.974	7.51	3.613	19.54	7.812	9.90	4.125
1977	8.67	3.232	11.47	4.027	11.20	8.687	11.10	4.583
1978	14.68	3.706	14.18	4.598	18.18	10.266	15.02	5.271
1979	14.69	4.250	19.01	5.472	20.87	12.409	18.90	6.267
1980	12.92	4.799	14.75	6.279	12.63	13.976	14.12	7.152
1981	13.46	5.445	4.96	6.590	2.19	14.282	5.41	7.539
1982	10.38	6.010	11.82	7.369	-3.05	13.846	8.87	8.208
1983	16.00	6.972	7.35	7.911	-0.26	13.810	7.13	8.793
1984	9.99	7.669	5.62	8.356	-6.65	12.892	4.11	9.154

Summary Statistics

Compound Annual Return	8.49%		7.66%		9.60%		8.06%	
Arithmetic Mean Return	8.57		7.73		10.70		8.42	
Standard Deviation of Annual Returns	4.16		3.80		7.74		3.71	

Note: All indexes are initialized at 1.000 on December 31, 1959 so that they can be compared. All real estate is assumed to be unleveraged. The composite is a value-weighted average of the three types (two types before 1960) of real estate.

Sources: For 1947–1959, returns are taken from Roger G. Ibbotson and Laurence B. Siegel, "Real Esate Returns: A Comparison with Other Investments," *AREUEA Journal,* Fall 1984, p. 239 (Appendix A). For 1960–1984, returns are taken from Roger G. Ibbotson, Laurence B. Siegel, and Kathryn S. Love, "World Wealth: Market Values and Returns," *Journal of Portfolio Management,* Fall 1985, Table 2. The authors linked (compounded) the returns to form indexes.

returns were about 9.6 percent and 8.5 percent, respectively. In the mid-1980s, farmland prices dropped sharply, but not enough to eradicate the superior past performance.

All three real estate sector indexes had relatively little variability from year to year, as shown by the low standard deviations in the summary statistics at the bottom of Table 13.1. The standard deviations are biased downward, however, as described below. While standard deviations *within* the three sectors are probably comparable, returns on real estate are only roughly comparable with those of other assets, such as stocks, bonds, and cash. Consequently, real estate's low standard deviations relative to other assets do not necessarily indicate that real estate is less risky. Moreover, since most real estate is leveraged, the risks of real estate investment are greatly increased.

The Diversification Potential of Real Estate

Statistical analysis suggests that real estate provides diversification to holders of financial assets. As shown in Table 13.2, composite returns on real estate have low and sometimes even negative correlations with all types of stocks and bonds. By contrast, real estate returns are highly correlated with U.S. Treasury bills and inflation. Real estate thus helps diversify the risk of financial assets.

Business real estate has a slightly higher correlation with the stock market and thus provides less diversification than holdings in other real estate sectors. This correlation was also evident during the stock market's declines of 1969–1970 and 1973–1974, when the returns on business real estate lagged behind returns on residences. In years when the stock market did well, returns on business real estate kept pace with or

Table 13.2. Cross Correlations of Real Estate Sector and Composite Total Returns with Various Other Assets, 1947–1984

	Real Estate Sector			Real Estate Composite
	Business*	Residential	Farmland	
S & P 500 Common Stocks	0.14	–0.08	–0.05	–0.06
Small Company Stocks	0.16	0.04	0.02	0.06
Long-Term Corporate Bonds	0.05	0.06	–0.31	–0.08
Long-Term Government Bonds	0.04	0.06	–0.33	–0.09
U.S. Treasury Bills	0.68	0.53	–0.10	0.38
Inflation Rates	0.57	0.80	0.50	0.85

* Correlations with business real estate are for 1960-1984.

Source: Table 13.1 for real estate returns; *Stocks, Bonds, Bills, and Inflation: 1986 Yearbook*, Ibbotson Associates, Chicago, for other assets.

exceeded those for residential property. These patterns suggest that business real estate probably contains some of the business risk of the economy.

While investors can use real estate to diversify the risk of holding financial assets, they may find it hard to diversify within the category of real estate. An owner-occupied house is often a large component of the individual investor's wealth. Many individual investors cannot afford more than one house, and thus they are unable to diversify their real estate holdings. Even if individuals invest in real estate partnerships, they may find their real estate undiversified unless they participate in more than one. On the other hand, institutional investors, with large funds at their disposal, can more easily diversify their real estate holdings.

For large investors with the resources to diversify within the real estate sector, adding farmland to residential and business properties provides an additional hedge against changes in the real estate market. Statistically, business and residential real estate tend to move together. Business and residential property returns have a correlation of roughly 0.5 with each other, while each has a low correlation with farmland returns, less than 0.3 in both cases.

Measuring Real Estate Returns

The returns in this chapter are not measured with the same accuracy as returns on other assets. Capital appreciation returns on real estate are based on appraised values instead of transaction prices. The use of appraisal values in estimating returns tends to smooth, or reduce, the standard deviation of the returns. Appraisals are usually based on three approaches:

- Discounted cash flows
- Replacement cost
- Transaction prices of comparable properties

The present value of future discounted cash flows only approximates market value because cash flows and the discount rate are difficult to estimate; thus, price estimates are somewhat inaccurate. The replacement cost and comparable sales methods both smooth returns because they depend on previous price data—in the first case, costs, and in the second, transactions—from various past time periods to estimate market values.

Marketability also complicates the comparison of returns across assets.

Most stocks, bonds, and cash equivalents are instantaneously market-able, or convertible into cash, with relatively low search and transaction costs. Reported returns for these assets, based on price quotations, are therefore very close to realizable returns. Real estate is unlike stocks, bonds, and cash in this regard, since it cannot be sold instantaneously at the quoted or appraised price.

Thus both appraisal inaccuracies and marketability costs must be considered when comparing real estate returns with those on stocks, bonds, and other homogeneous assets, traded in centralized, continuous auction markets. In general, real estate is riskier than statistical measures such as standard deviation would suggest.

A new attempt to measure business real estate returns has been made by the Frank Russell Company (FRC) for the National Council of Real Estate Investment Fiduciaries. The FRC Property Index is a benchmark used nationally to measure the performance of institutional real estate portfolios. Presented in Table 13.3, this index measures both capital appreciation and income returns on 900 large properties owned by 30 investment managers. As of year-end 1985, it had a compound annual return of 14.5 percent over the preceding 8 years, compared with returns on a leading stock market index, the S&P 500 with dividends reinvested, of 15.6 percent and returns on a bond index of 10.1 percent over the same period. While the FRC Property Index is subject to the same types of downward biases of standard deviation as other indexes, it improves upon them somewhat by incorporating a very large number of properties, reducing other measurement errors. Subindexes by geographic region and by property type are presented, showing the diversity of returns on different types of real estate.

Inflation and Real Estate Returns

Inflation has both direct and indirect effects on real estate returns. A property's appreciation is often due in part to a rise in the general level of prices. Thus, inflation increases the nominal prices of real estate, directly affecting its nominal returns. But inflation also has an indirect effect on real estate returns through taxes.

Leverage, Taxes, and Inflation

The returns for unleveraged real estate characterize the performance of the asset and enable comparisons with other assets. In practice, however, most investors hold real estate in leveraged form. Typically, a fixed debt

Table 13.3. FRC Property Index: Annual Total Returns (in Percent) and Year-End Indexes (December 31, 1977 = 1.000) by Region and Property Type

	All Properties (Composite)		East		Midwest		South		West	
Year	Return	Index	Return	Index	Return	Index	Return	Index	Return	Index
1977		1.000		1.000		1.000		1.000		1.000
1978	15.9 %	1.159	23.8 %	1.238	8.2 %	1.082	13.2 %	1.132	17.6 %	1.176
1979	20.6	1.398	26.9	1.572	11.8	1.210	23.6	1.399	20.4	1.416
1980	17.9	1.648	27.2	2.000	12.2	1.358	9.9	1.539	20.9	1.712
1981	16.6	1.922	17.2	2.344	12.6	1.529	14.8	1.767	20.7	2.066
1982	9.3	2.101	7.5	2.519	8.0	1.652	12.5	1.985	9.2	2.256
1983	13.3	2.380	18.2	2.976	9.5	1.809	10.4	2.193	14.4	2.580
1984	12.9	2.688	18.4	3.524	12.7	2.037	9.4	2.398	12.4	2.900
1985	9.8	2.950	11.8	3.937	11.7	2.263	7.0	2.583	9.4	3.172

	Apartments		Hotels		Industrial		Office		Retail	
Year	Return	Index	Return	Index	Return	Index	Return	Index	Return	Index
1977		1.000		1.000		1.000		1.000		1.000
1978	16.7 %	1.167	28.1 %	1.281	13.9 %	1.139	21.0 %	1.210	10.5 %	1.105
1979	32.3	1.543	73.4	2.221	19.0	1.355	19.4	1.445	12.3	1.240
1980	17.1	1.807	13.3	2.517	16.1	1.573	25.5	1.813	13.1	1.403
1981	13.7	2.054	10.6	2.785	17.4	1.847	20.4	2.184	11.0	1.557
1982	15.4	2.370	10.5	3.076	9.7	2.026	9.6	2.393	7.1	1.668
1983	14.5	2.714	11.8	3.438	13.7	2.303	12.1	2.685	15.6	1.928
1984	12.0	3.039	9.7	3.769	12.9	2.601	12.4	3.016	15.0	2.217
1985	8.0	3.282	4.5	3.939	11.8	2.906	8.6	3.276	11.5	2.474

Summary Statistics of Composite Index, 1978-1985

	Compound Return	Standard Deviation
Total return	14.5 %	3.7 %
Income	8.0	0.5
Capital appreciation	6.1	3.1

Note: The FRC Property Index and subindices are constructed using returns on unleveraged properties before deduction of management fees. As of the starting date, 236 properties were in the data base; as of the ending date, over 900. Property data are collected by the Frank Russell Company from numerous investment managers and are aggregated to produce these indices.

Source: *FRC Property Index,* Fourth Quarter 1985, published by the Frank Russell Company, Tacoma, Wash., and the National Council of Real Estate Investment Fiduciaries (NCREIF).

claim, or mortgage, and a variable equity claim, or the right to potential capital appreciation and residual income, are held by separate investors.

At the time of this writing, the U.S. tax system has undergone a major restructuring. Although there is presently no tax rate differential between capital gains and ordinary income, there will always be one major distinction: capital gains can be deferred, and their realization timed by the holder. By contrast, ordinary income is earned and reported each year. Thus, even with major tax restructuring, capital gains are preferable to ordinary income.

Inflation's tax effects can be either positive, reducing the investor's income, or negative, actually providing investors with tax shelter benefits. The simplest example of a detrimental inflation tax is the tax on a real property's nominal capital gain. When inflation alone causes price appreciation, the investor has no gain in real terms, yet pays a tax on the "gain" if the property is sold. In past versions of the U.S. tax code, this positive tax has been calculated at capital gains rates, which were lower than ordinary rates.

The inflation tax may be negative or beneficial, actually increasing the after-tax return of investors after leverage is considered. Lenders, or mortgagees, who anticipate higher inflation raise mortgage rates. If real estate equity holders leverage their properties, they may be able to deduct the higher interest payments, reducing their taxes each year. If a cash loss, a tax benefit from the interest expense (if permitted under the tax code), and a potential (inflated and deferred) capital gain net of tax are all combined, an investor may do better with higher inflation.

Were the investor a homeowner, the higher inflation might be even more beneficial. The implicit rent would presumably be the same, but the homeowner would not receive it in cash, and so would not declare it as income. The tax on any capital gains may be deferred practically indefinitely, and homeowners can still deduct mortgage interest. On the other hand, unlike a landlord, a homeowner does not deduct depreciation and maintenance. If the homeowner's undeclared, implicit rent exceeds the landlord's depreciation and maintenance expenses, then there is a tax incentive to own rather than rent even when renter, homeowner, and landlord are in the same tax bracket.

Paradoxically, both investors and homeowners have been able to make money while seeming to lose money in real estate. The high interest rate expenses each year are offset by deferred capital gains, saving taxes overall. The negative inflation tax has been a subsidy through the tax system and has benefited investors in high tax brackets. Low inflation has been less beneficial than high inflation because real estate is a better tax shelter in high inflation. In general, then, low rates of inflation have hurt real estate owners while high rates of inflation have helped real estate owners.

Very high rates of inflation, however, may not be increasingly beneficial. When inflation is very high, long-term interest rates rise correspondingly, and consumers cannot afford the high mortgage payment. This drives the price of real estate down. Innovations in mortgage financing, begun in the late 1970s and early 1980s, may reduce the impact of high mortgage rates if they occur in the future.

In addition to its effects on real estate prices and the taxes paid by homeowners and investors, inflation transfers wealth between real estate equity and mortgage holders. If inflation rises unexpectedly, those holding fixed claims like mortgages lose ground in real terms, while those holding residual equity claims benefit. During the mid-1980s, mortgage rates have fallen dramatically.

A Statistical Look at Inflation and Real Estate Returns

In Table 13.4, total returns on unleveraged real estate are regressed on U.S. inflation. As indicated in the table, the betas of all three sectors— farms, residences, and business—are slightly less than 1. If inflation rates had a one for one effect on real estate returns, their beta coefficients on inflation would be 1, indicating that inflation and real estate returns move in tandem. However, a beta of less than 1 indicates that these returns do not change by the full amount of the change in inflation.

Yet the differences between these betas and 1 are statistically significant only for business real estate. The beta of farm property on inflation is very near to 1—0.93—while the beta of residential real estate is only slightly more than one standard deviation below 1. Thus unleveraged real estate appears to be a good inflation hedge.

Since a real estate mortgage acts economically like a long-term bond, the rate of return on the mortgage, when regressed on the inflation rate, would be negative. Moreover, mortgages generally comprise more than half—and in some sectors as much as 80 percent—of real estate's value. Thus, *leveraged* real estate is likely to have a beta substantially greater than 1 when regressed on inflation. That is, the increased risk caused by leverage exaggerates inflation's effects on real estate.

Individual investors gain more from real estate's tax treatment than

Table 13.4. Real Estate Total Returns Regressed on Inflation Rates, 1960–1984

	Alpha (%)	Alpha T Statistic	Beta	Standard Error of Beta	Adjusted R^2	Standard Deviation of Residuals	1st-order Autocorr. of Residuals
U.S. Business Real Estate	5.08	4.01	0.66	0.20	0.30	3.56	0.44
U.S. Residential Real Estate	4.61	5.26	0.81	0.14	0.59	2.47	-0.08
U.S. Farm Real Estate	7.18	2.72	0.93	0.41	0.15	7.43	0.46
U.S. Real Estate Composite	5.23	7.53	0.80	0.11	0.70	1.95	0.13

Source: Roger G. Ibbotson, Laurence B. Siegel, and Kathryn S. Love, "World Wealth: Market Values and Returns," *Journal of Portfolio Management,* Fall 1985.

corporations or institutions, particularly those handling tax-exempt funds. If the price of real estate includes its tax advantages, investors unable to use these benefits should find real estate relatively more costly. Thus, pension funds do not gain the tax benefits from leveraging real estate and usually hold mortgages, perhaps with equity "kickers," a participation in the income from the property financed.

Returning to unleveraged real estate, the farm, residential, and business real estate sectors all had positive alphas, meaning that inflation-adjusted returns on real estate were positive. The results show that the R squareds of the three sectors are relatively high; the figures suggest that inflation explains 59 percent of variation of the returns on residential real estate, 30 percent on business property, and 15 percent on farmland. For the unleveraged real estate composite, inflation explains 70 percent of the variation of the return.

The serial correlation of real estate returns, unlike that of stocks and bonds, is high. A high serial correlation means that when returns on real estate in the prior period are high, those in the next period tend to be high as well; likewise, when returns are low in the previous period, those in the following period are likely to be low. Yet high correlations may be an artificial result caused by appraisal smoothing. Furthermore, the serial correlation of inflation-adjusted, or real, returns for real estate is much closer to zero. This indicates that the high observed serial correlation of nominal real estate returns is largely caused by the high serial correlation of inflation.

What Will Future Returns on Real Estate Be?

Economists generally believe that assets like real estate are fairly priced in the market. That is, returns are commensurate with the risks and other costs that investors must bear. Since real estate has a unique set of risks and costs, it is instructive to examine those that significantly affect its returns.

First it should be pointed out that the two major pricing models in modern portfolio theory—the *capital asset pricing model* (CAPM) and *arbitrage pricing theory* (APT)—have limited usefulness in determining real estate returns. Both models assume perfect arbitrage conditions, with no cash constraints, under which any mispricing will be instantly arbitraged away. Real estate markets do not even approximate these conditions. The nonrisk characteristics of real estate—taxes, marketability, and information costs—have a greater role in determining expected returns, and may be more important than those factors pertaining to risk. In the NET framework, investors pursue returns *net* of all investor-specific costs. The expected returns for real estate are determined by summing its risk and nonrisk pricing factors.

Discount Rates, Cost of Capital, and Expected Returns

Expected returns in real estate as from other securities can be viewed from three economic perspectives. When considering the asset side of the balance sheet, values are computed using a *discount rate,* or expected returns on the asset, in a present-value model. Looking at the liability and equity side, market-required returns are usually described using a weighted-average *cost of capital.* In the calculations of investors, this number is called the *expected return* before investor-specific costs. Although three different names are used, the concepts are essentially identical.

Economists most often use CAPM and APT to address directly the cost of capital, whether for real estate or other assets. Real estate investors typically use this rate as the discount rate when appraising properties using the present-value or income methods of valuation. For forecasting real estate returns, the concept of expected returns is most appropriate, and it is used in the following discussion. Here, the long-term expected return of real estate is forecast in equilibrium, without considering whether real estate is over- or underpriced.

Factors Dictating High Expected Returns on Real Estate

Many characteristics of real estate indicate that it should have higher expected returns than other assets in equilibrium. Probably the most significant characteristic is its risks. But nonrisk attributes of real estate also increase its expected return. Specifically, investors must pay relatively high search, transaction, and marketability costs associated with real estate.

Risk. The risk attributes of real estate include market risk, interest rate risk, and residual risk. Since real estate activity is related to some extent to business activity, equity market risk is to some extent correlated with real estate returns. In addition, inflation risk has very important effects on real estate returns, as described earlier. Finally, residual risk is endemic to real estate. Because most properties are large relative to investors' wealth and are not easily divided, investors often hold highly undiversified portfolios of real estate, burdening them with residual risk.

Most asset pricing models ignore residual risk, but the market appears to demand some premium for assuming it, and to receive such a premium when it is costly, difficult, or impossible to diversify. Overall, real estate risk has been higher than that of bonds, but lower than that of stocks.

Information and Transaction Cost.   The heterogeneity of real estate parcels makes the cost of acquiring information about them very high. A real estate property is unique; the physical and socioeconomic characteristics, as well as local market values, differ for like properties in separate locations. Further, investors may incur information costs for properties not acquired, and they seek returns to compensate them for these costs too.

Because real estate brokers typically work for commission alone, the transactions costs of real estate are also large, primarily to compensate brokers for the risks of their business. These large costs must be borne by real estate investors, and make for higher expected returns before investor-specific costs.

Limited Marketability.   Real estate has more limited marketability than many other investments. In fact, real estate is not readily marketable for three major reasons. First, the appraised price is only an approximation of the market price; a transaction price may differ substantially from appraised value. Second, each parcel of real estate has unique characteristics which increase the cost of locating a buyer; while one share of IBM stock is as good as another, no two office buildings are truly alike. Finally, even after the buyer and seller locate each other, they may need time to agree on the price and to structure what is frequently a complex transaction. Investors price this limited marketability differently; for example, real estate brokers may find this cost easier to bear than those not in the business.

Factors Dictating Low Returns on Real Estate

Other characteristics of real estate dictate lower expected returns, including: control attributes, tax benefits, certain evidence of low risk, ease of obtaining leverage, and gains from diversification. Since real estate's diversification potential and its lower measured risk than common stocks have already been described, the other three are discussed here.

Control.   Because of real estate's large unit cost, investors typically control entire properties. Whether the homeowner owns a house or the general partner owns and manages an investment property, those who own real estate equity often have a high degree of control over their investments. The control attribute is valued differently across investors; many want and will pay for control, while a few prefer to avoid its responsibilities and liabilities. Generally, though, control is desirable and results in higher prices, which translate to lower expected returns.

Taxes. As discussed previously, the tax attributes of real estate equity in an inflationary setting may be very beneficial. Moreover, the tax system is structured so that both real estate equity and mortgages have a natural, tax-determined clientele. Under a changing tax system, the effects will not be as strong.

Traditionally, individuals and partnerships, rather than corporations, have held real estate equity, which confers large personal tax benefits; deductibility of mortgage interest and real property taxes has made home ownership advantageous, while provisions for accelerated depreciation of real property also have encouraged real estate equity investment. Pension funds and other tax-exempt institutions have held the bulk of real estate mortgages, which paid high interest rates because they yielded highly taxable income. Tax-exempt institutions have been able to capture these rates yet avoid taxes entirely. This cornucopia of tax benefits almost surely has lowered the before-tax expected return on real estate.

Ease of Leverage. Finally, real estate is easy to leverage. Because real estate has a fixed location, it is relatively easy to identify, locate, and seize if the borrower defaults. Thus lenders almost always consider it to be good collateral.

Investment Advice

Real estate is a complex investment vehicle, and many books have been written explaining how to buy and sell real estate. A full explanation requires a book-length treatment. But a few rules for individuals are offered here:

1. Hold some real estate to diversify your portfolio.

Real estate provides considerable portfolio diversification for investors. The near-zero correlations of real estate with other assets mean that investors can reduce the risk in their portfolios by holding some real estate. However, it is difficult to diversify across real estate properties.

2. Buy real estate to hedge inflation.

In the last 25 years, real estate has provided a better inflation hedge than any other asset except Treasury bills. Under provisions of the U.S.

tax code, higher rates of inflation are probably more beneficial to real estate holders than low rates. Nevertheless, when inflation and corresponding mortgages reach double digits, the benefits of real estate as a hedge may be reduced. Still, in a world where inflation is uncertain, real estate may be attractive to investors who want to maximize their real expected returns.

3. Own your own home.

Unless you move frequently or are in a very low tax bracket, investing in your own home is likely to be one of the best investments you can make. Not only will your taxes be lower, but the forced saving inherent in a mortgage builds wealth over time.

4. Consider the benefits and costs of landlordship carefully.

Many fortunes have been made in real estate. This has induced many novice investors to buy apartment buildings, condominiums, and houses, thus entering the real estate business. In the 1970s, this strategy rewarded almost everyone who tried it, but much more skill and attention is likely to be required in the future because lower inflation and reduced tax benefits will produce lower after-tax returns.

5. Buy real estate limited partnership interests from a reputable dealer.

With the virtual elimination of the tax shelter aspect of limited partnerships, limited partnerships should be evaluated on their investment prospects alone. The best and worst deals may be available in little-known markets, but blatant rip-offs are rare in limited partnerships assembled by the top firms. Stick to the blue chips unless you have special knowledge of real estate.

6. Buy for the long term.

Brokerage, transactions, and search costs eat up short-run profits. If you might need your money out in a hurry, don't invest in real estate.

7. Use your comparative advantages.

The expected returns on real estate should be high enough to compensate investors for its associated risks, limited marketability, and high transaction and information costs. Counterbalancing these factors, real estate's desirable features of control, tax shelter in owner-occupied and owner-managed real estate, diversification, and leverage lower the expected return in equilibrium. These factors can work for or against you. For example, information costs are lower for local investors. The insightful investor will often be able to identify growing or declining areas before prices move radically. Great profit opportunities exist in the malleable character of America's cities and suburbs. But the less well-informed investor should be very careful of "buying at the top of the market."

Above all, remember that, as every prospectus says, past results are not a guarantee of future performance. In 1978, California house prices were rising at 3 percent a month. Four years later they were falling at the same rate. In general, assets, including real estate, are fairly priced, and it is difficult to make accurate forecasts of future trends. The spectacular returns of U.S. real estate over the last 3 decades are the result of favorable tax treatment and high, unanticipated inflation. With less inflation, lower tax rates, and a new tax system, these returns are unlikely to continue. There is, however, the possibility of improving your returns, which is probably greater for real estate than for any other asset. Real estate is one investment arena where there are returns to skill, and it is indeed possible to gain the performance advantage.

Suggested Reading

Arnold, Alvin L., Mike E. Miles, and Charles H. Wurtzebach: *Modern Real Estate*, Warren, Gorham, and Lamont, Boston, 1980. A good introductory textbook on real estate for those unfamiliar with basic issues.

Downs, Anthony: *The Revolution in Real Estate Finance*, Brookings Institution, Washington, D.C., 1985. A new analysis by a founder of modern real estate economics, now serving as a senior fellow in the Brookings Economic Studies program.

Ibbotson, Roger G., and Laurence B. Siegel: "Real Estate Returns: A Comparison with Other Investments," *AREUEA Journal*, vol. 12, no. 3, Fall 1984. This entire journal issue is devoted to the subject of institutional real estate investment, and is recommended for the institutional investment professional. The Ibbotson and Siegel article introduces the topic, which is studied by other authors in detail.

Musgrave, John C.: *Survey of Current Business*, U.S. Department of Commerce, Washington, D.C., various issues. Provides the estimates of the quantity of housing and business real estate over different time periods that were used in this chapter.

U.S. Department of Agriculture: "Income and Balance Sheet Statistics," *Economic Indicators of the Farm Sector*, Washington, D.C., annual. Gives annual prices per farmland acre, along with farmland income statistics.

14
Tangible Assets

Shortly after Hitler came to power in the 1930s, Walter Aufhauser, son of the Munich banker Martin Aufhauser, approached an American print collector about the purchase of some prints. When the collector saw a list of those for sale, he was astonished. The 300 pieces were a world-famous collection of fifteenth-century metal cuts and woodcuts. After months of negotiation, he bought the group, providing Martin Aufhauser with the funds to begin life anew in the United States when he was forced to flee Germany. Tangibles like this collection are portable and retain value in times of economic and political hardship.

Tangibles Defined

Tangibles are physical assets that can be touched and moved. They also are functional or useful; in economic terms, tangibles have consumption value. Many tangibles are bought principally for use or pleasure, which are nonpecuniary benefits to the holder. Presumably the Aufhauser family purchased its prints to display and enjoy, not to fund a flight to freedom. Often referred to as "real" assets, tangibles in the broadest sense include everything of value other than financial securities like stocks and bonds.

Tangibles encompass both durables like cars and valuable objects like art. The most common tangible assets, in which a large proportion of the U.S. population is able to, and does, invest, are durable goods such as automobiles, major appliances, audio and video systems, and clothing. Most investments, however, are made in tangible assets like gold and silver (covered in Chapter 12), real estate (covered in Chapter 13), gems, art, antiques, coins, and stamps.

Tangibles as Investments

If tangible assets serve their owners in nonmonetary ways, their status as investments might be questioned. In contrast to financial assets, tangible assets may have two kinds of returns. Like financial assets, some tangibles have a monetary return, usually in the form of capital appreciation realized at the end of the asset's holding period. Unlike financial assets, however, all tangibles also have a nonmonetary or nonpecuniary return, the pleasure or utility of owning and using the asset. Tangibles which have significant monetary returns and which are traded in sizable markets are most often held for investment.

Investment-grade tangibles, in particular, have pecuniary value over and above their original function. Although the Aufhauser prints had aesthetic value, they were redeemed for cash—probably far in excess of their original cost. Yet even if tangible assets are valuable as investments, they may still serve their original function. Antique tables can still adorn a home, rare musical instruments can still be played, and old books can still be read. Ironically as an artifact's value increases, it often ceases to be used as originally intended; rare Greek vases are more often encased in museums than filled with flowers.

Tangible assets are distinguished from other investments by three characteristics:

- Limited marketability
- High maintenance costs
- Nonpecuniary returns

These three characteristics all affect the expected monetary returns on tangibles.

Limited Marketability

Tangibles are not readily marketable in part because of their indivisibility. An investor holding IBM stock can easily sell some shares without altering the value of those that remain, while an investor holding a rare Stradivarius violin must sell it as a whole to receive its maximum value. Thus the indivisibility of tangibles limits their marketability.

Tangible assets also have high transaction costs that reduce marketability. Because tangibles are often unique, finding a buyer takes time. Thus brokers charge high commissions or dealer fees. In addition, investors themselves have high search costs, which include the long wait to find a willing buyer at a given price or the sharp price reduction necessary to reduce the wait. Finally, investors must pay higher transaction costs to buy and sell a tangible asset; its authenticity, quality, and in some cases provenance (the names and reputations of the previous owners) must be verified, all of which is expensive. While there can be high dealer fees for some other types of assets, high search and transaction costs are more frequently borne when selling tangibles.

High Maintenance Costs

Because tangible assets are physical objects, they also have high maintenance costs, which vary widely from asset to asset. Art objects like paintings, for example, require special handling to protect them from damage and special care to maintain their pristine condition. On the other hand, coins require less constant attention.

Insurance is another necessary maintenance cost. Assets like a diamond or a rare coin must be insured; however, the insurance cost will be lower if the asset is stored in a bank vault than if it is displayed in the owner's home to provide a nonpecuniary return.

Nonpecuniary Returns

Most important, many tangible assets—unlike other investments—offer a nonpecuniary return. This return can be practical utility, aesthetic enjoyment, or both. While not investments in the traditional sense, durable goods like cars or televisions have as their primary return their usefulness or function. Art objects, by contrast, have an aesthetic return.

Because an investor makes a subjective judgment about a tangible's nonpecuniary return, the investor who prizes the particular object most will own it. Station wagons provide high nonpecuniary returns only to large families, and skis provide the same only to athletic people with access to snowy hillsides. If these two "investors" traded their station wagons for skis on a dollar-for-dollar basis, both would be much worse off. Similarly, art objects also are held by those who value their particular characteristics most. Since no two investors enjoy a particular piece of art in the same way, this nonpecuniary return will differ across investors. But if many people enjoy a similar nonpecuniary return from an art object, the investor can conceivably obtain a monetary return by renting the object to someone else and sacrificing the nonpecuniary return.

Thus, while tangibles can be regarded as investments like any other, they have special characteristics of limited marketability, high maintenance costs, and nonpecuniary benefits. These pricing factors affect their expected returns.

Total Expected Returns
from Tangibles

In a financial sense, an asset's total return has two components: the change in price of the asset over time and the income earned from the asset while held. Unless they are rented out, cash income from most tangible assets is zero. Thus, the total financial return from investment-grade tangibles is generally equal to their capital appreciation. More broadly, the *net* investment return from a tangible asset is equal to its capital appreciation, minus the owner's search, transaction, and maintenance costs, plus the owner's nonpecuniary benefits.

The particular characteristics of a tangible asset affect its price. For example, if an asset's maintenance or transaction costs are high, the demand for that asset will be lower, thus lowering the price of acquiring the asset and raising its expected return before investor-specific costs. In other words, if investors are required to take on the higher costs of holding the asset, then they will demand a higher monetary return on their investment. Conversely, if the nonpecuniary benefits from holding the asset are high, investors' demand for the asset tends to be higher, and thus the price of acquiring the asset rises and the expected monetary return is lower.

When considered over time, returns on tangible assets are highest in periods when other assets perform poorly. Tangible assets are like car insurance in this regard. During a time when a car owner has no accidents, no "fires and thefts," car insurance has a poor return. After an accident, on the other hand, car insurance provides excellent returns. In fact, tangible assets like gold and antiques had high returns in the inflationary 1970s, when stocks and bonds did poorly. In the 1980s, stocks and bonds performed well, while returns on tangible assets were lower and often negative.

Durable Goods

Many individuals throughout the world invest more of their resources in durable goods than in financial assets. Durables are bought because the owner needs or wants the usefulness of objects such as automobiles, appliances, and clothing. In economic terms, people "invest" in these tangible assets and rent to themselves.

One primary durable good held by inhabitants of developed countries is automobiles. Consumers in the United States, Western Europe, and Australia appear to be the biggest investors in this asset, as Table 14.1 shows. In 1980, the United States had 1.8 persons per car; Australia, 2.4; West Germany, 2.6; France, 2.8; and the United Kingdom, 3.6. Few Chinese, on the other hand, own autos; there were 18,673 persons per car in that country.

According to the economist John C. Musgrave, U.S. durables amounted to $1235.5 billion, or 4.5 percent of total world wealth in 1984. This number includes automobiles, furniture, appliances, and other personal effects. A rough estimate of the value of foreign durables can be obtained by assuming that the proportion of automobiles to other

Table 14.1. Car Registrations around the World

Continent/Country*	Cars (000)	Population per Car
Europe	124.200	6.0
France	19,150	2.8
Romania	240	93.0
U.S.S.R.	8,255	32.0
United Kingdom	15,438	3.6
West Germany	23,236	2.6
Asia	31,883	78.0
China	55	18,673.0
Hong Kong	226	192.0
India	930	718.0
Japan	23,660	4.9
Singapore	164	15.0
Africa	6,330	72.0
Egypt	428	98.0
South Africa	2,456	12.0
Zaire	44	641.0
Oceania	7,415	3.2
Australia	5,950	2.4
South America	14,234	17.0
Brazil	8,213	15.0
Colombia	348	79.0
North and Central America	136,450	2.6
Haiti	31	182.0
Mexico	3,360	21.0
United States	121,724	1.8
WORLD TOTAL	320,513	14.0

* Representative countries are listed for each region. Totals for regions include more than just the countries shown.

Source: Car registrations in 1980 from *World Motor Vehicle Data*, 1982 ed., Motor Vehicle Manufacturers Association of the U.S., Inc. (300 New Center Building, Detroit, MI 48202). Population for figuring population-per-car from the same sources as used to construct Table 2.1.

durables is the same in foreign countries as it is in the U.S. Estimated in this way, foreign durables amounted to $2243.7 billion or 8.1 percent of world wealth in that year. Putting the figures together, roughly 13 percent of the world's wealth is held in durables.

Durables are usually expected to depreciate rather than appreciate in value. After much repair expense, they eventually fall apart, and thus their expected capital appreciation is negative. Recall also that the nonpecuniary "income" return of durables is their usefulness to the holder. Consequently, this nonpecuniary income alone must be sufficient to make the total return competitive with other opportunities for spending or investing.

Art and Other Valuables

While durables have functional value, art and artifacts have value that is mostly subjective and aesthetic. Why else would a painting at a local street fair sell for a few dollars while Cézanne's *Peasant in a Blue Blouse* goes for $3.9 million? Art's value is determined by buyers and sellers in the market, and depends in part on fashion, trends, and economic conditions, in addition to the work's intrinsic characteristics, such as its quality, authorship, rarity, and condition.

Measuring Returns on Art Objects

Although much of art's return comes from aesthetic enjoyment, it can also provide a monetary return. A distress sale price during the midst of World War II is not comparable with the same object's sale price in the postwar period. Likewise, a sale price in the inflationary 1970s is not strictly comparable to one in the 1980s, with its low inflation. But return indexes for art are likely to be biased upward. Paintings that have fallen in price are much less likely to be put up for sale, and are less likely to be negotiated through reputable dealers like Christie's or Sotheby's, where accurate prices would be recorded. Thus returns tend to be computed using mostly paintings that have risen in value, which does not produce a good indication of the average returns of artwork.

With those caveats, the Sotheby index of art prices rose from 100 in 1975 to 336 in 1985, a compound annual rate of return of 13 percent. For comparison, stocks provided a total return of 14.3 percent per year over the same period and had no aesthetic return. Data on sales at Sotheby's have also been used by J. Patrick Cooney of Citibank to derive returns for earlier periods. Cooney's index of Old Master paintings rose at an annual rate of 15.4 percent from 1970 to 1980. Impressionist paintings rose at a rate of 10.4 percent, and Modern paintings at a 13.6 percent rate over the same period. Note, however, that these calculations are for a period which was very favorable to tangible as opposed to financial assets.

Since each art object is unique and art markets are highly segmented, annual returns on individual paintings may vary greatly. In Table 14.2,

Table 14.2. Recent Sotheby's London Sales of Old Master Paintings (1979–1980)

Detail	Purchase Date	Purchase Price	Sale Date	Sale Price	Annual Growth Rate
The Madonna, Eusebio da San Giorgio	6-12-68	£ 450	7-16-80	£1,600	11.1%
Still Life, J.B.S. Chardin	6-12-68	4,000	7-16-80	8,500	6.5
Christ and the Adulteress, DeMura	6-12-68	2,500	4-16-80	3,000	1.5
St. Joseph and the Infant *Christ,* Guido Reni	6-12-68	600	4-16-80	3,800	16.6
Venice. Piazzetta Seen *From the South East,* Luca Carlevaris	3-26-69	12,000	7-16-80	38,000	11.0
Venice Piazzetta Seen From *the North,* Luca Carlevaris	3-26-69	15,000	7-16-80	40,000	9.3
An Arctic Scene: Dutch *Whalers off Greenland,* Abraham Storck	3-26-69	1,600	12-12-79	18,000	17.4
Raphael's Dream, Breughel the Elder & Hans Rottenhammer	6-25-69	5,200	12-12-79	40,000	22.6
Portico and Courtyard of *a Venetian Palace,* Franesco Guardi	6-25-69	13,650	12-12-79	50,000	15.5
Cascade at Tivoli, Claude Joseph Vernet	7-12-72	6,500	12-12-79	36,000	27.7
Italian Landscape with *Waterfall and Italian* *Landscape with Castle* (pair), Hendrick van Lint	12-10-75	9,500	12-12-79	11,000	3.7
The Wings of a Triptych: The *Annunciation with 4 Saints,* Alvaro Portoghese	1-22-76	8,900	12-12-79	14,000	16.3
A Coastal Scene, Ludolf Bakhuizen	8-12-76	8,600	7-16-80	15,000	21.9

Source: *Encyclopedia of Investments,* edited by Marshall E. Blume and Jack P. Friedman, Warren, Gorham, and Lamont, Boston, 1982, p. 604.

for example, returns on Old Master paintings sold at Sotheby's are compared. De Mura's *Christ and the Adulteress* had an annual growth rate of 1.5 percent, while Vernet's *Cascade at Tivoli* had an annual growth rate of 27.7 percent. Although not presented in this table, American artist Everett Shinn's *Saturday Night—Ringling Hotel, Sarasota Florida* grew at an annual rate of 46.5 percent. Old Master paintings have been valued highly for a long time, dampening recent returns, while American art has lately come into fashion, providing huge recent returns. When unique objects are traded in highly segmented markets, prices and returns vary widely.

Other Valuables as Investments

Although the purchase and sale of paintings dominate the world of tangibles in overall dollar value and publicity, other types of valuables are also held for investment. These include artifacts such as stamps, coins, books, gems, rugs, and furniture.

Stamp collectors in the United States number over 30 million. Because stamp collecting is the largest hobby in this country, the market for stamps is broad and relatively liquid. Like stamps, coins carry the imprint of history and can be an investment as well as a hobby. Both stamps and coins are small, portable, and easily stored. Unlike stamps, however, many coins contain valuable metals, which serve as a store of value. Because of their metallic content, coin prices tend to track those of gold and silver or other metals from which they are made.

Like stamps and coins, books and records have value for their intellectual and historical associations. They can also be an attractive investment. Consider the Houghton collection of rare books, sold at Christie's of London in 1979 and 1980. Arthur A. Houghton, Jr., paid $290,000 over 40 years to collect the books, which brought $1,865,583 when sold.

Gems—including emeralds, rubies, sapphires, and especially diamonds—are primarily objects of beauty. In addition, they are one of the world's oldest stores of value. Like prices of other tangibles, gem prices soared in the inflationary 1970s and plunged in the disinflationary 1980s.

While more popular in Europe than in the United States until the 1950s, Oriental rugs are now valued as art throughout the world. Such rugs are handmade of natural fibers, commonly wool or silk. Produced only in the Near, Middle, or Far East or the Balkans, these rugs are made by almost the same methods used 2000 years ago, and are astonishingly durable. Machine-woven rugs, while functional, have little investment value.

As they have sought Oriental rugs, Europeans have long held fine furniture as a hedge against economic unrest. With the dramatic rise in the value of antiques in the 1970s, American investors have also begun to consider period furniture as a serious investment.

Historical Returns on Tangibles

Compound annual returns on art and other valuables are shown on the left side of Table 14.3 for the decade of the 1970s, and on the right for

Table 14.3. Returns on Tangibles versus Returns on Financial Assets in the 1970s and 1980s

| | June 1970 to June 1980 | | | June 1980 to June 1985 | |
	Return*	Rank		Return*	Rank
Oil	34.7%	1	Stocks	15.2%	1
Gold	31.6	2	Bonds	13.2	2
U.S. Coins	27.7	3	Treasury Bills	12.0	3
Silver	23.7	4	CPI	5.7	4
Stamps	21.8	5	Housing	4.3	5
Chinese Ceramics	21.6	6	Old Masters	1.5	6
Diamonds	15.3	7	Diamonds	1.2	7
U.S. Farmland	14.0	8	Chinese Ceramics	1.0	8
Old Masters	13.1	9	U.S. Coins	0.1	9
Housing	10.2	10	Stamps	0.1	10
CPI	7.7	11	U.S. Farmland	(1.7)	11
Treasury Bills	7.7	12	Oil	(5.4)	12
Foreign Exchange	7.3	13	Foreign Exchange	(7.9)	13
Bonds	6.6	14	Gold	(11.0)	14
Stocks	6.1	15	Silver	(15.9)	15

*Compound annual returns.

Source: Salomon Brothers Inc., "Stock Research; Investment Policy," June 6, 1985, Figure 3.

the 1980s. The decade of the 1970s roughly corresponds to the tangibles boom that accompanied accelerating inflation. Oil, gold, U.S. coins, silver, and stamps had the highest compound returns over the decade, above 20 percent. All of the tangible assets on the list performed better than any financial assets in this inflationary decade.

During rapid disinflation, however, returns on financial assets greatly exceeded those on tangibles. For 1980 to 1985, bonds, stocks, and Treasury bills had higher returns than every category of tangible asset. The worst-performing tangibles have suffered huge losses in the 1980s. Thus, over the long run, including both favorable and unfavorable periods for tangibles, investors should expect a return commensurate with the risk and nonrisk costs and benefits of tangible assets.

Investment Advice

Some tangible assets make attractive investments. First and foremost, many provide aesthetic satisfaction to their owners. In addition, tangibles can give holders prestige, pride, and "psychological income." Assets like stamps, books, coins, and furniture also have historical interest. More practically, tangibles are portable and some are easily stored. Others can be owned in relative secrecy; in case of war, their owners can retain a source of wealth, as the Aufhausers did. As investments, tangibles also are a hedge against inflation and thus can offer attractive returns in an inflationary setting. The negative correlation between returns on financial and tangible assets suggests that, for diversification, investors might hold both kinds of assets.

Yet tangible investments also have disadvantages. The main difficulty with some tangibles is their lack of liquidity, particularly in the short term. For example, markets for stamps and Old Master paintings, while somewhat liquid, are narrower than those for even relatively obscure stocks and bonds. The market for many tangibles is also highly volatile. Changes in taste, major discoveries affecting supply, and general economic conditions such as a recession or a financial-assets boom can make investments in tangibles very risky.

In addition, the markets for tangible assets are segmented. Prices are difficult to determine because close comparables rarely exist. Determining authenticity and avoiding fraud often require the knowledge or assistance of a specialist. All this suggests that nonspecialized investors may find themselves at considerable disadvantage and risk in this market. Consequently, their search and transaction costs are high. In general, the high transaction costs and limited liquidity of tangibles lead rational investors to make long-term rather than short-term investments in these assets.

The physicality of tangibles also decreases their attractiveness as an investment. High maintenance costs are sometimes incurred to avoid deterioration. Valuables like fine furniture age and fall apart; they are not designed to be an investment in the sense that stocks and bonds are. Tangibles also should be insured against theft and damage. Furthermore, when tangibles are moved across international boundaries, import and export tariffs may also reduce their returns. Finally, unlike income from many financial investments, the "income" from tangible assets cannot generally be reinvested to compound their returns.

In evaluating tangibles, investors should not confuse investment with consumption. As a result of their special characteristics, tangibles should be bought by investors who receive special pleasure from them. Since such assets are priced by people who like them the most, this nonpecuniary income is part of the return. An investor who does not receive as much nonpecuniary return will have overpaid for the asset. For the same reasons, tangibles are not appropriate for institutions, aside from museums. In essence, investors should carefully consider whether the expected pecuniary and their own nonpecuniary returns from a particular tangible asset will cover its many costs.

Suggested Reading

Blume, Marshall E., and Jack P. Friedman (eds.): *Encyclopedia of Investments*, Warren, Gorham and Lamont, Boston, 1982. This book of readings describes various aspects of investing in objects such as art, furniture, coins, and stamps, as well as more traditional assets.

Keen, Geraldine: *Money and Art, A Study Based on The Times-Sotheby Index*, G. P. Putnam's Sons, New York, 1971. An overview of how art markets work and what past returns have been.

Taylor, William M.: "The Estimation of Quality-Adjusted Rates of Return in Stamp Auctions," *Journal of Finance*, vol. 38, no. 4, September 1983, pp. 1095–1110. Deals with the technical problem of how to estimate returns on assets of differing quality, traded in discontinuous markets.

15

Options and Futures

Markets for derivative securities like options and futures are important because they enable investors with different attitudes toward risk to contract with each other. Like insurance markets, these side markets allow one group of investors to pay another group for assuming a given risk. Further, in options and futures markets, investors can

- Take positions opposite to their portfolios to hedge against unfavorable price changes
- Lock in current gains without selling the underlying assets
- Generate current income from an asset

On the other hand, risk-taking investors can use these markets to speculate on future price moves for potential profits. Those who wish to speculate can be compensated for assuming risk, and those with more conservative objectives can obtain risk protection for a price.

Primary markets match capital users with capital providers, and secondary markets allow investors to trade their capital positions with other investors. Side markets for options and futures, however, serve primarily to shift risk. No capital is used or provided here except for capital to fill margin requirements; the underlying assets themselves need not be traded. In addition to risk shifting, side markets also function to increase capital liquidity and facilitate pricing.

Options

Before discussing how options are used, a little background on the mechanics and terminology of options and the parties to them is in order.

Option Terminology

An *option* can be defined as a contract that gives the holder, or buyer, the right to buy or sell a certain amount of a given underlying asset at a fixed price—called the *exercise price,* or *strike price*—up to an *expiration,* or *maturity,* date. The two principal types of option contracts are "calls" and "puts." A *call option* is the right to "call away" a specific amount of the underlying asset from the seller, that is, the right to buy the asset at a fixed price. Conversely, a *put option* is a right to sell the underlying asset at a fixed price.

Before standardized contracts came into existence, options had high trading costs because each had to be individually negotiated by the parties and drafted by attorneys. While options can still be negotiated over the counter, most trading now is done in options that are registered or *listed* on various exchanges. Listed options have standard terms, including exercise price and expiration, or maturity, date. The *price* of the option is the amount paid for the option and includes the option premium. The *option premium* is the amount that the option buyer pays the seller for the right to decide later whether or not to buy (if a call) or sell (if a put) the underlying asset. The total price of an option equals the premium plus the *exercise value,* which is the amount of profit (if any) that would be realized if the option were exercised immediately. The terms *seller, maker, writer,* and *issuer* are associated with both puts and calls and are synonymous: all mean the seller of the asset.

The *buyer* or *holder* of a call anticipates that the price of the underlying asset will rise, and the seller of the call expects that it will not. With a put, the buyer's and seller's expectations are reversed; the buyer of a put is betting on a fall in the market price of the underlying asset, while the seller of a put expects that the price will not fall.

A Call Option Example

Call options are more common than puts. In essence, the seller or writer of a call option must sell the underlying asset at the exercise price if the buyer wants to have it, but the buyer of the call does not have to buy the asset. For granting this one-sided right, the option writer demands a payment, or premium, which the buyer is willing to pay. For example, a call option to buy a hundred shares of IBM stock at a strike price of $155 expiring in 2 months might cost $6 when the stock itself is selling at $155. In return for this $6 premium, the seller of the call option must tender the stock at $155 when the buyer chooses, up to the expiration date, regardless of where the stock's market price goes. The buyer of that call has the right, but not the obligation, to buy the IBM shares for $155 until the expiration date.

If the market price of IBM stays at $155 or falls below that amount, the buyer of the call has nothing to gain by exercising the option, and it will expire unexercised, and the buyer will then have lost the money paid for the option. However, if the market price of IBM goes up, the option is valuable. The call buyer has the right to buy the stock at $155, and can then sell the stock in the market at the same time for a higher price, making money on the difference.

If the option is exercised when the stock price is $165, the call buyer will have paid an option premium of $6, but makes $10 on the purchase and sale of the underlying stock ($165 received for the share, less the $155 cost of the share bought from the option writer). Thus the call buyer gains $4. The call writer loses the same $4, since he or she had to deliver the share of stock at $155 when the market price was $165; thus the seller loses $10, less the $6 price of the option received. On a contract of 100 shares, one makes and the other loses $400.

A Put Option Example

The seller, or *writer,* of a put option must buy the underlying asset if the contractual terms are fulfilled, but the buyer of a put does not have to sell the underlying asset. Consider again the situation in which IBM stock is selling at $155. The buyer of a put on IBM with an exercise price of $140 can sell the IBM stock to the put writer for $140 at any time until the expiration date. The put seller receives, say, a $1 premium for writing the option. The buyer of the put may, but does not have to, sell the stock for $140. Of course, this option is valuable only if the price of IBM stock falls below $140; since this drop is unlikely during the 2-month option period, the price of the option is only $1. The buyer of either a put or call can also resell the option before expiration.

Option Markets

Options are available on a wide variety of assets, particularly major stocks, stock indexes, government debt securities, and foreign currencies. In the mid-1980s, the Chicago Board Options Exchange (CBOE) is by far the largest market for stock options and stock index options; in fact, it is larger than all other markets for these securities combined. Over 100 different option contracts are listed on this exchange.

Other option markets are the American, New York, Pacific, and Philadelphia Stock Exchanges. Stock options are also traded internationally. In addition to stock and stock index options, financial options exist on bonds and foreign currencies. Among options on a single stock, IBM options had the highest CBOE volume in 1985. Trading volume of the most popular issues is given in Table 15.1.

Table 15.1. The Most Popular Options in 1985

Contract	Exchange	Approximate Average Daily Volume
Standard & Poor's 100	CBOE	360,000
Major Market Index	AMEX	45,000
IBM Corp	CBOE	39,000
Foreign Currencies	PSE	15,000
Merrill Lynch	AMEX	11,000

CBOE = Chicago Board Options Exchange
AMEX = American Stock Exchange
PSE = Pacific Stock Exchange

Source: Information provided by the exchange named.

A stock index option is based on the level of a specific stock index; these options are settled at the exercise price in cash. Indexes, and consequently options on those indexes, track different segments of the stock market. The S&P 100 index is a value-weighted portfolio of the 100 largest U.S. companies tracked by Standard and Poor's, and thus captures large market moves. Other indexes, like the Computer Technology Index, are sensitive to price changes in particular industrial sectors. During the mid-1980s, the S&P 100 Stock Index option is by far the most actively traded of all option contracts, undoubtedly because the index tracks the movement of the largest and most widely held U.S. companies. It has several times the volume of the next most active option, the Major Market Index. Options on stock indexes are gaining popularity, probably because they provide relatively inexpensive portfolio hedging and diversification.

Option Pricing

Limits on the Value of a Call Option. While the price of an option is determined in the market by many factors, the upper and lower limits of that price are relatively easy to see. Let's examine an IBM call option of any striking price.

What is the maximum value of such an option? Since the call can be converted to a share of IBM stock only upon payment of the exercise price, the option is clearly less valuable than the stock itself. Because the option is only a means to obtain the stock, the option would never sell for more than the stock. Thus the value of the stock is the maximum value of any IBM call. In fact, the key determinant of an option's price is the price of the underlying asset or security.

What, then, is the minimum value of an IBM call option? Since the call buyer cannot be forced to exercise the option at a loss and does have the power to exercise it if there is a gain, it must have some positive value. Thus, at minimum, the option's value is zero. Furthermore, the price of an option is greater than or equal to the price of the stock at the time the option is written minus the exercise price, since the option could be exercised immediately for this difference.

The Movement of Option Prices.   Expressions have evolved to designate the value of options at various points in time. An option is *in-the-money* if the current market price of the underlying asset is above the option's exercise price. When IBM's market price is $160 and the call option's strike price is $155, this option is "in-the-money $5," and should sell for at least that amount. The expression *at-the-money* (or *on-the-money*) means that the market price of the underlying asset is the same as the exercise price of the option. If both the market and strike price were $155, the option would be at-the-money, and the option price would be equal to the premium, i.e., the value of the right to exercise at $155 if the stock moves.

Finally, if a call option is *out-of-the-money,* the current market price of the underlying asset is below the exercise price of the option. Even these options have premium value today since the stock may move in-the-money before expiration. Contracts in-the-money and at-the-money trade most actively. An option's price is equal to its premium if the option is at- or out-of-the-money. The price includes the premium plus the exercise value (the value if exercised now) if the option is in-the-money. Call options which are in-, at-, and out-of-the-money are illustrated in Figure 15.1.

If capital markets are in equilibrium, call options must be priced in such a way that the average return on a perfectly hedged portfolio having no market risk equals the risk-free rate. Fischer Black and Myron Scholes have derived the relationship between the call price and the underlying stock price, known as the Black-Scholes formula. The mathematical formula has six inputs:

- The stock price
- The exercise price
- The present value of the stock's dividends
- The risk-free rate of interest

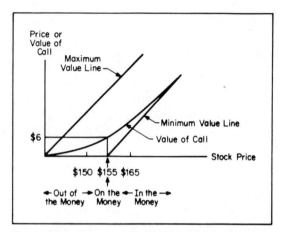

Figure 15.1. The value of a $155 call on IBM. (The *maximum value line:* the value of the call cannot exceed the value of the stock. The *minimum value line:* the value of the call equals the payoff if exercised immediately. The value of a call is related to six factors: the stock price, the exercise price, the present value of the stock's dividends, the risk-free rate of interest, the option's expiration date, and the standard deviation of the price of the stock per unit of time.)

- The option's expiration date
- The standard deviation of the price of the stock per unit of time

Using this formula under conventional assumptions, the value of the call option can be determined precisely.

The price of a put option can be derived from the price of the call. Under three conditions, the price of the put equals the price of the call plus the price of a riskless discount bond, less the price of the stock. These conditions are

1. The put, call, and bond all have the same maturity date.
2. The put, call, and bond have the same exercise price (par value for the bond).
3. The put and call can be exercised only at maturity.

Since option traders actually use the Black-Scholes formula in trading and tend to arbitrage away profit opportunities, the prices of options are extremely close to their values as measured by the formula. Option prices are quoted in the financial pages of major newspapers; in Figure 15.2, the presentation of option quotes is explained.

Exercise Price: For calls, the price at which the option buyer may acquire the stock from the option writer. For puts, the price at which the option buyer may sell the stock to the option writer.

Stock Price: The day's closing price of the underlying stock (the stock on which the option is written).

Option: The name of the underlying security.

Last Option Price: The option's closing price for the day, per share of underlying stock. Most option contracts are for 100 shares, so in the example the actual price of the option contract is 100 x $7 = $700.

Option Expiration Month: The date after which the option can no longer be exercised.

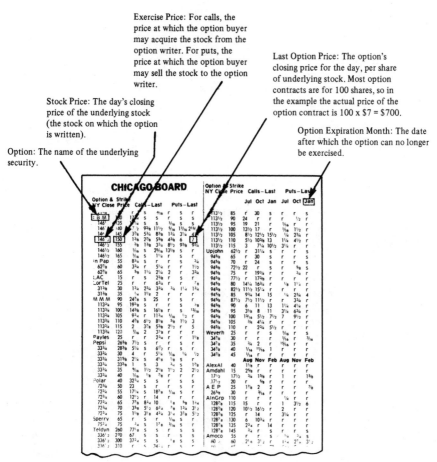

Figure 15.2. How to read options quotes. (*Reprinted by permission of* The Wall Street Journal, © *Dow Jones & Company, Inc. 1986. All rights reserved.*)

Futures

Futures are very different from options. With an option, only one party is obligated to buy or sell. A future is a contract, entered into by two parties, for one to sell and the other to buy an underlying asset at a predetermined price on a specific future date. Both parties must perform under this contract. If the future contract is not traded before expiration, the price specified in the future contract is actually paid when the asset is delivered. Future contracts exist for commodities, financial instruments, stock indexes, and currency. Futures are grouped together with options because both are side markets where risk, not capital, is traded. Further, both markets are "zero sum games"—each dollar of profit to one market participant is a dollar of loss to another. This is in contrast to the primary and secondary capital markets, where all participants gain on average over the long run (a "positive sum game").

The contractual terms for futures contracts, like those for listed options, are standardized; futures markets exist to determine only the price of the various contracts. The exchanges standardize the terms. This standardization allows for greater ease in trading and increases marketability.

Futures Terminology

Profits and losses on futures contracts are recognized daily, when traders' positions are *marked to the market*. This means that the gains or losses on all open futures positions are calculated at the close of each trading day and then posted to each investor's account. Profits from a gain are transferred to the investor's margin account immediately, and losses are deducted from it immediately.

Margins function as performance bonds in futures trading. If the losses are sufficient to bring the margin account below an acceptable level, investors must replenish their accounts to keep their positions in the market open. The demand to replenish the account is referred to as a *margin call*.

Of various future contracts, commodity futures were the first to be publicly traded in the United States. A *commodity* is defined as an article of trade or commerce that can be transported. This asset class consists largely of agricultural products, such as grains and meats, and mining products like petroleum and metals. The most active farm products are corn, wheat, and soybeans; the major industrial product is oil; and the most important metal is gold.

The commodities and stock exchanges have associated *clearinghouses* that take the opposite side of each futures contract as soon as trading is complete, thus guaranteeing performance of the parties, reducing credit risk, and making the futures market more liquid. The parties assume only the default risk of the exchange's inability to complete the contract. The London Metals Exchange's failure to perform on certain contracts in the mid-1980s suggests that this default risk can be real.

Types of Futures Markets

Commodities. Commodity contracts cover standardized units of a given commodity. Uniform terms such as the place of delivery (Chicago) and quality of the commodity (Number 2 red wheat) are spelled out far in advance of the delivery. The quantity of the commodity is also predetermined; one contract of corn is equal to 5000 bushels, one contract of live cattle is equal to 40,000 pounds, and one contract of hogs is equal to 38,000 pounds. Finally, the maturity date, or delivery month, is specified in the contract itself, as in a contract for December corn or a contract of May wheat. Thus, as with other futures, the only market variable in commodity futures is price.

Less than 3 percent of all commodities futures end in delivery. Individuals who have no commercial interest in the underlying commodities and who actively buy and sell commodities futures are referred to as *speculators*. The ultimate buyers and sellers of the commodities, called *hedgers,* pay to shift the risk of price fluctuations to other hedgers or to these investors.

Financial Futures.   Like other futures contracts, financial futures are firm commitments to buy or sell a specific financial instrument during a specified month at the current price established in a continuous auction market. Futures include contracts on the later delivery of fixed-income securities, stock indexes, and foreign currencies. In 1985, Treasury bond futures had an average daily volume of about 155,000 trades, about half the CBOE's daily activity. These bonds were by far the most active financial future, probably because brokerage firms and institutional investors use them to hedge their fixed-income portfolios. Treasury bond futures had a little less than three times the volume of the next most active future—the S&P 500, with an average volume of 57,000 trades daily. Eurodollars, gold, and soybeans were also high-volume futures contracts, as Table 15.2 suggests.

Options on Futures.   Recently, options on futures contracts have been listed on public exchanges. In such a contract, the buyer has an option to call or put the futures contract for a security, currency, or index. Upon exercise, the option writer pays the buyer the difference between the current price of the future contract and the exercise price of the option. In the mid-1980s, options on futures are being traded on major futures exchanges. The most important contracts are options on Treasury bond futures, stock index futures, gold futures, and foreign currency futures.

The Pricing of Futures

Buying a future on an asset like gold is much like buying the gold now for future delivery, and the approximate price of such a future can be derived. If gold were purchased now, the investor would have expended

Table 15.2. The Most Popular Futures in 1985

Contract	Exchange*	Approximate Average Daily Volume
Treasury Bonds	CBT	155,000
Standard & Poor's 500	CME	57,000
Eurodollars	CME	35,000
Gold	CMX	31,000
Soybeans	CBT	29,000
West German marks	CME	26,000

*CME = Chicago Mercantile Exchange.
CBT = Chicago Board of Trade .
CMX = Chicago Monetary Exchange.
Source: Information provided by the exchange named.

an amount equal to its price. Alternatively, the investor could buy a future on gold and invest his or her funds in Treasury bills, earning the riskless rate of interest until the gold is delivered and the payment is made. Therefore, today, the price of the future is equal to the price of the underlying asset, plus interest accrued at the riskless rate, less storage and handling costs. The only differences between the two alternatives are

- The delay of delivery
- The taxes
- The storage
- The transaction costs

Like option prices, future contract prices are quoted in major newspapers; the presentation of such quotes is explained in Figure 15.3.

Hedging with Futures

Commercial firms like producers, merchants, processors, storers, and exporters are typically hedgers in commodities markets. Producers include grain and livestock farmers, oil drillers, and mining companies, while end users include cereal and meat processors, oil refiners, and industrial users of metals.

Consider an example of commodity trading in grain futures in which two hedgers contract with one another. In January, an Iowa farmer may sell futures on September wheat at $3 per bushel, and, at the same time, the Kellogg Company of Battle Creek, Michigan, may buy such a future. Both do this to reduce business risk. If the price falls to $2 in September, the farmer gains, and the cereal producer loses, $5000 ($1 times 5000 bushels per contract) by this early price negotiation.

Frequently, investors are also involved in commodities contracts. Suppose investors learn in July that drought has ruined the September wheat crop in Kansas. Consequently, they believe that wheat will become

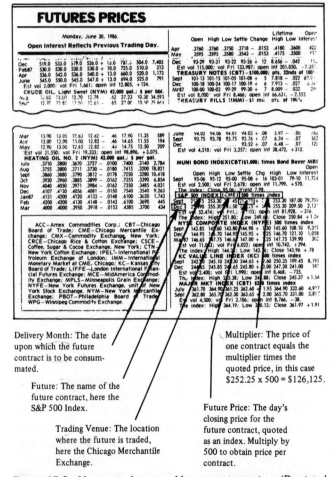

Figure 15.3. How to read quotes of futures contract prices. (*Reprinted by permission of* The Wall Street Journal, © *Dow Jones & Company, Inc. 1986. All rights reserved.*)

increasingly valuable, and buy future contracts on September wheat which are then selling at $4. If wheat futures rise to $5, the investors will profit by the $1 increase.

Using Options and Futures

Hedging

Options and futures contracts can be used to accomplish various objectives. Conservative investors hedge, or protect their current positions, by writing options or selling futures. In taking a position opposite to the one they hold, investors obtain protection against market swings and reduce the volatility of the underlying returns. For example, a hedger like a farmer who owns grain might sell a grain future contract. Because the value of this inventory usually moves with the commodity's future price, this position provides a hedge. Any increase in the grain's price will be offset by a comparable loss on the future contract. Similarly, any decrease in grain's price will be offset by a gain in the value of the future contract. Risk reduction can also be obtained by writing a call; the call itself produces a return to compensate for losses on the underlying asset. The call writer receives a premium for giving up some upside potential on the underlying security.

Portfolio Insurance

A strategy even more conservative than writing options is to buy puts on a portfolio to limit losses. If an option is available on a stock index that perfectly matches the investor's equity portfolio, the investor can obtain portfolio insurance by buying a put on the index. If the value of the index falls below the exercise price of the put, the investor can exercise the put at a profit. This will compensate for any loss in the protected portfolio. The put thus protects the portfolio from downside risk, ensuring that losses will be limited.

Hayne Leland and Mark Rubinstein were the first to realize that securities could be traded to provide "portfolio insurance" similar to that obtained by buying puts. Portfolio insurance can be accomplished by constructing a synthetic put, which adjusts the mix of stocks and bonds or stocks and cash in the portfolio to replicate a put on the portfolio. If the market falls in value, the strategy provides an offsetting gain that limits losses. If the market rises in value, the strategy produces the entire gain, less the synthetic insurance premium, and less trading costs. Portfolio insurance is one of a number of trading strategies called *dynamic asset allocation,* in which assets are traded to achieve various forms of portfolio protection rather than explicitly to beat the market.

While just a few years ago pension funds did not use options and futures at all, now they have billions of dollars in portfolios protected by portfolio insurance. Typically the synthetic put is constructed not by buying and selling stocks, bonds, and cash, but by buying and selling related futures. By committing in advance to buy and sell futures, the funds' managers lock in returns at that date. While losing some possibility of gains if conditions become more favorable, they gain assurance that returns will reach a minimum level, and they limit losses. Portfolio insurance became popular because it provides a way to ensure that the portfolio will always have returns above some specified minimum.

Market Timing

Some investors use options and futures to try to make money on movements of the market as a whole, or to "time the market." One method is to shift from high- to low-beta securities before market declines, and to move from low- to high-beta securities before rises. This can be accomplished in a much easier way using options and futures. Investors might own stocks representing segments of the market and buy index options, or index futures. Because institutional investors control large portfolios of stock, they often try to take advantage of these positions to time the market. But all these strategies depend on the ability to forecast market movements. It is difficult to make a profit by timing the market on average after costs.

Speculation

Finally, investors use options and futures for speculation because these contracts provide a high degree of leverage. This is true because option prices are only a fraction of the total price of the asset optioned, and because futures contracts are purchased on margin. Consequently, options and futures are ideal speculative instruments, with potentially high returns. For example, if investors believe they have early knowledge of a new computer that IBM will introduce, they could buy 100 shares of IBM at $155 per share ($15,500 total) or they could buy options on 100 shares of IBM with a strike price of $155, for $6 per share ($600 total). If the stock's market price zooms up to $175 per share, the buyer of the shares makes $2000 on an outlay of $15,500, a 12.9 percent return. However, the option buyer makes roughly a 333.3 percent return. The approximate equality of the stock's and the option's absolute price changes means that relative to the option's price, the return can be large.

Investors' returns from speculating in options and futures are volatile, ranging from spectacularly high to extremely negative. Option buyers' losses are limited to −100 percent, or the loss of their purchase price; in futures markets, investors can lose more than the margin money they put up. Because contracts are leveraged and because expectations about a particular commodity's supply and demand change rapidly, dramatic fluctuations occur in the value of investors' accounts. Individuals can buy and sell options or futures to assume this risk in hopes of profiting from the market's fluctuations.

Investment Advice

Options and future contracts offer you as an investor the opportunity to shift risks. Options can be priced using financial models that begin with the Black-Scholes formula. The key pricing factor of an option is the price of the underlying security. Options and futures can be used to speculate, to time the market, or to hedge.

When using them to speculate, beware. Options and futures returns are extremely leveraged and very risky. If you buy either calls or puts, you can lose no more than *all* of your investment. If you write uncovered calls or puts, you can lose *more than all* of your initial margin. If you buy or sell uncovered futures, you can also lose more than your entire initial margin.

You can also time the market with index options and index futures. The investor who is bullish on the market either buys calls, writes puts, or buys futures. The investor who is bearish either buys puts, writes calls, or sells futures. Timers usually coordinate their options and futures positions with their overall portfolios. They adjust their positions in options and futures instead of trading the underlying securities.

To hedge, you may follow one of three strategies. You may write calls. This guarantees a small profit, while you forgo large gains. You may also buy puts. In this case, you are insured against large losses. And finally, you may achieve portfolio insurance by either buying puts or through futures trading systems which replicate put positions.

Suggested Reading

Black, Fischer, and Myron Scholes: "The Pricing of Options and Corporate Liabilities," *Journal of Political Economy*, vol. 81, no. 3, May–June 1973, pp. 637–654. The classic work which derives the option pricing model.
Cox, John C., and Mark Rubinstein: *Option Markets*, Prentice-Hall, Inc., Englewood Cliffs, N.J., 1985. Presents options theory and gives a detailed description of how options are used in practice.

Figlewski, Stephen, in collaboration with Kose John and John Merrick: *Hedging with Financial Futures for Institutional Investors: From Theory to Practice,* Ballinger Publishing Co., Cambridge, Mass., 1986. Describes how financial futures can be used in various trading strategies.

Leland, Hayne E., and Mark Rubinstein: "Replicating Options with Positions in Stocks and Cash," *Financial Analysts Journal,* July–August 1981. Clearly presents synthetic portfolio insurance.

PART 5

Constructing Your Portfolio

16

Investing: The Institutional Portfolio

Managers of institutional portfolios invest money held by pension funds, insurance companies, endowments, foundations, mutual funds, and wealthy individuals. This chapter covers pension funds, endowments, and foundations since these particular funds have a common theme: their investments are exempt from taxation.

Because most institutional portfolios are large, have long time horizons, and are accorded tax-exempt status, institutional investors have similar goals and find it economical to hire full-time money managers to invest these funds. Until recently, such managers took a limited view of the world's capital markets, and therefore did not fully exploit all investment possibilities. This chapter provides a framework that will allow institutional investors to improve investment results by taking a global approach to capital markets.

The Evolution of Pension Fund Management

Pension assets comprise by far the largest part of institutional investments. Pension assets include money to fund the retirement benefits for employees of corporations, states, and municipalities. This is money contributed over the years into corporate, union, and government-sponsored pension and profit-sharing plans. Such portfolios summed to approximately $1.3 trillion at the beginning of 1986.

Pension funds are deferred wages, intended to be paid as retirement benefits. Upon retirement, an employee is entitled to either a lump sum or a guaranteed pension annuity for a period of time, which is usually the employee's life. In return, employers expect that employees will settle for a lower current wage than they might otherwise demand. The U.S. government has granted these investments tax-exempt status to encourage workers and employers to contribute to private pension plans.

The Development of Pension Plans

The first private pension plan was established in the United States for employees of American Express in 1875. This plan and others like it were intended to secure the loyalty of workers, particularly those who had served the same company for years and were valuable to it, and possibly to competitors too.

In the late nineteenth century, most pension, accident, or sickness benefits paid to employees were acts of corporate charity. The formalization of pension plans secured the work force against economic ruin and was thus socially desirable. Few plans, however, had assets designated for these purposes. Payments to retired or disabled workers were usually made from general corporate funds, and thus were backed solely by the firm's ability to pay.

Since the 1920s, segregated accounts to hold dedicated pension assets have become more prevalent. As the pool of dedicated funds grew, more and more plan sponsors hired money managers to actively manage the funds in these accounts. Corporations found that prudent management of pension assets could enhance the value of the funds both to the firm and to its employees.

Until recently, pension funds were protected only by trust law and state legislation. Under "prudent man" rules, those who managed the money of others were held to the standard of care of a "prudent man," not merely a "reasonable man." Consequently, pension investments were conservative and income-oriented. Investment attention was focused on individual assets, the traditional concern of trust law, not the total portfolio.

ERISA's Effect on Pension Fund Management

The beginning of the 1960s was a milestone period for the management of institutional portfolios. In academia, modern portfolio theory was evolving, emphasizing the construction of "efficient portfolios." Researchers found that the interrelationships of individual securities were even more important in determining the risk of a portfolio than the risks of the individual assets. Concern thus shifted from the risk of individual securities to the risk of the total portfolio.

Many of the new portfolio management ideas were incorporated into the Employee Retirement Income Security Act of 1974 (ERISA). This landmark act swept away the conflicting patchwork of "prudent man" rules and substituted professional standards which emphasized the total portfolio. As a result of this legislation, nontraditional assets such as real estate, international securities, and venture capital could now legally be held in pension portfolios. Intensive academic research on portfolio management, the availability of computing power, and the ERISA legislation caused dramatic changes in the composition of institutional portfolios.

Basically, there are two types of pension plans. One type promises specified benefits, typically in the form of a monthly retirement pension, based on levels of compensation and years of service. Contributions to the plan are actuarially calculated to provide the promised benefits. This is referred to as a *defined-benefit pension plan*. The second type is a *defined contribution plan*. In this case, the employer promises a specific contribution on behalf of each participant, usually expressed as a percentage of compensation. These contributions are unrelated to the employer's profits.

By the end of 1985, nearly 23,000 employee benefit funds existed in the United States. In Table 16.1, the types of assets held by such corpo-

Table 16.1. Asset Class Breakdowns for Major Institutional Fund Categories, 1985

Asset Classes	Institutional Fund Categories		
	Corporate	Union	Government
Cash Equivalents	8.5%	14.0%	9.6%
Bonds	23.3	40.4	43.2
Guaranteed Investment Contracts	8.5	6.2	0.5
Mortgages	0.9	6.7	11.9
Equity	49.8	28.3	32.1
Real Estate Equity	3.9	2.7	2.0
International	1.5	0.2	0.5
Venture Capital	0.4	0.1	0.1
Oil and Gas	0.1	0.0	0.0
General Insurance Account	3.1	1.4	0.1
	100.0%	100.0%	100.0%

Source: *Money Market Directory*, Money Market Directories Inc., Charlottesville, Virginia, 1986, p. xiv.

rate, union, and government pension funds are described. Note that each of the three types of funds holds only a small percentage of its assets in real estate, venture capital, and international stocks and bonds. Most pension funds are concentrated in traditional assets like U.S. stocks, bonds, and cash equivalents. Of the three types of pension funds, corporate plans have the most aggressive, or riskiest, positions due to their greater emphasis on equities.

A Decision-Making Framework for Portfolio Construction

To the degree that large pension plans represent institutional portfolios generally, such portfolios have earned embarrassingly low returns. Table 16.2, for example, shows that the median large plan performed worse than all assets and portfolios except Treasury bills over the last 16 years. Furthermore, such plans have received little reward for the risks assumed; the Sharpe ratio of the median large pension plan, which is a measure of the amount of return obtained per unit of risk, is the lowest on the table. As a result, pension funds have lost ground relative to other investors over the period. This unfortunate performance is the result of a focus on individual assets rather than the aggregate portfolio; by toiling around in the roots, plan sponsors and their money managers hoped that they could make the overall portfolio grow. As the results show, this approach has been ineffective.

Institutional investors should address the investment decisions that will have the biggest impact on their portfolios' overall performance. In particular, they should give attention to four critical decisions:

1. Which asset classes to include in the portfolio
2. What policy weights to assign to those classes over the long term
3. What short-term strategic weights to assign to these classes
4. Which manager(s) and management strategies to use within and/or across asset classes

The first two decisions are issues of policy and lead to the creation of benchmarks for the portfolio. The last two involve active management, specifically market timing and security selection.

Table 16.2. Median Large Pension Plan Performance, December
31, 1969 to December 31, 1985

| Asset Class or Portfolio | Annualized | | | Annualized | |
	Geometric Return	Arithmetic Return	Standard Deviation	Sharpe Ratio[1]	Coefficient Of Variation[2]
Median Large Plan[3]	8.30%	9.33%	13.84%	0.033	1.48
Wilshire 5000 Index[4]	10.36	12.30	19.01	0.132	1.55
S&P 500 Index[5]	10.08	11.72	17.54	0.127	1.50
Int'l. Equity	11.65	13.57	19.02	0.200	1.40
Venture Capital	12.70	21.17	41.06	0.118	1.94
Domestic Bonds	9.52	9.91	8.77	0.191	0.89
Int'l. Dollar Bonds	10.21	10.46	7.01	0.337	0.67
Nondollar Bonds	10.20	10.90	11.71	0.202	1.07
U.S. Real Estate	10.86	10.88	1.83	1.646	0.17
30 Day T-Bills	7.84	7.85	1.42	0.000	0.18
Multiple Markets Index[6]	11.34	12.20	12.75	0.274	1.05
Personal Consumption Deflator[7]	6.43	6.44	1.41	NA	0.22

[1]The Sharpe ratio is a measure of risk-adjusted return. With a high Sharpe ratio, the asset class or portfolio offers high return for its risk, and higher ratios are desirable. It is computed as (geometric return less the 30-day Treasury bill return) divided by the standard deviation of those returns.

[2]The coefficient of variation is also a measure of risk-adjusted return. With a high coefficient of variation, the asset class or portfolio has high risk for its return, and a low ratio is desirable. It is computed as the standard deviation of the return over the arithmetic mean return.

[3]SEI Funds Evaluation Services produces a data base with quarterly returns of large pension plans called the "Large Plan Universe."

[4]The Wilshire 5000 Index is an index of total returns on 5,000 common stocks listed on the NYSE, AMEX, and OTC.

[5]The S&P 500 Index is an index of the market prices of 500 major U.S. stocks, as selected by Standard and Poor's. This index has been adjusted to include reinvestment of dividends. It thus gives an indication of total returns on major U.S. equities.

[6]The Multiple Markets Index is an index of expected returns on a portfolio of various asset classes typically held by institutional investors, with weightings determined by optimization procedures.

[7]The personal consumption deflator is a measure of inflation rates used to convert nominal to real GNP. This measure is different from the CPI.

The Conceptual Matrix

These four key decisions can be viewed as a matrix, which is illustrated in Figure 16.1. This matrix is divided into four quadrants, each representing a key decision.

The bottom right-hand portion, or Quadrant I, is labeled *policy return*. In this case, the policy return is the fund's benchmark return over the long-term planning horizon. Policy decisions concern both the asset classes included in the portfolio and the normal, or policy, weights to assign to them. The policy return is computed as the sum of returns for

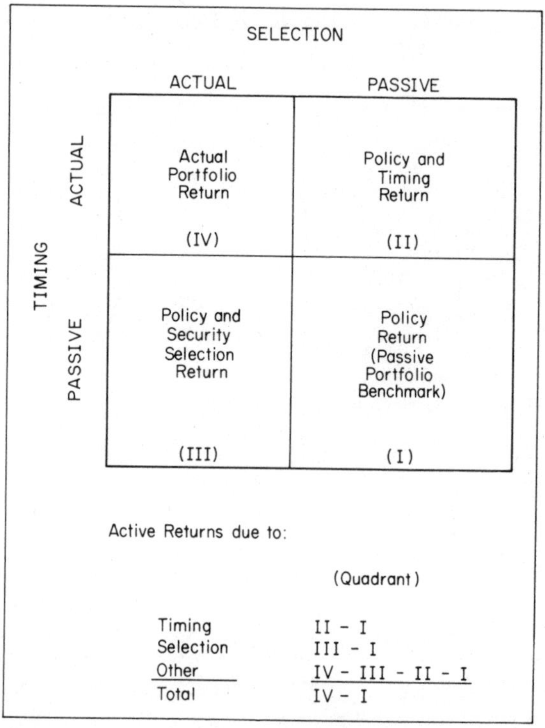

Figure 16.1. A simplified framework for return accountability.

all asset classes included in the portfolio, where each class's return is its *policy weight* times its *benchmark return.* (The benchmark return for an asset class is the return on a diversified, well-constructed index of the securities in that class.)

The upper right-hand corner, or Quadrant II, is called the *policy and timing return. Timing* in this instance is the strategic under- or over-weighting of an asset class relative to its policy weight. By altering the policy weights, timing temporarily changes the mix of assets in the portfolio to enhance returns or reduce risk. Thus the asset mix is altered in an attempt to achieve incremental returns relative to the policy return. Mathematically, the return from "policy plus timing" is the sum of the returns for all asset classes, where each class's return is its *actual weight* times its *benchmark return.*

The lower left-hand corner, or Quadrant III, is the returns from *policy and security selection. Security selection* is an attempt to select securities within an asset class which outperform the class. Mathematically, the return from policy and security selection is the sum of returns for all asset classes, where each class's return is its *actual return* times its *policy weight.*

The upper left-hand corner, or Quadrant IV, shows the actual return of the portfolio for the period. This is computed by summing the returns of all asset classes, where each class's return is its *actual weight* for the period times its *actual return.*

Historical Returns on Institutional Portfolios, Evaluated with the Matrix

To what extent can the four key investment decisions, represented by the four corners of the matrix, explain returns on institutional portfolios? To answer this question, returns on 91 corporate pension plans, those in SEI Corporation's Large Plan Universe, are analyzed. Since no data on policy weights exist, the 10-year average weights for each asset class in each plan are used. Those derived weights are shown in Table 16.3.

Returns from active management are shown in Table 16.4 and derived from the mean returns for each of the four quadrants. These pension plans as a group lost an average of 0.66 percent per year when the weights of the asset classes were altered through time, and 0.36

Table 16.3. Asset Classes as a Percentage of the Portfolios of Ninety-One Large Pension Plans, 1974–1983

All Asset Classes	Average	Minimum	Maximum	Standard Deviation
Common Stock	57.5%	32.3%	86.5%	10.9%
Bonds	21.4	0.0	43.0	9.0
Cash Equivalents	12.4	1.8	33.1	5.0
Other	8.6	0.0	53.5	8.3
	100.0%			
Stocks, Bonds, and Cash Only				
Common Stock	62.9%	37.9%	89.3%	10.6%
Bonds	23.4	0.0	51.3	9.4
Cash Equivalents	13.6	2.0	35.0	5.2
	100.0%			

Source: SEI Corp. Large Plan Universe.

Table 16.4. Returns on Ninety-One Large Pension Plans, 1974–1983

Source of Return	Mean Annualized Return
I. Policy Return	10.11%
II. Policy/Timing Return	9.44
III. Policy/Selection Return	9.75
IV. Actual Return	9.01
Returns from Active Management due to:	
Timing (II − I)	−0.66%
Security Selection (III − I)	−0.36
Other (IV − III − II − I)	−0.07
Total (IV − I)	−1.10 %

Definitions:
Policy return is the benchmark return assuming long-term class weights and traditional asset classes. *Timing* is the short-term alteration of weights of asset classes. *Security selection* is choosing assets within an asset class that outperform the class. *Actual return* is the real class weights times the actual return on the class.

percent per year from selection of securities within the asset classes. The cross product of timing and selection, called *other,* resulted in an additional loss of 0.07 percent per year. As a result of such management efforts, these 91 plans experienced an overall annual *loss* of 1.10 percent per year relative to a benchmark. To make matters worse, investors paid fees to managers for these services. Clearly, the management of institutional portfolios needs dramatic improvement.

The power of the key investment decisions to affect the returns of pension plans is illustrated by the analysis of variance in Table 16.5. The percentages were calculated by regressing each plan's actual total return, Quadrant IV, against returns as described above for the other quadrants. *Policy returns,* Quadrant I, explains on average 93.6 percent of the total variation in actual return, with a range of 75.5 to 98.6 percent. The returns due to Quadrant II, *policy plus timing,* added modestly to the explained variance, with 95.3 percent, as did *policy and security selection,* with 97.8 percent. Thus the total returns of these pension plans are most affected by decisions concerning investment policy; active management, while important, adds far less to a plan's returns than do policy decisions.

Table 16.5. Variances on Ninety-One Large Pension Plans, 1974–1983

Source of Return	Percent of Return Variance Explained by Activity
I. Policy Return	93.6 %
II. Policy/Timing Return	95.3
III. Policy/Selection Return	97.8
IV. Actual Return	100.0 %

Variance Explained by Various Investment Activities				
	Average	Minimum	Maximum	Standard Deviation
Policy	93.6%	75.5%	98.6%	4.4%
Policy/Timing	95.3	78.7	98.7	2.9
Policy/Selection	97.8	80.6	99.8	3.1
Actual Return	100.0	100.0	100.0	0.0

Note: This table is based on 91 regression equations. For the resulting r-squareds, a minimum, maximum, and average were computed. The estimated standard deviation of the residual is shown.

Policy Decisions Concerning Portfolio Construction

The 10-year average performance of the SEI group of 91 pension plans was dismal, and calls attention to the need for better management. This can best be achieved by focusing on policy decisions about asset classes and policy weights, rather than on security selection.

Policy Decisions on Asset Classes

The first policy decision is which asset classes to include in the portfolio. What is required is a broad criterion applied uniformly across classes to distinguish appropriate from inappropriate assets. The goal is to select classes that provide satisfactory returns for their associated risks. Satisfactory returns can result from high average returns on the asset class or from a manager's extraordinary skill in achieving good returns on certain assets in a poor market. The first is easier than the second.

The primary asset classes currently held in institutional portfolios presumably merit consideration. In the United States, those asset classes include domestic stocks, bonds, real estate, venture capital, and cash equivalents, as well as foreign stocks and dollar-denominated and non-dollar-denominated bonds.

Decisions on Policy Weights

The second key decision is what policy weights to assign to the asset classes. The *weight* is the percentage of the portfolio to be invested in each asset class. A *policy weight* is the weight used in the absence of any specific insights about the short-term performance of the class. The policy weight is also the appropriate default weight, or the percentage of the portfolio normally held in the asset class.

Policy weights are set in one of three ways. In the first approach, the proportions of the asset classes in the world portfolio are determined and used as weights. The second method uses information about the investor's unique circumstances to set weights. In the third approach, risk/return optimization determines policy weights.

The Market-Value Approach.   When using the market-value approach, the market-value weights of all investment-grade asset classes are determined, and their percentages computed; these percentages become policy weights. As shown in Figure 16.2, the world's investment assets as a percentage of the total in 1985 were: 18.1 percent U.S. stocks, 20.8 percent dollar-denominated bonds, 11.6 percent U.S. real estate, 8.0 percent U.S. cash equivalents, 14.9 percent foreign stocks, and 26.6 percent international bonds. Using this approach, these percentages would become the policy weights.

The assumptions underlying the capital asset pricing model, described

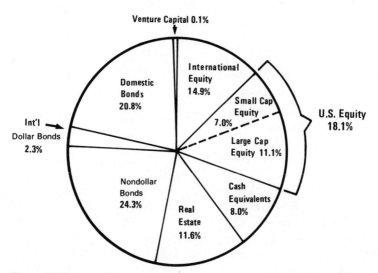

Figure 16.2. Investable capital market as of December 31, 1985—$13.7 trillion.

in Chapter 4, suggest that market-value weights are appropriate. According to this theory, every investor should hold the market portfolio to minimize risk relative to return.

Customized Policy Approach. The second method of setting policy weights is based on new equilibrium theory, also described in Chapter 4. According to this theory, investors have different tax situations, institutional constraints, and time horizons. With the customized approach, investors must analyze such factors as their tax situations, investment skills, and time horizons to determine whether they have any unique characteristics. Institutional investors must also understand their organization's attitude toward risk, future liabilities, and integration of plan assets with corporate assets.

An institution's tolerance for risk varies in part with its time horizon. An organization with a long-term focus may be willing to assume some high-risk investments. The nature of the institution's liabilities and its policy toward these obligations can also differ. Some firms, for example, carefully estimate future cash outflows and buy assets that match the duration of these liabilities. Finally, the way in which pension assets fit into the corporation's assets can also be unique. A real estate construction company, for example, may want to avoid real estate in its pension portfolio because the corporation is already exposed to risks associated with real estate. If the real estate market does poorly, its business will suffer; therefore its pension plan should be weighted away from real estate so that it will not suffer too.

Risk/Return Optimization. A third approach to setting policy weights was initially proposed by Harry Markowitz and is referred to as *portfolio optimization*. With portfolio optimization, or *mean-variance optimization* as it is sometimes called, a frontier of portfolios is constructed which offer an array of risk/return possibilities, with minimum risk for a given expected return. No one portfolio dominates any other, and if the equilibrium risk/return relationships change, dynamic asset allocation policies would be required.

Optimization is a quantitative approach to the problem of determining policy weights. While the answers are apparently very precise, they are quite sensitive to changes in inputs and to the form of inputs themselves. Optimization is most effective when investors have either short or relatively undefined time horizons.

One example of the optimization approach is the Multiple Markets Index (MMI), developed by First Chicago Investment Advisors. The inputs for the MMI model are described in Tables 16.6 and 16.7. The forecasted returns and correlations in these tables were developed by

Table 16.6. Illustrative Long-Term Expectations:
Optimization Inputs*

	Geometric Return	Less Passive Fee	Realizable Geometric Return**	Risk**
Large Cap Stocks	12.30%	.10%	12.20%	16.50%
Small Cap Stocks	14.05	.20	13.85	22.00
Int'l. Stocks	12.85	.25	12.60	20.50
Venture Capital	21.50	2.00	19.50	40.00
Domestic Bonds	8.80	.10	8.70	8.50
Int'l Dollar Bonds	8.75	.10	8.65	8.00
Nondollar Bonds	8.80	.15	8.65	11.00
Real Estate	11.30	.80	10.50	14.00
T-Bills	6.50	.00	6.50	1.50

*Assumes 5% inflation and a 1.5% real risk-free rate.
**Optimization inputs.

Source: First Chicago Investment Advisors, early 1986 forecasts.

First Chicago, and differ from historical returns and correlations presented elsewhere in this book. In the MMI example, two constraints are placed on the optimization. First, all weights are required to be nonnegative, and second, the maximum weight for venture capital is set at 5 percent to allow for this asset's small size relative to the world market. From the array of possible portfolios, a portfolio with risk equal to that of the typical pension fund (assumed to be 60 percent stocks and 40 percent bonds) is selected as the MMI, which gives the suggested policy weights for pension plans.

Table 16.7. Long-Term Forecasts of Correlations
between Asset Classes

	1	2	3	4	5	6	7	8	9
1. Large Capitalization Equity	1.00								
2. Small Capitalization Equity	.85	1.00							
3. International Equity	.55	.55	1.00						
4. Venture Capital	.40	.45	.55	1.00					
5. Domestic Bonds	.45	.40	.30	.15	1.00				
6. International Dollar Bonds	.45	.40	.35	.20	.90	1.00			
7. Nondollar Fixed Income	.15	.25	.75	.40	.40	.40	1.00		
8. Real Estate	.50	.55	.50	.45	.30	.35	.30	1.00	
9. Cash Equivalents	.00	.00	.00	.00	.00	.00	.00	.00	1.00

Source: First Chicago Investment Advisors, early 1986. These forecasts are based on historical correlations, such as those presented in Table 3.2, as well as judgment about future trends.

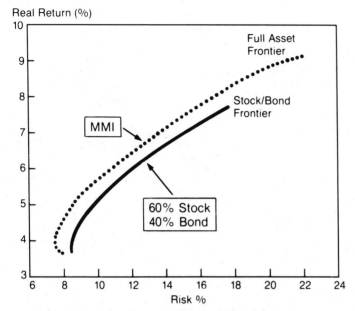

Real Return (%)

Risk %

Figure 16.3. Attainable efficient frontiers (includes passive fee).

The required returns, standard deviations, and correlation coefficients used in the optimization process are all long-term estimates of First Chicago Investment Advisors. Long-term estimates are used because the process of setting policy requires continuity. Policy weights should not be upset by short-term fluctuations in capital markets.

In Figure 16.3, an array of risk/return portfolios are graphed. The lower line, called the *stock/bond frontier,* is the risk/return mix from all possible combinations of stocks and bonds in a portfolio. The upper line, called *the MMI full asset frontier,* reflects the return and risk combinations available from all investment-grade assets. Clearly, the full asset frontier offers more return per unit of risk than the limited stock/bond frontier. Furthermore, the full asset frontier gives a wider range of risk/ return options. Together, these are powerful arguments for taking a global approach to investing.

An index, such as the MMI, used to set policy weights should have risk similar to that of the typical pension plan. The MMI policy weights are 45 percent domestic stocks, 19 percent dollar-denominated fixed-income securities, 15 percent U.S. real estate, 5 percent U.S. venture capital, 10 percent foreign stocks, and 6 percent foreign bonds. As Figure 16.4 shows, the MMI performed much better than the typical large plan with no additional risk.

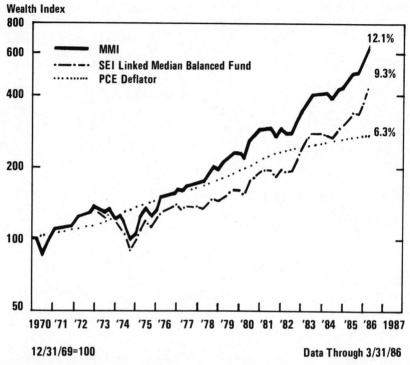

Figure 16.4. Multiple Markets Index. (*Source: First Chicago Investment Advisors.*)

Active Management of Portfolios

Strategic Allocation to Set Short-Term Policy

Occasionally, the asset mix of a portfolio determined by investment policy may be shifted to take advantage of short-term opportunities in the marketplace. This is called *strategic asset allocation,* or market timing. Opportunities might arise from the underpricing of certain assets relative to the market. When current investments promise returns in excess of policy benchmarks, the portfolio can be altered temporarily to capture these anticipated profits.

To constrain strategic asset allocation, policy decisions must be made regarding minimum and maximum positions of asset classes in the portfolio. For example, policy benchmarks and strategic ranges used by First Chicago Investment Advisors are illustrated in Table 16.8. Factors which

Table 16.8. Sample Asset Allocation Guidelines

	Policy Norm*	Current Strategy	Strategy Ranges
Common Stocks	55%	X	30% – 80%
Domestic Equity	45	X	20% – 75%
Large Cap.	30	X	15% – 45%
Special Equity	15	X	5% – 30%
International Equity	10	X	5% – 15%
Venture Capital	5	X	3% – 6%
Fixed Income	25	X	10% – 40%
Domestic Bond	15	X	5% – 30%
Int'l Dollar Bonds	4	X	2% – 10%
Nondollar Bonds	6	X	2% – 10%
Real Estate Equity	15	X	12% – 18%
Cash Management	0	X	0% – 45%
	100%	100%	

•Multiple Markets Index Weights.

Source: First Chicago Investment Advisors.

may influence the size of ranges are the opportunities presented by shifts in capital markets, assumptions about transaction and other costs, and determination of the extent to which the portfolio should be altered to profit from special opportunities.

Approaches to Strategic Asset Allocation

Institutional investors primarily use four techniques to determine when to make short-term adjustments in their portfolios:

- Business cycle anticipation
- Liquidity anticipation
- Technical analysis
- Comparative valuation of assets

The First Three Techniques. Using the first method, the manager tries to anticipate how investment markets will react to business cycle recoveries and recessions. In the second, the liquidity technique, the manager shifts from financial to real assets just before the money supply increases due to changes in Federal Reserve policy or overseas investment. This causes prices of financial assets to fall and those of real assets to rise. In the third system, managers attempt to use the past returns of asset classes to identify trends and patterns.

Comparative Valuation of Assets. The first three methods of strategic asset allocation all depend to some extent on the fourth approach, the comparative valuation of asset classes. In this technique, expectations of returns for various asset classes are compared objectively to each other and to policy benchmarks. Long-term equilibrium returns on various classes of assets can be used to judge the relative attractiveness of current returns on asset classes.

The global investor who can speak all languages and interpret information from all sources is best suited to use comparative valuation. Nevertheless, the language of finance is most useful in this endeavor, particularly if quantitative measures of risk and reward are used to set policy weights.

When comparative valuation of assets is undertaken, common macroeconomic assumptions should be used. In computing the values of various asset classes, factors such as economic growth, inflation, business risk, and interest rate risk should be held constant across all classes. If the bond market is valued using a 5 percent expected inflation figure while the real estate market is valued with 10 percent expected inflation, erroneous results will be generated.

To make smart short-term decisions about strategic asset allocation, money managers should have many attributes:

1. They ought to be able to integrate their strategic framework with basic policy assumptions.

2. They should have an accurate assessment of their ability to capture profit opportunities.

3. They ought to be knowledgeable about capital markets, broadly defined, i.e., to have perspective on the relative attractiveness of various assets in those markets.

4. They should tightly control macroeconomic assumptions for all asset classes.

5. They ought to have in-depth knowledge about individual asset classes.

6. They should obtain the inputs used for comparative valuation of asset classes from independent sources.

7. They ought to have a long-term perspective in which to interpret ongoing performance results.

Implementation of Investment Policies

Book after book has been written about how to pick winning stocks or how to make a killing in real estate. Such advice is avoided here. The performance advantage comes from allocating funds between asset classes and across countries, not from selecting individual securities. Let's now focus on practical aspects of handling tax-exempt portfolios.

Asset Returns as Benchmarks for Security Selection

The goal of security selection is to build a portfolio of individual assets with returns that exceed benchmarks for their classes—for instance, the Wilshire 5000 (a broad index of returns on 5000 common stocks) or the Shearson Lehman Government/Corporate Bond Index (a widely used index of returns on a portfolio of U.S. bonds). Most managers of institutional portfolios spend the greatest portion of their time and effort trying to beat such benchmarks. While important, this function may receive disproportionate attention.

In fact, policy benchmarks should be used to establish hurdle rates for comparative valuation of individual securities. The equilibrium returns of various asset classes, already used for policy benchmarks, can also be used as hurdle rates to choose securities that offer unusual opportunities. When securities are expected to earn a short-term rate of return equivalent to their equilibrium rates, managers should hold the default or neutral portion of such securities.

Use of Multiple Investment Managers

Many plan sponsors use several money managers to invest funds in similar assets. There is one sponsor who employs approximately 30 managers for U.S. stocks alone. Yet multiple managers may be costly. Plan sponsors give several rationalizations to justify the extra costs associated with multiple managers.

First, some plan sponsors believe that using multiple managers is the best way to diversify the risk of errors in judgment and to gain access to the knowledge of many professionals. Managers who specialize in submarkets may, in fact, have special insights. By implication, the argument runs, a collection of these specialists will be less prone to serious errors than any one manager. In the second place, plan sponsors may divide funds among money managers to give them all incentives to perform. After receiving a large fee for managing a whole pension plan's assets, a small investment manager may be more interested in planning an extended vacation than in working hard to provide superior results for the client. Therefore, the plan sponsor maximizes each manager's performance by distributing funds among various managers and encouraging competition.

On the other hand, the use of multiple managers has important drawbacks. First, the plan sponsor incurs extra transaction and fee-related costs. Second, such division may diversify away not only random errors but also valuable opportunities. Finally, the plan sponsor may be foreclosing the opportunity for coordinated judgments about the overall portfolio, with the result being a collection of uncoordinated investments or, possibly, a "closet index fund" differing little from a passive portfolio except in having high costs.

The Importance of a Coordinated Approach to the Total Portfolio

If institutional funds are handled by multiple managers, no one manager can make consistent estimates of macroeconomic factors affecting the entire portfolio. With the advent of arbitrage pricing theory (APT), described in Chapter 4, a few plan sponsors have become interested in the development of "factor" portfolios. APT suggests that security returns may—in differing degrees—be sensitive to various factors, such as inflation or the stock market. The ability to make value-added judgments on the basis of such factors may become important to future profits. Investors who successfully adjust the factor exposure of their aggregate portfolios over time may be able to earn the highest risk-adjusted returns. More importantly, portfolios in which factor correlations are not identified have unplanned and unrewarded risks. While statistical tests indicate that such factors do exist, the practical applications of the theory are not yet clear.

The authors contend that institutional managers should focus on the aggregate portfolio. Factors such as inflation trends, tax changes, and interest rate fluctuations should affect investment decisions at all levels—policy determination, strategic asset allocation, and security selection. When several managers handle different parts of an institution's portfolio, these thematic opportunities may be lost. It is difficult if not impossible for several managers to use macroeconomic information consistently.

Most very large plans, with billions of dollars under management, need an integrated approach. Selection of specific securities contributes less and less to the returns of such portfolios as their size increases. Yet institutions with large pension portfolios are most likely to use multiple managers, and thus least likely to have a consistent, coordinated approach to pension investments. Large plan sponsors need managers who focus on critical decisions, those with the greatest impact on aggregate wealth. A theme-based or factor-based investment approach has a greater potential effect on the returns of large portfolios than security-by-security analysis.

Investment Advice

To be a successful institutional investor, you should focus on four key decisions:

- What asset classes to include in your portfolio
- What policy weights to assign to those classes
- How to adjust those weights to capture possible short-run profit opportunities
- How to select securities within each asset class

The first of these decisions is by far the most important, explaining over 93 percent of the variation in portfolio performance.

While making these decisions, you should maintain a global perspective on capital markets, across assets and across borders. Intimate knowledge of each market is desirable but by no means essential. You can invest in a variety of securities in each class to diversify your exposure to each market's risks. Investors who put all of their investment eggs in one basket—be it one asset class or one country—assume far greater risks than those who diversify. To take the conservative approach, you should diversify across countries and among asset classes. If global investing and diversification among asset classes are your long-term policy objectives, you can use benchmark returns and policy weights based on these principles. You can also use them as the basis for strategic allocation decisions, to capture short-term profit opportunities.

Suggested Reading

Periodicals and Directories

Institutional Investor, Institutional Investor Systems, New York. A monthly trade journal on institutional investment.

Pensions and Investment Age, Crain Communications Inc., Chicago. A biweekly publication for institutional portfolio managers.

Money Market Directory, 1986, Money Market Directories Inc., Charlottesville, Va., 1986. This annual directory contains names and addresses of pension plan sponsors, money managers, research firms, and other money management professionals.

Books and Articles

Brinson, Gary P., L. Randolph Hood, Jr., and L. Gilbert Beebower: "The Determinants of Portolio Performance," *Financial Analysts Journal,* July–August 1986, pp. 39–44. The performance measurement techniques in this chapter are detailed here.

Brinson, Gary P., Jeffrey J. Diermeier, and Gary G. Schlarbaum: "A Composite Portfolio Benchmark for Pension Plans," *Financial Analysts Journal,* March–April 1986, pp. 15–24. Describes the Multiple Markets Index, which measures the composite performance of nine asset classes generally available to institutional investors.

Latimer, Murray W.: *Industrial Pension Systems,* Industrial Relations Counselors, New York, 1932. The first comprehensive review of the U.S. pension system, detailing the inception of modern pension plans.

Markowitz, Harry M.: *Portfolio Selection: Efficient Diversification of Investments,* John Wiley and Sons, Inc., New York, 1959. Classic study presenting the mathematics of diversification.

17

Investing: The Taxable Portfolio

Historical returns from various investment markets are described and their characteristics identified to provide the basis for sound financial advice. While the previous chapter discusses the management of an institutional portfolio, this one covers the management of a personal portfolio. Both the typical size of investments and the tax status of the returns on these portfolios differ.

While the dollar volume of typical transactions in institutional portfolios is much higher than those in individual portfolios, it is the different tax status of their income that has the most impact on investment choices. Unlike the returns earned by pension funds and most other institutional funds, those earned by individuals are subject to tax. Consequently, individuals have their own investment incentives and opportunities. The 12 guidelines outlined below are tailored to individual portfolios, and provide a synthesis of the findings presented in earlier chapters.

1. Know that background in economic history, grasp of economic concepts, and analysis make an informed investor.

Equilibrium and efficient markets. When markets are in equilibrium, the supply of an asset equals demand for it. When markets are efficient, the price of an asset reflects its true, underlying value. Both the capital asset pricing model and arbitrage pricing theory are useful in understanding price relationships when equilibrium exists and markets are efficient.

Since assets are usually efficiently priced, you should generally be suspicious of claims that an investment offers extraordinary profits. If opportunities exist, you must also act quickly. However, what appears to be a profit opportunity may really be an investment with hidden risks.

In practice, markets may be somewhat inefficient because investors must pay for information, there are costs to arbitrage, and investors have differing and in some cases misperceived abilities. If you can find these inefficient niches speedily, you can make money until others discover them too.

Risk and return. Recognize the relationship between asset characteristics such as risk and the asset's returns. In general, you can expect that your returns will vary with an investment's risk and other characteristics, such as its tax attributes, transaction costs, and marketability. While historically some assets have had superior returns over some periods—returns cannot be fully explained by their risk and other characteristics—in the long run there appears to be a direct relationship between the economic characteristics of assets and the returns they have produced. All of this indicates that you should invest with a long-term horizon to weather the economic ups and downs.

2. Know yourself.

Investment objectives. Perhaps the first step in financial self-knowledge is to identify your objectives, financial goals, and investment horizons. The next step is to take a financial inventory, enumerating all of your financial assets. This inventory will not only help you identify your assets and liabilities, but it can also be used to revise your will or assist your heirs.

Mental compartments. Another aspect of self-knowledge is understanding how your mental compartments work. Mental compartments such as those described in Chapter 8 help people to stifle spending impulses and set financial priorities. Yet mental compartments may have unforeseen costs. You should dispassionately evaluate the costs of your mental compartments against their benefits.

Risk tolerance. Because there is a long-run relationship between risk and return, the more risk you assume, the higher, potentially, the returns you will eventually reap. Your attitude toward risk really has two parts: a factual and a psychological one. Considering your financial assets and the present value of your labor income together, you have a factual basis for determining the amount of risk that you and your family can afford to take. The other aspect of risk is your psychological tolerance for living on the edge. Ultimately, you should make investments that allow you to sleep at night.

Comparative advantages. Finally, financial self-knowledge involves using your comparative advantages. Your special advantage may be access to information, free time, or special skills. You will want to make the most of your personal advantages.

3. Minimize taxes.

It is extremely important to understand the tax consequences of your investment decisions before such decisions are made, not afterwards. If your situation is straightforward, you might evaluate the tax effects yourself. Consult a reputable tax advisor if you are in doubt or if your situation is at all complicated.

Marginal bracket. Nevertheless, the basic facts of taxes should be familiar to all investors. First, you should know your marginal bracket. This is the rate at which your last dollar of income is taxed in a given year. Note that your bracket will change with inflation and your income. Remember also *only the last dollars* of your investment returns are taxed at your marginal tax rate.

Deferred capital gains. The timing of capital gains and losses is an important investment consideration. You have some control over when you realize capital gains, and they can have significant tax consequences. In addition, you should take the present value of money into account when you defer taxes. The longer that taxes can be deferred, the smaller is the present value of your tax liability.

Taxable versus tax-exempt income. A basic understanding of taxes is also necessary if you are to know when to seek taxable as opposed to tax-exempt interest income. Those in high tax brackets benefit much more from tax-exempt income. Investors in a low bracket ought to seek taxable interest, which to them provides higher, not lower, after-tax income.

Tax-advantaged investments. Despite recent reforms, the tax code is still designed to provide incentives for certain behavior that is deemed beneficial to public policy. Those who want to make the best use of their financial resources ought to use all the breaks that investors are given. Features such as low tax rates on certain investments and deductible retirement accounts provide a means to lower taxable income. Although many tax shelters have been eliminated or reduced, investors should pay careful attention to those that remain. Consult a reputable tax planner for current information.

4. Minimize transaction costs.

Buy-and-hold strategies. You should consider a buy-and-hold strategy to minimize transactions costs. When your stockbroker moves you in and out of investments rapidly to capture profit opportunities, probably only he or she will get rich—from your commissions. Furthermore, if you trade large amounts of illiquid assets, you will also incur the bid-asked spread (that is, pay the asked, or higher, price when you buy and receive the bid, or lower, price when you sell) as another transaction cost.

Vehicles that minimize transaction costs. As more and more investors recognize that heavy trading seldom produces high returns, products and services have been developed to help investors minimize transactions costs. Among these are discount brokers, no-load funds, and dividend reinvestment plans. You should use them unless you have compelling financial reasons not to.

Decisions that minimize transaction costs. But there are other ways to minimize transaction costs. For example, you should make volume purchases when possible. If you trade stocks in round lots of 100 shares, the brokerage commissions will be lower. You should also negotiate with various brokers if you anticipate a large trade. You might also try to avoid real estate commissions by buying or selling your home yourself, with the help of a lawyer.

5. Diversify.

Economists generally believe that there are two kinds of risk: diversifiable and nondiversifiable. Since the average investor can diversify his or her portfolio and avoid diversifiable risk, such an investor is only compensated with higher returns for undiversifiable risk, i.e., the risk present after the investor's portfolio has become fully diversified.

Diversification across asset classes. Many tables in this book, such as those in Chapter 3, illustrate the historical correlations between returns on various asset classes. Since you receive no additional compensation for lack of diversification, you must diversify into several types of investments to have the highest average returns. For most investors, this means holding some of your portfolio in stocks, bonds, cash, and real estate.

Diversification within asset classes. But it is also important to diversify within an asset class. The investor who accumulates a large position in one stock through profit sharing and holds no other investments takes a much greater risk that the firm will do poorly than the investor who holds only 10 percent of his or her portfolio in such a stock.

Geographic diversification. Apart from asset classes, you should also consider diversifying geographically. This may mean holding stocks of companies in Japan as well as the United States; it may mean buying a home in Philadelphia and an apartment building in Phoenix; or it may mean holding CDs in various banks to get the $100,000 maximum of federal deposit insurance from each one.

6. Emphasize common stocks.

U.S. equities. Although U.S. equities may not always be the investment with the best returns, their expected return is always high, and long-run investors with diversified stock portfolios have excellent chances of achieving their goals. While stocks have a higher level of risk than other investments, equities' risk has paid off handsomely with higher returns. Furthermore, higher-risk equities, such as OTC stocks, have had higher returns than stocks traded on the NYSE.

International equities. Yet the economic and historical circumstances so favorable to U.S. equities in the past are not guaranteed to recur. Thus, you may wish to diversify further and also bet on the world economy by investing in international equities.

Profit opportunities in equities. Careful analysis now confirms that equity returns follow close to a random walk. That is, returns in one year are nearly independent of returns in the previous year. In general, then, it is difficult to outguess the market. Yet in some circumstances, patterns recur that have yet to be explained by market efficiency. Empirical studies of equities point to excess returns on stocks with small capitalization, as well as those with low price/earnings ratios and those that are unfashionable or analyzed by few researchers. Other economists have noticed that buying stocks to capture their dividends and then reselling them, or buying stocks in December and selling them in January, can offer above average returns.

Minimizing equity risks. Large investors should consider using options and futures to hedge their portfolios against risk and to create portfolio insurance, as described in Chapter 15. Small investors can use mutual funds to achieve diversified equity investments with small amounts of capital and minimal monitoring of their accounts.

7. Consider owning some bonds.

Bonds offer a fixed stream of cash flows, and they may have high expected real rates of return. Special types such as floating-rate bonds have good principal stability because interest rates are adjusted to levels just above Treasury bill yields every 6 months.

Bond investment mechanics. Bond investments call for specific considerations. First, you should understand bond terminology (see Chapter 9). For example, it is essential to recognize that a bond's yield to maturity is not its approximate return unless the bond is held to maturity. If interest rates fall, bond prices rise and you may realize a capital gain. On the other hand, if rates rise, bond prices fall and you may have a capital loss. These both affect your actual returns.

Investment horizons and bond duration. Next, you should determine your investment horizon, and invest in bonds that are compatible with that time frame. You may wish to use the concept of bond duration to match your investment horizon precisely, and to measure the interest rate and price risk that you are assuming. Some investors who try to forecast interest rate swings may also wish to use options and futures. Remember, however, that the use of options and futures can add substantial risk to your portfolio.

Tax-exempt bonds.   Finally, if you are in a high tax bracket, you may wish to take advantage of tax-exempt bonds. Many municipal bonds are A-rated or better, making them a good credit risk. Municipal bonds can also be bought in mutual funds, with a small initial investment.

8. Monitor your cash holdings.

Cash balances.   Of course, you need some cash to spend, but be careful not to hold too much. You pay a price for having a liquid investment like currency or banking accounts; you give up yield.

Money market funds.   Even for your liquid cash, you should consider various alternatives to see which offers the best returns. Money market funds usually provide a better return than various bank accounts. Such funds have the advantage of safety, high yields, right to withdraw without penalties, and they earn interest until checks clear.

Like all investments, your cash resources are affected by inflation. Holding cash in money market funds provides a hedge against inflation, because the yields on the underlying assets change with changes in inflation. This is less true for fixed-rate accounts, CDs, or longer-term investments.

Tax-free money funds.   Most interest income on cash investments is taxable, but if you are in a high tax bracket, you should consider the alternatives, such as tax-exempt money market funds.

9. Own some real estate.

A house as an investment.   Particularly for investors in a high bracket, owning a house or condominium has been a smart investment after tax. However, low-bracket investors, such as young people just beginning their careers, will be better off renting, as will the family that must move often and incur numerous real estate commissions and mortgage closing fees. Even aside from taxes, your home is a good investment. With most real estate investments, you must pay a manager, who may be careless, or worse. Or you might have to put up with calls about broken plumbing at 3 a.m. With your own home, you do not need to monitor anyone but yourself. In economic terms, there are no conflicts of interest between the principal and agent with this investment.

Real estate as a tax shelter.   Under past versions of the U.S. tax code, all leveraged real estate has been a good tax shelter. It has been one of the few investments that allowed buyers to recover their costs before they sold, through depreciation. As before, mortgage interest is deductible. But the 1986 tax revision makes landlordship less attractive than before. Owning rental property is recommended for investors who take an active role in its management, so that losses are deductible from ordinary income. *Check the latest tax code changes.*

Real estate as a diversifier. Real estate helps you reduce the risk of your portfolio. When other assets do poorly, real estate tends to do well, and vice versa; that is, real estate returns have low correlations with returns of other assets. Thus, by holding some real estate, you reduce the overall risk of your portfolio and improve your average returns. Nevertheless, you might find it hard to diversify within the category of real estate, since real estate parcels are large in dollar value. Syndications, investment trusts, and limited partnerships are among the vehicles enabling small investors to hold diversified real estate equity.

10. Hold tangibles only if you enjoy them.

The pleasure of tangible assets. Tangible assets like art, coins, stamps, books, furniture, and rugs are objects of beauty and of historical interest. They can give you prestige, pride, and "psychological income." Since such assets are priced by people who like them the most, this nonpecuniary income is part of their return. You should own tangibles primarily for the pleasure they bring.

Investment limitations of tangibles. While tangible assets have had spectacular returns in periods of high inflation, they are not generally smart investments if you do not enjoy their nonpecuniary benefits. They have no income to reinvest, and are costly to store and protect. Finally, without special expertise, it is difficult to judge good from bad quality, and to identify fakes.

Gold and silver. Gold and to a lesser extent silver are exceptions to the general rule of holding tangibles primarily for personal pleasure. They are exceptions in part because the market for monetary metals is relatively liquid, and also because these metals are a surrogate form of cash. As described in Chapter 12, gold and silver are insurance against catastrophic changes such as economic collapse or hyperinflation. They also can provide considerable portfolio diversification. But in the long run, the returns to gold and silver are likely to be similar to those of cash, although gold and silver will be much more volatile.

11. Be smart about investment mechanics.

Decision making and procrastination. You may be better off overall if you pay as much attention to how you make investments as to the ones you choose. First and foremost, you should not delay your investment decisions. If you are unsure what to do, see a financial advisor; but don't sit around with $40,000 in your checking account. Put it in a money market fund while you decide.

Monitoring investments. Next, spend some time keeping track of your money. Don't neglect to do tax planning prior to year end. Check promised returns against those received, and understand the discrepancies. Also, make sure your heirs are informed about the broad outlines of your financial situation.

Understanding investments. Just as you should understand the basic tax effects of investments, you should also understand how your investments work, and how fees will be charged. Recognize, for example, that if you invest in a tax shelter where the general partner's returns are largely initial commissions and fees, this partner has little incentive to minimize costs and maximize eventual capital gains. Also, check out thoroughly the investments that your friends recommend.

Investment advisors. If you delegate your investment decisions, make sure the advisor you choose is well qualified. Consider using several advisors, such as an accountant, an insurance broker, and a financial planner. Check what one tells you against what another says. And if you do use advisors, be honest with them. The advice may be inappropriate if your advisors do not fully understand your situation.

12. View the full opportunity set.

The most important lesson to be gained from this book is the importance of viewing the entire set of investment opportunities. Principally, the assets in this opportunity set are equities, bonds, cash, real estate, monetary metals, and tangibles. By diversifying across various asset classes, you minimize your risks and take advantage of each asset's desirable characteristics.

In addition, viewing the full opportunity set means looking at all asset classes from an international vantage point. The world's economy has become increasingly more integrated across countries. If you want to diversify, you can see from the size of international markets that foreign assets are far too significant to be ignored. Furthermore, there have been spectacular returns on some assets abroad; you may miss major profit opportunities if you do not maintain a global perspective. These trends suggest that you should expand your horizons to encompass all investment markets.

Suggested Reading

Commerce Clearing House, Inc.: *U.S. Master Tax Guide,* Chicago, annual. A technical treatment of tax issues, intended for tax accountants.

J. K. Lasser Tax Institute: *J. K. Lasser's Your Income Tax,* Simon & Schuster, Inc., New York, annual. A yearly publication describing the U.S. tax laws, with aids for tax planning, oriented to the individual.

Levine, Sumner (ed.): *Dow Jones-Irwin Business and Investment Almanac*, Dow Jones-Irwin, Homewood, Ill., annual. Compendium of business and investment facts, published each year.

Malkiel, Burton G.: *A Random Walk Down Wall Street*, 4th ed., W. W. Norton & Company, New York, 1985. A popularized account of stock market behavior, which also gives investment advice on all types of assets. The author is a prominent financial economist.

Porter, Sylvia: *Sylvia Porter's Money Book*, Avon Books, New York, 1980. A compilation of the basics of personal financial planning.

18
What the Future Holds

The search for investment value is essentially an appraisal of the future. Quite literally, investors care only about the future. The value of a security today is the sum of the discounted cash flows that it is expected to generate. In this purely mathematical sense, the past is irrelevant. Yet investors study the past extensively to learn about the patterns and relationships that have characterized capital markets and that might be expected to prevail in the future.

The Dynamism of the Market

The only certainty is change itself. This view, which has dominated the thinking of the last half of the twentieth century, may have impeded an appreciation of the past. But in regard to technology, finance, and science, if not also to human nature, change has in fact been the norm.

Capitalism is a powerful instrument of such change. Each year, new businesses displace old ones; in every generation, whole industries and technologies change. In Table 18.1, for example, the largest U.S. industries are ranked by the number of persons employed for 20-year periods from 1880 to 1980. In the 1880s, fiber product industries—cotton, wool, men's clothing, and lumber—were the top four in importance. By the 1920s, however, railroad manufacturers employed the most persons, and automobile producers were large enough to appear on the list. In 1940, railroad manufacturers disappeared from the top 10, steel moved into second place, and automobiles became the most important industrial sector. Aircraft manufacturers, a totally new sector, ranked second only to auto producers in 1960. By 1980, the upstart communications industry followed auto and aircraft manufacturers as the third most important sector.

Table 18.1. The Rise and Fall of Industries, 1880–1980 (Persons Employed, in Thousands)

1880		1900		1920	
Cotton goods	185.5	Machine & foundry	350.3	Railroad car shops	484.4
Woolen goods	161.6	Cotton goods	302.9	Machine & foundry	482.8
Men's clothing	160.8	Lumber	283.3	Lumber	481.0
Lumber	148.0	Iron & steel	220.5	Cotton goods	431.0
Machine & foundry	145.4	Men's clothing	191.0	Iron & steel	375.1
Iron & steel	141.0	Railroad car shops	173.7	Shipbuilding	344.0
Boots & shoes	133.8	Printing & publishing	163.0	Electrical equipment	212.4
Brick & tile	66.4	Boots & shoes	143.0	Boots & shoes	211.0
Furniture	59.3	Carpentry	124.0	Automobiles	210.6
Printing & publishing	58.5	Masonry	110.6	Men's clothing	175.2

1940		1960		1980	
Autos	397.5	Autos	694.5	Autos	714.3
Steel	368.9	Aircraft	679.2	Aircraft	580.5
Cotton goods	312.2	Steel	620.2	Communications	566.1
Lumber	285.2	Newspapers & periodicals	374.3	Electrical components	498.6
Footwear	218.0	Women's clothing	364.1	Newspapers & periodicals	491.8
Bakery goods	201.5	Lumber	349.3	Steel	489.9
Wool	140.0	Structural metal	328.4	Plastics	470.1
Meatpacking	120.0	Meat products	306.9	Structural metals	464.6
Paper products	110.6	Bakery goods	306.0	Women's clothing	456.4
Canned food	98.0	Commercial printing	302.2	Commercial printing	414.6

Source: The Manhattan Institute for Policy Research

In the year 2000, communications will undoubtedly still be a significant industry in the United States, although automobiles and steel may not be. If the past is any guide, the leading employer of the twenty-first century is probably not on the 1980 list, and several other new industries will undoubtedly appear. In fact, there is every reason to believe that changes in the structure of industry and employment will be even more rapid in the twenty-first century than they were in the twentieth.

The market economy's remarkable dynamism, as shown in the flux of significant industrial sectors in the United States, can be translated into an observation in political philosophy. About 50 years ago, the economist and Austrian finance minister Joseph Schumpeter wrote of the "creative destruction" wrought by market capitalism, which he defined as the unsentimental tearing down of nonadaptive traditions and their sudden replacement by new ideas and methods. More recently, the conservative essayist George Will, in his *Pursuit of Virtue and Other Tory Notions,* noted that "Manhattan, the capital of world economics, is . . . scary . . . to conservatives because commerce, although indispensable and endlessly creative, is—because of its revolutionary energy—inimical to existing institutions, always." Both men convey the same message: those who advocate a free-market economy must accept the changes that it brings.

Global Integration

Because capital markets, like other segments of the economy, are in flux, it is likely that prices in those markets do not yet reflect all future developments. The investor who correctly anticipates such developments can gain the performance advantage and earn returns above the market. For example, at the Crystal Palace exhibition in London during 1851, Albert, Consort of Britain, was prophetic. He was quoted as saying that as a result of the technologies displayed, humanity would eventually live under one figurative roof. In the following 60 years, inventions that would unify the world—the automobile, airplane, and telephone—came into being. In another 60 years, these discoveries became common parts of everyday life. If Prince Albert had turned his observation into an investment strategy, he might have become even wealthier than he was.

Yet technology has not yet unified nations completely, and the world is still deeply segmented. The migration of human resources, for example, is painfully restricted, even in the United States. In the sphere of investments, portfolios typically are constructed from one country's assets. The transition from a segmented to an integrated world is being caused by many forces. Chief among them is the basic illogic, or economic inefficiency, of borders. To date, the increase in multinational corporations is the primary indicator that borders have begun to break down.

When borders become more permeable and the cost of travel continues to fall, the world economy will become more efficient. This is because labor, capital, and other resources will migrate more quickly and cheaply to the places where they receive the highest wages and rents. Such migration greatly lessens the inequality of compensation among people of comparable skill. The breakdown of borders has important implications for investors who want to gain the performance advantage. This disintegration of borders causes a new integration in six areas.

1. Standards of Living

In a more integrated world economy, the gaps between rich and poor people will narrow, not widen. The richest countries have already achieved near zero population growth and their economic growth rates have fallen to very sedate levels. Meanwhile, some poor countries have fabulously high economic growth rates, like those observed a century ago in the United States and Europe. The 12 percent annual growth rate of the People's Republic of China is probably not sustainable, but it represents the kind of growth that can be achieved over short periods of time by an emerging economy. Thus standards of living are likely to become more uniform throughout the world.

2. Business

Most big businesses already have international divisions, and this trend is likely to continue. When profit opportunities exist abroad, Nestlé Co. has no incentive to limit chocolate sales to Switzerland, or even to Europe. Also, business in the future is likely to be subject to less regulation and taxation. Political entities that impose these burdens will be seen as uncompetitive. Finally, unprocessed information from throughout the world will be cheap and abundant, but sorting and interpreting it will be a key business activity.

3. Capital Markets

Capital markets of the future will almost certainly encompass new types of investment opportunities. As borders break down, markets become more integrated. Already, they are highly permeable; when the push of a button can send a billion dollars traveling through the foreign exchange markets, borders have only limited meaning. As securities come to be traded almost continuously, the character of their markets will be altered. The exchanges in New York, London, Tokyo, Singapore, and other cities may become literally interchangeable. Investors will execute trades where the terms are the most favorable at the moment. Exchanges as physical entities may even disintegrate. Some pundits have suggested, only half humorously, that the NYSE will disband within a generation; securities traders will then communicate by computer from their cottages on Cape Cod or from poolside in Puerto Vallarta.

4. Investments

As a result of this change in the business environment, investment portfolios will also become more international. In order to achieve significant diversification of risk, investors will have to hold securities from throughout the world. Also, as information on foreign markets becomes available, investors may wish to take advantage of profit opportunities abroad. Already, large institutional investors are increasing their international holdings, and fund managers like John Templeton are forming international mutual funds.

5. Language

For educated and scholarly people, mathematics and data have always stood as a kind of universal language. These languages are now being adopted by a much broader segment of society. Just as a knowledge of

Latin was required as evidence of competence in Western cultures during the nineteenth century, so a rudimentary understanding of computers and mathematics is required today and will be even more necessary tomorrow.

6. Culture

In a broader sense, Prince Albert's vision of humanity under one roof will become more of a reality. This phenomenon is, of course, already underway. Levi's blue jeans are worn by Soviet consumers, and McDonald's hamburgers are sold in practically every country. But there is a deeper level at which the world is becoming more integrated. The values of each culture are being disseminated to other cultures, creating more commonalities among peoples. The dissemination of values is imparted more by the consumption of cultural products, such as music and literature, than by formal learning. For example, radio programs that feature an Italian opera singer, a British rock band, and an American jazz quartet probably have more impact on third world countries than philosophical writing about the values of these cultures. In addition, the dissemination of values is carried out more by the business world than academia or government, since business is typically the medium for distributing cultural products.

The Performance Advantage

The investor who can anticipate the future can gain the performance advantage. An optimistic investor looking at these future trends will perceive the future to be a cornucopia, affording riches to those who simply participate. This investor has a choice of assets a thousand times broader than the most visionary capitalist of 1789 could have imagined.

The optimist also remembers that a dollar invested in U.S. equities at the founding of our country would have grown by now to almost $5 million. There is nothing to suggest that the reward for taking risk has changed dramatically, so that this result ought to be repeatable too, give or take a few orders of magnitude.

On the other hand, a pessimistic investor looking at the future would take a very different tack. He or she would note that a single tempest in the market, or a bad investment decision, could wipe out one's hard-earned capital. The crash of 1929–1932, the 1950–1981 collapse in bond prices, and various real estate, gold, and oil price bubbles provide plenty of examples in the United States alone. Pessimists also remember the many foreign markets where principal was wiped out by war or revolution, and they conclude that investing is a dangerous business indeed.

In forecasting the future, the pessimist also considers the possibility that most of the economic growth that will take place already has. Although poor people and poor countries aspire to become rich, there is no natural law saying that they will succeed, or that an investor can share in such success, should it occur. Moreover, political arrangements that militate against wealth building, such as communism, have proven difficult to shake.

The resolution of the optimist's and pessimist's dilemmas lies in realizing that diversification and knowledge provide investors with both safety and gains. By diversifying among asset classes, the investor obtains protection against events like the near-total loss of equity capital from 1929 to 1932; over that period, bonds went up slightly. By diversifying internationally, investors are much more likely to pick at least one winner country from among potential winners, losers, and in betweens.

Knowledge, like diversification, also provides investors with protection and profit, with safety and gains. Safety is achieved by understanding all of the risks of an investment, not just the most obvious ones. Investors can then distinguish real bargains from apparent ones with hidden risks. Gains are available to investors who can perceive value that is not discerned by the market. Since most capital markets are partially inefficient, and since certain of these markets are open to the application of knowledge, informed investors undoubtedly are the ones who can earn the biggest returns. By acquiring skills and information, as through diversification, investors gain the performance advantage.

Index[1]

[1]The letter T or F following a page number designates reference to a table or figure, respectively, on that page.

About the Authors

ROGER G. IBBOTSON, Ph.D., is Professor in the Practice of Finance at the Yale School of Management and president of Ibbotson Associates, Inc., a consulting firm specializing in economics, investments, and finance. Professor Ibbotson's research on asset returns has brought him international recognition as an investment authority, as well as the prestigious Graham & Dodd Scroll from the Financial Analysts Federation. A frequent contributor to leading journals, Ibbotson is the co-author with Rex Sinquefield of *Stocks, Bonds, and Inflation*.

GARY P. BRINSON, C.F.A., is president and chief executive officer of First Chicago Investment Advisors, a national investment management firm with over $9 billion in assets under management. Mr. Brinson has published several articles in investment journals and is a frequent lecturer at universities and investment forums. He is president of Fort Dearborn Income Securities, Inc., a member of the editorial advisory board of the *Journal of Portfolio Management*, and a trustee of the Institute of Chartered Financial Analysts.